THE DESERT
ANZACS

THE DESERT
ANZACS

THE FORGOTTEN CONFLICTS IN THE DESERTS OF MESOPOTAMIA, NORTH AFRICA AND PALESTINE

Barry Stone

hardie grant books
MELBOURNE · LONDON

Published in 2014 by Hardie Grant Books

Hardie Grant Books (Australia)
Ground Floor, Building 1
658 Church Street
Richmond, Victoria 3121
www.hardiegrant.com.au

Hardie Grant Books (UK)
Dudley House, North Suite
34–35 Southampton Street
London WC2E 7HF
www.hardiegrant.co.uk

A Cataloguing-in-Publication entry is available from the catalogue of
the National Library of Australia at www.nla.gov.au
The Desert Anzacs

ISBN 978174 270 7549

Cover design by Luke Causby, Blue Cork
Text design by Loupe Studio
Typeset in 11/15 pt ITC Bookman LT by Kirby Jones
Cover image courtesy of Australian War Memorial B02465
Printed in Australia by Griffin Press

Contents

A Story from Dad

'I joined the Air Training Corps at sixteen in 1942. My unit was the 1st Wireless Air Gunners School at Ballarat. I learned morse code and by the time I was eighteen I knew it backwards. But that didn't get me into the aircrew. They found I had a colour deficiency: I was colour-blind. When they rejected me for pilot training I said: 'Well come on, what else is there?' And they said 'Well, we've got the engineers.' I said ok, and I became a flight mechanic.

Our training was all directed towards Mustangs – and there wasn't any doubt we would have been up in the islands if the war had gone on another six months. We used to get Mustangs and Liberators in at Ballarat; they were flying through to Darwin. The way it worked was that if you did night flying you had the next day off, so I'd go in with the Liberator boys and say: 'Have you got a seat for me?' 'Ohhh yes,' they'd say.

One day we took off from Ballarat, and in next to no time we were over Port Phillip Bay and I headed for my favourite seat, the sling seat in the tail. But my comfort was quickly disturbed by a Kittyhawk that went past the tail – we were the target aircraft! Then the copilot came down after a while and said: 'The skipper wants you in the middle of the aircraft, we've got trouble. Take your parachute, you might need it.' So we clipped on our parachutes and reported to the middle of the aircraft and sat there with our chins on our knees and waited for the captain to say if we were going overboard or not. The Liberators had a nose wheel and one wheel under each wing, and the one under the left wing wouldn't come down. It'd come down partially but *wouldn't lock in. So the skipper started doing short dives and pull-outs to try and flick it back into place. By the time he made three goes at that, we were sitting there looking at each other with our parachutes on ready to go! After three attempts and pull-outs – and they were sharp pull-outs – he managed to get it back in so we didn't have to go overboard after all.*

– Donald Charles Stone, my wonderful father
9 November 1925 – 31 March 2013, Resurrection Sunday

Imperial Camel Corps Brigade formed in December 1916. (AWM B02465)

Introduction

I am proudest of my thirty fights in that I did not have any of our own blood shed.

– Lieutenant Colonel Thomas Edward Lawrence (of Arabia),
Seven Pillars of Wisdom

Albert Einstein once asked his friend and fellow physicist Niels Bohr if he believed that the moon could be considered to exist if nobody was looking at it. Bohr replied that to prove something does not exist observation is required, therefore how can the question be answered if the only way to answer it involves nobody looking to see if it is there? The question is philosophical in nature, an interesting conundrum, but is valid nonetheless and just as much at home in the lap of the historian as the philosopher. If an event occurred but no one bothered to write it down, if no knowledge of it is passed on and it cannot be 'seen' historically, did it ever in fact happen? And would it really matter if it had? History is not the 99.9 per cent of every action and interaction that has ever occurred in the world and was never written down. It is only the 0.1 per cent that has been.

Einstein's question suggests the victory of Alexander the Great over Darius III at the Battle of Issus, the triumph of Hannibal over the Romans at Carthage, or the storming of the beaches by our Anzacs at Gallipoli could one day be considered not to have happened if no one had thought to write them down. The latter may sound absurd to us just a few generations on, but fast forward three hundred years and look again. Great deeds can be lost to us, they can sink in the ocean of time amid the continual unfolding of the present. Would there have been a crucifixion if there was no New Testament? History is not about what we do not know, or what we guess at, or what has been lost. It is only about what *can* be known. The rest is just fluff.

Though the Charge of the Light Horse is the stuff of legend, the desert campaigns in Mesopotamia, the Mediterranean and North Africa in both world wars are mostly forgotten theatres of war. And so we need to be especially grateful to the men and women of these campaigns who wrote things down. This book is an attempt to capture the thoughts and reminiscences of our men and women in uniform who fought in the sands of North Africa and throughout the Middle East from our first-ever overseas deployment to the Sudan in 1885 through the campaigns in the Great War and finally to the Siege of Tobruk in 1941. Of course while impressions and events cannot be lost once recorded, the scourge of a dusty, dank existence being 'forever archived' always lingers. So they are resuscitated here – and the narrative is theirs alone.

Thankfully, Patrick Hamilton of the 4th Australian Light Horse Field Ambulance Unit wrote things down. So too did the lyrical war journalist, poet and wanderer Hector Dinning and the bulletproof, pioneering pilot Thomas White of our serendipitous Half Flight. Keast Burke, a wireless operator in Mesopotamia, wrote things down, and so did nurses Alice King, May Tilton and Agnes Bennett. Because they and many others wrote things down, those things became real and knowable. They *happened.* And so they entered into history. Our history.

George Berrie of the 6th Light Horse Regiment wrote things down too. Unfortunately, though, his reminiscences of the Great War weren't published until 1949, just three years after the end of yet another world war. By this time the public was weary of conflict, and so his book, *Morale*, never really flew off the shelves. And that is a pity.

It is anything but a traditional narrative. Told in the third person, *Morale* has as its central character 'the Bushman', a Light Horseman whose name you are never told despite the story being plainly autobiographical. The Bushman served in a unit that was known only as 'the Regiment', and all the Turks were 'Jackos'. The book is dedicated to the author's close friend and fellow Light Horseman, 'Snow', who was with him through thick and thin. Snow's background isn't given up easily, but Berrie acknowledges that he was something of an outlaw in the regiment: a man who once told a sergeant he 'wasn't fit to hold *one* stripe, let alone three!' Soldiering didn't come as easily to Snow as it did others; he was a bit of a misfit. One night he was ordered out on sentry duty and ended up blundering into a troop of Turkish cavalry that required the dispatching of half a squadron to get him back. 'Next time I go to a war I'll be a good soldier,' Snow confided to Berrie late one star-encrusted night in Palestine in May 1917. 'I won't stow away, or desert either.'

Berrie was unconcerned with unit numbers, ranks, designations, even names and backgrounds – the sort of things that most accounts of men at war are awash with. But one thing he did know well was the day-to-day life of the Light Horseman, the medic and the cook. *Morale* is filled with incidental moments and unnamed characters that make it a tribute to every man who ever served, an achievement made all the more possible thanks to its deliberate embracing of anonymity, a literary equivalent to the Tomb of the Unknown Soldier.

Of course a little digging into Berrie's own experience immediately reveals the whole story. The regiment was the 6th Light Horse, and they had seen it all: Suvla, Sari Bair, Gallipoli, Romani, Rafa, Gaza–Beersheba, the Jordan Valley. One hundred and eleven of its men were killed and 461 were wounded. Berrie knew all about the grief of war, but by the time he put pen to paper thirty years after returning home all of the 'obvious stuff' had been sufficiently told, and there was no need to tell it all again. So instead *Morale* reads like a sort of non-fiction novel, a literary genre unheard of at the time and an approach to storytelling that wouldn't be fully realised until Truman Capote published *In Cold Blood* in 1966. By not concerning himself with the usual stuff of battlefield reminiscences such as statistics, troop strengths, strategies and tactics, weapons and logistics, he was free to construct a personal account that, by the time the final page is turned, gives the reader an uncommon insight into war by revealing it obliquely, by talking of what soldiers did with the 90 per cent of their time that was spent *not* shooting at the enemy, as opposed to the 10 per cent that was. It is an approach I have tried to emulate here.

When you read *Morale,* or the poetic reminiscences of the Australian war correspondent Hector Dinning or Keast Burke's triumphal look at the life of a signalman in *With Horse and Morse in Mesopotamia,* you see through the horror of war to its banalities and its ironies. You see its lulls and its bad food and the heat and dust of the desert and the things that made our diggers laugh and think of home. And you see the beauty that exists everywhere in the world, even on the periphery of war. Dinning in particular had a singular eye for beauty. Such was his love of the vibrant street life of foreign cities he eschewed even the grand monuments of Ancient Egypt because all they did, he said disparagingly, was speak to the dead and so were a distraction from 'the occupation of first importance, the looking upon the living'. Dinning wrote of sunsets and bazaars, of merchants and artisans and spice-laden alleyways, and of alfresco cafes in Cairo where he drank mud coffees at sidewalk tables eighty years before it became *de rigueur* in Australia. He thought the veiled women of Cairo, Jerusalem and Damascus 'tantalising', able to hide their bodies under their burkas but not their alluring shapes. 'I wonder if Muslim husbands know,' he wrote without malice in 1917, 'what inciting suggestiveness lies in the figures of their veiled wives, and that the veil only heightens it. The veil is the merest spur to free love. I believe it is designed to be a cheek.'

Dinning also had a deep admiration for the men of the Light Horse, with whom he had travelled and seen so much. They were, he wrote in *Nile to Aleppo* (1920) 'a modest people ... in many ways an unsophisticated people. They are plain ... loving their horses, careless of danger. It was nothing to them that Napoleon had traversed Sinai and fought where they fought; it was of more importance that their horses should have water and food.'

What follows is a collection of vignettes rather than panoramas, an emotive and personal view of war and of the everyday stuff that happened beyond the pale of conflict. All the usual suspects are here – the Suez Canal, Romani, Gaza, Cairo, Jerusalem and Tobruk – but they share equal stage with other, lonelier places such as Kut, Baku and Basra. For anyone who thinks the Sinai is remote enough, spare a thought for the men of the 1st Pack Wireless Signal Troop as they stepped off the *Teesta* in March 1916 onto Mesopotamian soil without a soul to welcome them. And what of the mysterious Dunsterforce – the 'Hush-Hush Army' – whose elite volunteers had no idea what they were volunteering for but who set off on an adventure through Persia all the way to the Russian Caucasus and back that packed enough of a mix of drama, myth and legend that it rivalled the exploits of T. E. Lawrence himself.

And who remembers that Turks and Australians once joined forces and bivouacked together one night at a railway siding at Ziza in the Jordan Valley in September 1918 to bolster their combined firepower as a deterrent against thousands of marauding Bedouins? Just another overlooked moment that, despite being documented well enough, is nowhere more powerfully preserved as in *Ziza*, that monumental oil on canvas by the war artist Harold Septimus Power, one of the first of a distinguished array of artists, sculptors and photographers who have been cataloguing and preserving our military history for almost a hundred years – the longest-running and largest art-commissioning project in our nation's history.

And then there are the stories that should be recorded but have not, like 'Rat of Tobruk' Joe Madeley of the 2/13th Battalion, Australian 9th Division. While he was in his trench one frosty night some Germans began to sing 'Lili Marlene', its melody drifting across the flatness of the desert and over the Australian lines. 'It felt,' Joe said, 'like the Germans were right there with us' and his unit clapped in appreciation as the last note faded into the night. In reply one of our diggers, a young baritone named Peter Robinson whose name you'll struggle to find in the history books, sang 'Silent Night'. When he finished, the applause from the German lines was the most wonderful sound Joe heard during the entire siege. The song was of course an old German hymn, and the audience, crouching beyond the footlights out there in the dark, thought he'd sung it just fine. Just another moment, now firmly embedded in our history, that lays bare the insanity and the waste of war.

Chapter One
The Hell of the Desert

The 'cafard' of the Foreign Legion, a near relative to tropical madness, is a collective name for all the inconceivable stupidities, excesses and crimes which tormented nerves can commit. The English language has no word for this condition. In 'le çafard' murder hides, and suicide and mutiny too; it means self-mutilation and planless flights out into the desert; it is the height of madness and the depth of despair.

– Erwin Rosen, *In the Foreign Legion*

Erwin Carle – Rosen was a pseudonym – was a German–American author who joined the French Foreign Legion in October 1905 and deserted its ranks pretty much as soon as he was able to the year after. Born in 1876 in Karlsruhe, Germany, Carle was sent by his father to the United States as a teenager to, by his own admission, 'get straightened out'. He lived first as a farmhand and occasional cowpoke in Texas then fell into journalism, working for a German newspaper in Missouri before moving to San Francisco. He covered the Spanish–American War in 1898, travelling extensively as a reporter throughout Central and South America and joined the French Foreign Legion in North Africa in 1905, after his fiancée dumped him.

Never much of a believer in the Legion's motto 'March or Die', Carle popularised the term *'le cafard'* in his 1910 book *In the Foreign Legion*, a scathing account of his misspent months serving alongside the squalid collection of vagabonds and misfits that were his fellow legionnaires. In French a *cafard* is a cockroach, but it wasn't until legionnaires in the scattered French colonies throughout Algeria and Morocco took to shooting them to relieve their boredom did the term begin to be used to describe a kind of persistent restlessness, purposelessness, apathy, depression and even madness – the kind of madness only a legionnaire could know, born of isolation and marches of hundreds of kilometres over desert sands, done for no other reason than because that is simply what legionnaires did. Carle spoke of how men on sentry duty would all of a sudden run off into the desert screaming, while others would cover their faces and begin to weep when asked how they were feeling.

There were no such ambiguities in the wars our diggers fought in the deserts of the Middle East and North Africa. The threats, whether from Ottomans, Nazis or Italians were clear and defined. They were 'just' wars: wars to stop aggression – though in the case of the Afrika Korps in North Africa, a fight with a surprising absence of enmity. It was a 'war without hate' according to the late author and Londoner John Bierman, a phrase echoed time and again by our World War II diggers.

Ask any who served there, though, if the heat and the flies and the scorpions and the sand had the potential to bring out *le cafard*. Reports by British censors in Egypt in 1941 spoke of the 'fear of desert lunacy becoming more likely among those who have served long unbroken periods in the desert'. That monotony was the 'greatest curse of life' whose effect varied 'according to individual temperament'. Is it any wonder? If sentry duty and long pointless marches across desert sands in times of peace were sufficient to invite the onset of a troubled mind, what added torments could fighting a war let loose?

Nine-tenths of the human body is water. Humans can survive for weeks without food, but take water from us and we perish in days. Our bodies are overwhelmingly sensitive to its presence. We need only lose a miserly half a per cent of our body weight through dehydration and we begin to feel thirsty. If we deliberately go without water and lose, say, 2 per cent of our weight in an act of voluntary dehydration, our *entire stomach* won't possess the necessary volume, on one filling, to resupply our body's flagging needs. When dehydration reaches 5 per cent of body weight we become fatigued, we lose our appetite, we become irritable, our pulse rate increases, we feel dizzy and our speech begins to slur. Lose 10 per cent and walking is no longer possible. At 12 per cent the tongue swells, the mouth loses its sensory capacity, and we can no longer swallow. Urinating becomes painful, your skin begins to shrink back over your bones, your eyes sink into their sockets, delirium sets in, and your blood thickens as water is drawn from it by a body desperately trying to distribute the precious fluid elsewhere. One of the functions of blood is to draw heat away from the body's interior and upwards to the surface. No longer able to redistribute the heat we naturally generate, the body's temperature inexorably rises, resulting in uncontrollable convulsions. And then you die. In the deserts of North Africa and the Middle East, where you can lose up to 7 litres of precious sweat in twenty-four hours even when blissfully at rest and not having to fight a war, all of the above can happen in less than half a day.

In the desert water can, however, occasionally appear from under its blanket of sand when it might look as though there isn't any to be had for miles. In the Great War the first encampment for the men of the 6th Light Horse Regiment after having crossed from the Sinai Peninsula into Palestine was at a nothing place called Sheikh Zuweid, a small village on the shores of the Mediterranean. Straight away the men could see the ground had changed. The vegetation was different to the Sinai – there were places you could stand and have one foot on typical desert sands and the other on well-grassed soil. But the real surprise lay underneath. A few troopers had begun to dig a trench just in from the beach, and to the amazement of everyone fresh water had seeped into it. Minutes later a remarkable scene was being played out: a line of horses was at the trench, and at the same time the horses hind feet were being lapped by the warm, salty water of the Mediterranean they were drinking fresh water from a hole in the sand.

When it rained in the desert the excitement of the troops was almost incidental when compared to that of their horses. In December 1916 a heavy downpour over Mageibra in the Sinai saw the horses of the 6th Light Horse bucking and rearing with delight so much that the anchors and ropes of the horse lines, normally more than enough to keep them tethered in their places, were ripped from the ground as entire troops of horses broke free and encircled the camp with heads and tails uplifted in triumph, galloping defiantly.

In the desert campaigns in North Africa in World War II water became so scarce you couldn't even wash your shirts – not that you'd have bothered because all it took was a day for them to become dark with sweat and encrusted with dust. Showers were rarely taken alone. Your mate stood by you, poured water sparingly into his open hands then rubbed it over your body while you worked up a lather with a bar of soap and a flannel. Most however, preferred to drink all of the water they had and relied on an occasional swim in the ocean for their bathing.

Water was so precious that Captain Vernon Northwood of A Company, 2/28th Battalion, Australian 9th Division took to shaving with water he'd spat out after brushing his teeth:

I used to shave in a tobacco tin; and after cleaning my teeth I'd spit the water back into the tin and shave in it. I had a little piece of sponge. We shaved every day, to avoid sores while the men took their boots off and walked around in the sand to clean their feet.

The British considered the absence of water so potentially catastrophic that they formed a squad of water diviners from within the Royal Engineers. 'We've found at least a dozen men who claimed to be able to discover springs and hidden streams by the old-fashioned hazel twig method,' one optimistic officer wrote home in a letter. As a backup there were also several mobile purifying plants each capable of making more than 10,000 litres of drinkable water every hour as well as a pellet that could mask the water's questionable taste and turn it into something akin to – if you believed the hype – spring water. The Germans, by contrast, came to North Africa better equipped as regards the provision of drinking water, with centrifugal pumps, mobile water purification units, motor-driven water filters, water distillation plants and even a laboratory for water analysis.

The problem of not enough water was exacerbated by the nature of the war itself. Because of the continual advance and retreat of Axis and Allied forces back and forth along the coast many water wells had been salted and re-salted by both sides prior to their retreats to deny drinking water to the enemy on their heels. The Australian 9th Division dug in at Tobruk were being given water that was only borderline palatable and that led to a large number of intestinal diseases. The Germans for the most part had better access to wells and their ration was between 4 and 5 litres per man per day.

What concerned the Germans more than water, however, was fuel. A tank's three crew members required just 12 litres of water a day. The tanks they drove needed 22 litres of water per day – and 50 litres of precious fuel. The problem of adequate supplies of petrol to fuel his armour bedevilled Field Marshal Erwin Rommel throughout the campaign. 'The bravest men can do nothing without guns,' Rommel wrote in his diary in 1942. 'The guns can do nothing without plenty of ammunition, and neither guns nor ammunition are of much use in mobile warfare unless there are vehicles with sufficient petrol to haul them around.' Axis ground forces consumed an average of 132 tonnes of fuel per day in early 1942, and the mileage of armoured vehicles was predictably appalling. A medium-sized armoured car averaged just 3 kilometres per litre, and a light armoured car 5 kilometres per litre. Miserable enough until one considers the fuel efficiency of a tank – just 500 metres per litre for Mark III and Mark IV Panzers!

Scarcity was not the only water problem. When heavy rains came in Libya and the Western Desert, as they did every October, water would accumulate in depressions and lowlands and make them all but impassable, while empty wadis had the potential to be the conduit for torrents of wild water capable of washing away tents and even vehicles. During the German retreat from Alamein in 1942 a Panzer unit became so bogged down in mud that the tanks had to be destroyed. On that occasion, however, the rain was a blessing, preventing the Allies from pursuing them along the coastal road out of Alamein and allowing them to continue their retreat.

It's easy to look back through newsreels and photographs and get a skewed idea of what it must have been like chasing Rommel and his Afrika Korps back and forth along the ribbon-like coastal plains of North Africa in 1942, or of the 4th Light Horse Brigade galloping towards the water wells of Beersheba. Photographs focus on a few scant degrees of vision and capture the 'big' things well, such as tanks, tents, staff cars, men, weapons and buildings. But what they don't often reveal are the very small things, the unseen things – the things that make fighting a war in the desert almost unbearable even on those days when there isn't an enemy to shoot at. Things like heat, sweat, exhaustion, sandstorms ... and flies.

In North Africa in 1942 army censors estimated that half of all the letters being written home by soldiers referred at least in part to the constant plague of flies: unending swarms that were unimaginably infuriating and all but prevented rest during daylight hours in the 'fly season', which began in March and reached its peak in the summer months of June, July and August. The problem was always there, even without a war, only now exacerbated by the presence of the dead and decomposing bodies that littered the battlefields. In Jonathan Fennel's 2011 book *Combat and Morale in the North Africa Campaign* the author quoted an observation in July 1942 by army censors whose job it was to vet the letters being written home:

> *Overshadowing the loss of Tobruk, the German offensive in Russia, the possibility of a second front – unanimously condemned as the chief enemy and worse than Rommel were the millions of flies that are worrying the troops in the front line from dawn to dusk. As an officer remarked: 'We can beat Rommel, but not the flies.'*

Flies are attracted to moisture, and desert-born flies seem drawn to it more than most, which is not a good thing considering the one substance all men in the desert produced in abundance was sweat. The human body begins to sweat when the temperature nudges 29 degrees Celsius. In the desert – even at rest in the shade of a tree – the body sweats around 220 millilitres every hour! Flies were attracted to soldiers' eyes, mouths and nostrils, and swarmed in plague-like proportions around their food. Eating was a case of seeing how few flies you managed to swallow along with your tinned bully beef. Some men made tiny paper spills and filled them with paraffin, which they'd pour over the vast armadas of flies that liked congregating on the roofs of their dugouts, and then lit them. Lieutenant G. F. Morrison of the British 7th Battalion put it best in one of the 54 letters he wrote home to his mother that are now held in the archives of the British Imperial War Museum: 'You can kill about 200 at one go in one dugout that way – marvellous!! It's lovely to hear them crackling and popping, like chestnuts on a fire!'

Flies have lived long in the memory of Joe Madeley of the 2/13th Battalion, one of the legendary Rats of Tobruk. 'God knows, the flies!' he told me during a visit to his home on the New South Wales Central Coast in early 2013.

> *If you went to sneeze and forgot to cover your mouth you'd choke on the bloody things. And the maggots! Well this one chap in Alamein was hit just beside the eye, and we couldn't get him out for a while, we just couldn't get him out. And when we finally did get him out, well, the maggots had already got into the wound. It sounds awful but actually it was the best thing that could've happened to him because what they did was they'd eaten away everything that had rotted. They'd cleaned him up! The medics said that he'd have lost his eye if it weren't for the maggots. Yep, they said it was the best thing that could've happened to him.*

There are few more efficient consumers of necrotic (dead) tissue than the maggot, and using maggots to clean wounds is as old as antiquity. During the Great War the American orthopaedic surgeon William Baer noticed that patients suffering gangrene and infections and wounded soldiers who staggered back into their positions after days spent untreated in no-man's-land had survived because maggots infesting their wounds had been busy cleaning up the bacteria. One soldier brought to Baer who had spent days unattended on the battlefield had a compound fracture of the femur and a ghastly abdominal wound. Baer noted that 'there was practically no bare bone to be seen and the internal structure of the wounded bone as well as the surrounding parts were entirely covered with the most beautiful pink tissue that one could imagine'. Baer later went on to conduct the first therapeutic experimentations in what he called 'maggot therapy' in the 1920s, and the use of maggots remained the singular most effective treatment in cleaning open wounds and preventing infection until the development of new strains of antibiotics in the 1940s.

In every war there has been the ever-present scourge of dysentery, a disease that in the twenty-first century, providing one has access to basic health care, is a mild and easily curable illness. An inflammation of the linings of the large intestines, it manifests itself as a chronically debilitating form of diarrhea thanks in most cases to the micro-organism *Shigella dysenteriae*, which infects human faeces and then is brought into contact with either food or drinking water. Dysentery can be viral, bacteriological, or parasitic in nature, and used to be called 'campaign fever' in the 1700s because of its tendency to run through armies in the field. It can strike anywhere at any time. In 1933 almost 2000 cases were reported at the World's Fair in Chicago after faulty plumbing in a city hotel led to the contamination of its drinking water. In 1962 a shipment of imported butter from China resulted in a 30,000-strong outbreak in East Berlin, which *TIME* magazine – in the best traditions of Cold War rhetoric and questionable journalism – labelled the 'Wall Disease'.

The prevalence of dysentery and diarrhea among the troops in Egypt in World War I was more or less proportional to the extent to which the fly problem was being addressed. Hospital wards in the Allied hospitals in Cairo represented scenes 'not unlike those in the Crimean War' according to those who worked there, with dysentery cases so rife nurses were run off their feet. By September 1942 it was being referred to as an epidemic, spread by new arrivals who were 'not sufficiently fly-minded'. The Australians around Tobruk, thanks in no small part to their strategy of 'making no-man's-land their own' via their deliberate tactic of aggressive patrolling, sometimes cheekily took their rubbish out at night and placed it near the German and Italian lines. They did this in part because it meant they didn't have to bury the stuff, but mostly so that the prevailing onshore winds would funnel the thousands of flies in each small pile of waste into the midst of the enemy!

But you could be as fly-minded as possible and still graze the back of your hand, or suffer a small scratch and so create a magnet for every winged creature for miles around. The Allies in the Western Desert in both wars were constantly getting abrasions and cuts to their skin that straight away became fodder for hordes of marauding flies. These so-called 'desert sores' (a diagnosis loosely applied to any localised septic skin lesion) were slow to heal and festered easily. Living in the midst of scores of motorised transports didn't help either, with tyres and tracks throwing up dust so fine it penetrated bandages and gauze, easily infecting cuts, abrasions and insect bites. By July 1917 the problem of a poor diet resulted in more than one in five men of the Anzac Mounted Division suffering 'Barcoo rot', scurvy-like septic sores resulting from food deficiencies. (Everyone knew what the sores were, but where the term 'barcoo' came from no one really knows. Banjo Patterson and Henry Lawson both spoke of it, and it may have been the Aboriginal word for Queensland's Victoria River. In the 1890s Rockhampton chemist Thomas Ingham claimed to have found a cure for it and even patented his discovery – an ointment made of carbolised eucalyptus.

For those men not accustomed to desert life, in World War II bothersome skin sores began to surface that first summer – around July of 1941 – and were more or less tolerated, just one more daily annoyance to suffer. By the time a cold cream had been developed to treat septic skin conditions the Battle of El Alamein had been fought and won, and the resultant advance westward by the Allied forces meant the cream never managed to catch up to the front lines. The New Zealand Division, however, found that an ointment made by crushing a tablet of sulphapyridine in two ounces of paraffin molle flavine (paraffin wax) and covering the wound with sticking plaster brought significant relief.

In his 1919 book *With Our Army in Palestine*, Antony Bluett of the Honourable Artillery Company, the British Army's oldest regiment incorporated by Royal Charter by King Henry VIII in 1537, reminds us that North Africa's flies were every bit as ubiquitous in the First World War as they were in the second:

> *The slightest scratch turned septic. It was the rule rather than the exception for units in the desert to have 50 per cent of their strength under treatment for septic sores. There was no help for it; active service is a messy business at best. It was appallingly difficult to give adequate treatment. Sand would get into the wound; if it were cleansed and covered up, the dry, healing air of the desert had no chance; if it were left open the flies made a bivouac of it – and the result can be imagined! There were men who were never without a bandage on some part of their person for months on end, and it was a common sight to see a man going about his daily work literally swathed in bandages.*
>
> *Infinitely worse than any other was the plague of flies. When we arrived at Ayun Musa there was not a fly to be seen. Within a week you would have thought that all the flies in the universe had congregated about us. They were everywhere. If you leave your tea uncovered for a minute the flies around you hastened to drown themselves in it! And as for jam! Successfully to eat a slice of bread and jam was a feat, and one requiring careful preparation. You had to make a tunnel of one hand, wave the required mouthful about with the other for a few seconds in order to disturb the flies on it, then pass it quickly through the*

tunnel and into the mouth before they could settle again.
One man nailed a piece of mosquito-netting to the front of
the mess table and with himself as the pole made a kind
of tent, so as to eat his food in comfort.

Not being able to eat in peace because of flies was one
thing; being struck down by sandfly fever, however, was
something else entirely. Egyptian sandflies are tiny and avoid
strong winds by flying close to the ground. They rarely travel
more than a few dozen metres from their breeding places,
and carry a parasite that gives its recipient three days of hell.
After an incubation of a few days the disease suddenly erupts.
Severe headaches, temperature of 39 degrees, extremely sore
eyes, aching limbs and a stiff neck are accompanied by nausea
and anorexia. The effects of the parasite were so debilitating
that patients often developed depressive symptoms that stayed
with them for days or even weeks after their symptoms were
gone.

During the Great War in the deserts of Mesopotamia
flies also made life a misery for the men of our signal corps.
'To describe them,' wrote one signalman in his diary, 'is to
hazard one's reputation for truth.' You couldn't eat without
swallowing them, they settled like clouds on everything, and
when you wrote a letter home it was said you 'couldn't see
the end of your pen'. Coming upon a squadron of mounted
cavalry one signalman wrote: 'I thought they were wearing
chain armour ... before I discovered that what looked like mail
was a steely blue metallic mesh of flies.' It was estimated that
one in twenty indistinguishable from the Australian house fly,
had a propensity to bite, and as a result were considered to be
'impregnated with vice'.

In the hospitals set up in the palaces and public buildings
of Egypt during the Great War the problem of the 'fly pest'
was ever present. Refuse and soiled dressings were placed in
sealed bins and any wet or moist ground around them sprayed

with sulphate of iron and sprinkled with lime chloride. Camel and horse manure was sprayed twice a day. Spit cups were covered, strips of sticky flypaper were hung from the ceilings of every ward, and food was covered by gauze paper or stored in fly-proofed mesh cupboards. Fly-proof netting for larger openings was in short supply and what could be sourced was heavy and cumbersome and the last thing you wanted to do in Egypt, especially in the warmer months, was cover over doors and windows and place a barrier to those longed-for afternoon breezes that were about the only aspect of the oppressive climate that made life tolerable.

In his 1999 memoir *Out of the Desert*, World War II veteran Sergeant John Blundell wrote this account of the horrors of sand, Saharan flies and scorpions while stationed at Gambat, 65 kilometres south of Tobruk:

> *Torments in the desert were many. Sand as fine as talcum powder routinely clogged our cameras and everything else. Driven by the hot southerly winds, the sand filled your nostrils and ears. There was no water to wash it off. The time spent there was inconceivable misery ... Then there were the flies. Flies by the millions. Pesky, irritating, ubiquitous flies that got into everything. Even when you talked you had to be careful they didn't fill your mouth or fly up your nose. Once I saw a rack of lamb, which was to be delivered to our cooks, sitting on the floor of a truck so covered with flies it looked as though they were trying to carry it off.*
>
> *The only sign of life was the scorpions ... they were not only plentiful, but they were big and dangerous. It was almost impossible to avoid them. One of their favourite places to collect was in boots after you'd taken them off at night. I could almost certainly count on two or three in each boot the next morning.*

Scorpions were rife in Mesopotamia in 1918 also, as this diary entry by one of our signal corps shows:

Our camping ground at Tekrit was honey-combed with scorpion holes from which, on warm nights, scorpions issued forth and inspected our blankets. There seemed to be several species – the longest being quite four inches long – horny tailed old warriors with stings like fair-sized fish hooks. One of the boys was bitten in the leg and, although taken to hospital and given several injections, he suffered agonies for two days.

And there were rats, too. Blundell quoted a mate in his unit who remarked on the size of the *actual* desert rats, known as *jerboas* in Libya, desert-dwelling rats quite distinct from the rats and mice that inhabited Libya's towns and cities: 'I don't think I've ever seen a rabbit with a long tail before.' Another of Blundell's fellow bombardiers swore the rats were so big they'd 'chew your leg off at night if you were unlucky enough to have one crawl into your tent'.

But more pervasive than the flies and the scorpions and the rats was the sand and dust, and anything that was in any way porous – such as people – was rendered useless when smothered in the choking sand of a sandstorm. As Kevin Robinson of the Australian 9th Division wrote in 1942,

When a sandstorm was blowing, the fine dust used to clog up everything; for instance the intakes on the carburettors [sic] on our trucks. The sand got in under the glass of your watch and it would stop. You couldn't shave or wash because the sand got into your skin ... a heavy one could blow for two days, and you might get them once a week. We got a hot meal once a day, after dark. If there was a sandstorm blowing, you couldn't eat the whole of the mess tin because the last spoonfuls were sand.

The sandstorms, when the really big ones came sweeping in, black and gargantuan, sounded like an express train. Bob Sykes of the British Eighth Army wrote of the first one he endured while sitting, shivering with fear in his dugout:

All oxygen seemed to go out of the air, and the flies were maddening and swarming. The heat was terrific and I sweated so the sand caked onto me – in my eyes, nose and ears. I sat down in my dugout and waited, thinking it would be over in a few minutes, but suddenly I nearly panicked – the sand was coming through every crack. I thought I would be buried. I fought my way out – the sand was whipping the skin off my face and hands. It was almost pitch black and I felt entirely alone. Then a light appeared and the sun began to look a dirty orange. The noise slowly abated and the wind died down: I had ridden out my first sandstorm.

In Alamein in 1942 Captain Peter Braithwaite, a medical officer with the 2/12th Battalion remembered when he tried to find his way from the officers' mess to his tent in the midst of a sandstorm: 'Once I tried to get to my tent from the officers' mess which was only about 50 yards and I finished up at the apex of the triangle instead of the other end of the base. I was 90 degrees out because of the total darkness.'

Sand constantly fouled Allied and Axis weapons alike, getting into gun breeches, optical equipment such as binoculars and rangefinders, the turret rings of tanks, playing merry hell with air-cooled engines of every kind, and ruining or at least interfering with everything else that required smooth, precise and unfettered movement. Lubricating oil only added to the problem, mixing with the sand to produce a sticky abrasive sort of gunk that saw entire tank turrets removed so that their rings could be cleaned. In the Afrika Korps the infantry were given sailcloth to wrap their rifle bolts and other moving parts in to protect them against the corrosive effects of sand.

It is difficult to imagine sand in these conditions being good for anything, but there was one exception. In 1942 men of the British Eighth Army and our own 9th Division, with hot meals tending to be difficult things to make happen in the middle of the desert, occasionally took to cooking their meals in their affectionately named 'Benghazi cookers' – tins with holes pried in the bottom using a bayonet, then half-filled with sand mixed with petrol to create a gooey, flammable paste. A match thrown into the tin produced a flame that would burn for around half an hour. No wonder, perhaps, that 30 per cent of accidental injuries during the North Africa campaign were the result of burns.

Sand and dust were so pervasive their presence even had the potential to determine where battles were fought. In North Africa in 1942 the dividing line between those areas of the desert that were vehicle friendly and those that were not was in a region in eastern Libya and western Egypt between the 29th and 30th latitude. To the south of the 29th latitude marked the beginning of a vast expanse of sand dunes, and to even consider crossing them was to invite the ire of your comrades. There was just no getting away from the consequences of sand, unless you were lucky enough to be a pilot and could spend a few hours above it.

In Mesopotamia in 1917 a diary entry by a member of Australia's 1st Pack Wireless Signal Troop described the choking dust of that campaign as 'fine and clinging, as soft as the powder that is sprinkled on a baby'. The only ground troops Australia sent to serve in Mesopotamia, the men of our wireless and signalling units, wrote of how they picked the dust off themselves 'in lumps and knobs from our cheeks, where it solidified the drops of perspiration that were continually running down our faces'.

But as bad as the sand and dust were in the Middle East in both wars, nowhere were they as bad as the Jordan Valley in

1917. Our Light Horsemen stationed there had a saying: 'For every gallon of water you had to drink at Romani, you needed two in the Jordan Valley.' The Australian war journalist Hector Dinning, in his wonderful 1920 account of life with the Light Horse, *Nile to Aleppo*, wrote of the Jordan Valley dust:

> *Men in the rear of a mounted column will see nothing either side for hours and scent nothing all day but the dry, strong smell of the powdered earth that parches them. They are powdered ashen and by the end of the march they feel the ghosts they look. Your hair is whitened by it, it has covered your body beneath your clothes; your lips hold ridges of thin mud the saliva has made; your ears are filled. But you cannot better it. You've got to stick it. Sometimes you sleep all night in a cloud of dust. Your blankets are laden with it. Your food is covered and you bite grit. Some light horsemen have resigned themselves to a life of dust until this war ends.*

Dust was also sucked into the engine cylinders of aircraft and took no time at all setting in motion the process of wear and the scoring of cylinders and pistons. In World War II air intake valves were often placed inside cars and vehicles in the hope this would deliver cleaner air to the engine. But all attempts to counter the effects of dust proved fruitless. The life of a Volkswagen engine in the desert was only 13,000 kilometres, compared to almost 70,000 kilometres in other dust-free theatres of the war. Tank engines suffered too. A Panzer Mark III engine that would be expected to run for up to 8000 kilometres in Europe had to be overhauled or changed after just 3500 kilometres in North Africa. Artillery pieces had muzzle protectors, and engines of all sizes required considerably more lubrication than in other less extreme environments. Dust also made it all but impossible to move large columns of men without signalling to the enemy precisely where you were, and attempts at camouflaging troop movements were all but impossible in the desert's open terrain.

The best time to move men was during the overwhelming blackness of a moonless night, even though men often had a hard time finding their way back to their tents after they'd pitched them. Then daylight would come, and the extreme sunlight reflected off the sand dunes and was so bright you couldn't buy or beg a pair of sunglasses. The midafternoon sun was so blinding it often proved impossible to tell a tank from an armoured car at a distance of 2 kilometres. Evening or during the day, in still air or in sandstorms, there wasn't a single element of the desert's environment that didn't present its own peculiar challenge.

The sandstorms were particularly ferocious and on a scale few could have imagined. Vast sand clouds were often blown in by the phenomenon Libyans called the *Ghibli*: dry, desiccating desert winds that came from nowhere and blew with such ferocity they overturned vehicles and brought offensive operations to a standstill. The electrical disturbances that accompanied them also played havoc with radio reception, caused compasses to behave erratically, and saw more than a few operations by the British Air Force, which enjoyed considerable air superiority, either scaled back or abandoned. A *Ghibli* usually came in from the south-east, reduced visibility to virtually zero, had the potential to last several days and in the process to move unimaginably large quantities of sand and all but bury the few roads along which supply lines had to be moved. In March 1941 Rommel himself wrote of one such encounter as he was making his way by car to his headquarters in Sirte:

> We really had no idea of the tremendous force of such a sandstorm. Huge clouds of a reddish blue hue obscured our vision and the car crawled slowly along the coastal road. Often the wind was so strong that one could not drive

at all. Sand dripped down the car windows like water. It was only with difficulty that we could breathe through a handkerchief held in front of the face and perspiration poured from our bodies in the unendurable heat. That was the ghibli.

In Egypt the winds were known as the *khamseen,* and in Morocco they called them *siroccos.* They were the *chiheli* in the northern Sahara, the *ouahdy* in the central Sahara, the *irifi* on the coast, and were the hot, moist winds of the *habub* when they blew across northern Sudan. They came in like clockwork every year, and were so thick with sand they could suffocate a camel. The Australian journalist Hector Dinning, who was with our troops in Egypt in the Great War, said they began so softly, almost like a zephyr, that the uninitiated would be seen giving thanks to Allah for the cooling breeze and before the hour was spent was 'calling out to Allah for deliverance'. They blew for days. Dinning spoke of men who were 'disgusted with having to continue to live', who 'couldn't smoke, couldn't speak, without swallowing the gale'. And then, on the third morning, the serene blue of a fresh desert sky smiled at you as though nothing had happened.

Sandstorms caused particular problems for pilots in World War II. While wind speeds on the ground reached 60–80 kilometres per hour, at heights above 900 metres the wind could be blowing at 150 kilometres per hour or more. Fortunately the terrain was mostly favourable if one had to make an emergency landing, which although not without risk was usually the preferred option for aircrews when the only other choice was bailing out and coming down somewhere where there wasn't a wing to shelter them from the blazing sun. And the Afrika Korps had a standing offer of gold pieces for any Arab who located Allied airmen and brought them back alive.

The almost complete absence of any meaningful infrastructure in the North African desert in World War II made fighting a war there very frustrating. The complete lack of railway lines so bedevilled the Germans that a study was made of what it would take to construct one: at least 60,000 tonnes of shipping space would have been needed for all of the locomotives, railway carriages, rails and sleepers, and a minimum of twelve uninterrupted months would be required to construct a line first from Tripoli to Benghazi and an additional three months for a secondary line to Derna, near Tobruk. The idea was shelved almost as soon as its logistics were realised.

To add to the sand and the dust and the wind and the absence of a railway there were the locusts, which were always threatening to breed and multiply and block out the sun with their unending cloud-like migrations. Alexander Aaronsohn, a Romanian-born Jew serving in the Ottoman Army in the Great War, wrote of their capacity for destruction:

> While I was travelling in the south, another menace to our people's welfare had appeared: the locusts. From the Sudan they came in tremendous hosts – black clouds of them that obscured the sun. It seemed as if Nature had joined in the conspiracy against us. These locusts were of the species known as the pilgrim, or wandering, locust; for forty years they had not come to Palestine, but now their visitation was like that of which the prophet Joel speaks in the Old Testament. They came full-grown, ripe for breeding; the ground was covered with the females digging in the soil and depositing their egg-packets, and we knew that when they hatched we should be overwhelmed, for there was not a foot of ground in which these eggs were not to be found. Not only was every green leaf devoured, but the very bark was peeled from the trees, which stood out white and lifeless, like skeletons. The fields were stripped to the ground, and the old men of our villages, who had given their lives to cultivating these gardens and vineyards, came out of the synagogues where they had been praying

*and wailing, and looked on the ruin with dimmed eyes.
Nothing was spared. The insects, in their fierce hunger,
tried to engulf everything in their way. I have seen Arab
babies, left by their mothers in the shade of some tree,
whose faces had been devoured by the oncoming swarms
of locusts before their screams had been heard. I have
seen the carcasses of animals hidden from sight by the
undulating, rustling blanket of insects'.*

In the Old Testament locusts were the eighth of ten
plagues sent down by Jehovah upon Egypt and its recalcitrant
pharaoh. In North Africa locusts live solitary lives in the
continent's grasslands, but unlike ants and bees that swarm
as a single organism, a locust's trigger for flight occurs only
when its hind legs are touched. This random contact signals
to the locust that its environment is becoming crowded, and
can lead to a sort of insect version of a nuclear chain reaction,
which begins with lots of initial close-knit groups that then
merge into one giant airborne cloud. On 3 April 1915 Herbert
Reynolds of the 9th Battery, 3rd Field Artillery Brigade had left
his encampment outside Cairo and had been marching into
the city when he encountered a locust swarm:

*All day a huge cloud of locusts have been overhead. One
cannot realise what a locust plague is until seeing one;
looking at the sun is like looking at the moon. The density
of the moving swarm of insects acts in the same manner
as a smoked glass. The whole sky seemed to be a moving
mass of them.*

The widespread loathing in respect to locusts was not of
course confined to our soldiery, but is universal and as old as
agriculture itself. In 1945 an Anti-Locust Unit was formed in
Palestine, and the men in it given the job of chasing swarms of
locusts wherever they might appear across the Arab world and

to poison as many of them as they could by feeding them bran embedded with insecticide. One of the greatest-ever locust hunters was the legendary Charles Cholmondeley, the 5th Marquess of Cholmondeley and a direct descendant of Robert Walpole, Great Britain's first prime minister. Cholmondeley spent years in the desert after World War II determined to be the man who would rid Arabia of every single living locust. It was always going to be an impossible task, but undeterred he would drive off into the desert, often for months at a time, and turn up in villages in places like Yemen that were so utterly remote and off the map it was said the village women would come out from their homes with straw to feed to his jeep.

Locusts were bad, but at least they came and went. The heat was always there. But as hot as it was, particularly in the summer months, the temperature did mercifully drop off the closer one got to the coast. Before 1942, the hottest day recorded in the Sahara was 58 degrees Celsius at Al Aziziya, 41 kilometres south-west of Tripoli in 1922, but this was an anomaly. Summer temperatures along the coastal belt – the area within which much of the North African campaign was fought in World War II – ranged from 32 to 38 degrees Celsius, uncomfortable but bearable providing one was properly provisioned. Unless you were unfortunate enough to be in a tank, which could get as hot as 71 degrees!

There are plenty of tales of tank crews eating scrambled eggs that were cooked on the exteriors of their machines. There are even stories of soldiers opening up their tins of bully beef only to have it drip out after being left in the sun and turning to liquid. The heat made it impossible to make accurate observations over the ground of more than a kilometre or so due to the vibration of the air from heat haze. Extreme heat also meant the density of the air was extremely low, which in turn meant aircraft needed far longer runways before they could generate enough lift to take off. Aircraft cockpits also had to be covered over so their instruments wouldn't be too hot to touch should their pilots need to hurriedly become airborne.

The real heat, though, was inland, on the other side of an unending escarpment and its adjoining plateau and beyond in the Qattara Depression, a giant 19,000 square kilometre sinkhole filled with salt pans and marshes with an average depth of 60 metres. Even today you can find wreckage of the cars and trucks of the Long Range Desert Group, the reconnaissance and raiding unit of the British Army (comprising some New Zealanders but no Australians) whose recruits were experts in desert navigation and survival techniques, men whom Rommel would later describe as doing more damage to his forces than any other single unit of comparable size.

Desert warfare is full of its own peculiarities that make fighting in them unlike that of any other campaign. At the conclusion of the desert campaigns of the Great War a report on the health of our soldiers noted that it was 'remarkable' that the cases of sickness were as low as they were considering the troops had little rest, no opportunity for recreation, a lack of shelter from the sun, makeshift sanitation, and were subject to the 'scantiness' of drinking water. 'Remarkable' was putting it mildly if a 30 May 1916 report by the Australian Light Horse Field Ambulance is accurate. At the camps of the 6th and 7th Light Horse, inspectors found flies were breeding unhindered in manure dumps, buried vegetables were laden with fly eggs, neither regiment had its required portable incinerators, there were twelve men to every bell tent and most had no change of underclothes. There was no muslin for fly-proofing of plates and pans, no grease traps or clean towels (not even in the officers' mess), and not only was the provisioning of troughs so cooks could wash their hands scant at best, there were no records detailing the health of the cooks or any real interest shown in keeping an eye on the general health of the men whose job it was to prepare the regiment's daily meals.

As if fighting the enemy in a desert wasn't penitence enough. You had to contend with the cooks as well.

Chapter Two
We Were Soldiers

Allah made the Sudan. And Allah laughed.

– old Sudanese proverb

Australia was an association of six colonies on the verge of Federation when the Boer War broke out in South Africa in 1899, and by the time the fighting there was done in 1902, we had become a nation. But while it may have been the first war in which Australians fought as a nation, it was not the first overseas conflict in which Australians participated, nor was it the first time an Australian government did all it could to ingratiate itself with the British by sending troops to fight in a conflict on the other side of the world. That rather dubious honour belongs to the New South Wales colonial government in a decision it made in February 1885 to send the New South Wales Contingent to help the British extricate themselves from a messy entanglement in the north African nation of Sudan. It was our country's first – and largely forgotten – commitment of troops to a foreign war.

British colonial forces had been on the losing end of a fight against an insurgency led by the charismatic Muhammad Ahmad, a religious leader who had proclaimed himself Mahdi – a redeemer and liberator of Islam. Ahmad had promised the people he would throw off the British-backed Turko–Egyptian rulers who had been repressing the Sudanese with an iron fist ever since the Egyptian ruler Muhammad Ali Pasha, with British acquiescence, invaded Sudan with 5000 troops in

1820 and established the era of Egyptian–Ottoman rule – the *Turkiyah*.

It can be assumed our troops knew little and likely cared even less about the tempestuous history of British colonial rule in Africa. That was certainly the case with Robert Weir. Born in the New South Wales coastal town of Gerringong, not far from Kiama on the state's south coast, Weir knew very little about Sudan and its troubled capital, Khartoum. He would have known nothing of its politics or that Khartoum, just forty years earlier, had been little more than a fishing village, a collection of grass and cone-shaped mud huts – *tukuls* – at the confluence of the Blue and White Nile rivers. He wouldn't have known of its origins, about how it was established originally as a military outpost and only really began to flourish in the late 1840s when the Turko–Egyptians sought to build their so-called 'equatorial empire'. He wouldn't have known about the city's burgeoning ivory trade, or that you could buy an elephant's tusk for upwards of 168 shillings – a huge sum at the time that attracted all sorts of undesirables and drifters to converge upon the place, adding to the already complex mix of competing political and economic interests.

Back in Australia, citizens were becoming increasingly conscious of the fact that the 'tyranny of distance' – which separated Australia from trouble in Europe and elsewhere – was no longer any guarantor of safety. The feeling was that foreign conflicts now carried with them the potential to wash up on distant shores. The capability of navies to cross oceans and take the fight to far-off enemies had been uppermost in the minds of our military planners ever since the Crimean War in 1854, a conflict that saw the construction of a series of coastal defences and gun emplacements at the entrances to harbours in Sydney, Hobart and Melbourne, among others, all built to deter a Russian fleet that never bothered to come, having better things to do than train its guns upon an emerging but insignificant British colony.

Travelling theatre troupes depicted the battles fought in foreign wars – from the American Civil War to the Franco–Prussian War and Britain's Zulu Wars in South Africa – in the form of illustrated panoramas, which they erected in towns up and down the east coast of Australia during the latter half of the nineteenth century. These exhibitions were heavily patronised by a populace fascinated with anything that shed light on what was happening beyond our shores, many of whom were first generation immigrants with families left behind in far-off lands. Information was getting to us faster than it ever had before. By the 1880s a telegram could bring news of foreign conflicts to our doorsteps within a single day, providing us with the ability to be proactive in world affairs. Suddenly we were in a position to do more than just sit on our collective behinds and reflect on what might have been. Now, at last, we could make a diplomatic response, assert some influence. Be a participant.

By the early 1880s, while Robert Weir was still a teenager, the situation in Sudan had become ripe for revolt. The Sudanese were happy to give their support to anyone who promised them greater autonomy. It all began getting out of hand from London's point of view in August 1882, when the British government sent troops to the Suez Canal in an attempt to restore stability to an increasingly unstable Egyptian government. The British General Charles George Gordon was sent to Khartoum by the British prime minister, William Gladstone, to extricate foreign nationals from the city, and under no circumstances was he to stay and defend it. But the popular military figure had some very different ideas regarding the possible consequences of retreat, fearing that if Britain pulled out then the empire could lose all of the Sudan, and eventually even Egypt, to the Mahdist uprising. So in an act of political defiance that would have made Douglas MacArthur proud, Gordon defied his commander-in-chief and chose to stay and fight.

The New South Wales colonial government sent troops to Sudan just three years shy of the 100th anniversary of British settlement. It was the first time a contingent of soldiers was sent to fight in an overseas war – if you exclude the 'Soldiers of Fortune' who went to fight with the Waikato Regiments in the Maori War in New Zealand in 1860. Our involvement began on 6 February 1885, when news reached the government of New South Wales of the defeat of the 7000 Egyptian and Sudanese troops under Gordon's command. The news was accompanied by a request for assistance. Gordon's garrison at Khartoum had endured a ten-month siege by 50,000 Dervish soldiers, finally succumbing late in the night of 25 January when the Mahdists crossed the River Nile and charged the city's walls. Gordon was killed. His head was severed, put on a stick and taken to the Mahdi as a spoil of war. His headless body was then dumped in the river, just two days before Gladstone's relief mission arrived.

The impact Gordon's death had in New South Wales was significant. 'When General Gordon was killed in the Sudan in 1885,' wrote Private Richard White, a former boot maker with the New South Wales Contingent's A Company, 'the colonies went into mourning. Melbourne school children wrote essays on "General Gordon as Hero", and statues were erected to commemorate his sacrifice to Empire.'

The day after New South Wales received its request for assistance, Major General Sir Edward Strickland was among the first to suggest sending an expeditionary force to the Sudan to help avenge Gordon's death. Acting premier William Dalley (the premier, Alexander Stuart, was convalescing in New Zealand and was none too keen on Sudanese intervention) also thought it a splendid idea, and immediately cabled London with an offer of troops. A reply in the affirmative arrived on 14 February, and without bothering to consult Parliament, which in any case was conveniently in recess, Dalley began preparations to raise a mixed force comprising infantry and artillery. It didn't matter to Dalley that the whole exercise was in clear violation of the Constitution, which prevented troops from being dispatched beyond our shores to fight in another country. One should never let a Constitution get in the way of a bloody good fight!

It was a decision without precedent, the first time that a British colony *anywhere* in the empire sent an armed force overseas to assist Mother England. *The Sydney Morning Herald* certainly seemed to appreciate the significance of the event and with just a hint of hyperbole – and no doubt egged on by Dalley in the form of a promise to send along a *Herald* reporter to cover the forthcoming bloodshed – called our offer of assistance 'almost unique in the history of the world'. To further sweeten the offer to London, Dalley cabled Gladstone and told him his government had plenty of money in its treasury and would be more than happy to meet all of the contingent's expenses.

Just why New South Wales, alone among the Australian colonies, was so enthusiastic about sending troops to Africa for a set of such ill-defined objectives and without a clear understanding of what awaited our troops on the ground is not clear but, if you do a little digging, hidden political motives begin to emerge. For Dalley at least, the benefits of putting so many lives in jeopardy were obvious. He wanted assistance from London in putting a brake on Victorian claims in the push towards federation, there were ongoing negotiations with the British government over a Royal Navy base at Sydney's Garden Island, and he wanted better terms and broader access to international money markets as well as freer trading terms in an era of growing protectionism.

Dalley wasn't exactly what you'd call a popular figure in the eyes of the government of William Gladstone ever since he suggested that Britain should give up northeastern New Guinea to colonial Germany and content itself with the southeast region of the country nearest to Australia. The idea was poorly received by Gladstone's expansionist parliamentarians, and it was felt in Sydney that it was time to claw back a measure of goodwill. What better way than to offer to join them in a foreign war? Never before, or since, had an Australian government's decision to send men to war been so blatantly political and unconscionably self-serving.

Oblivious to the politics, volunteers came to Sydney from every back road, from every pub and outhouse. In Bathurst, 2000 wellwishers gathered at the railway station (which had opened just nine years earlier) to see their fourteen volunteers off to Sydney. In Kiama Private Robert Weir, #392 of D company, was one of that region's nine volunteers who left for Sydney on the steamer *Illawarra*. In the 1880s Kiama was the largest of the local towns along the New South Wales south coast and, just as importantly, was the only one with a courthouse, which doubled as the enlistment and recruitment centre.

The eight men who departed Kiama with Robert Weir on that day were John Eppel, a twenty-one-year-old machinist; William Arnold, twenty-four years old and single; James Armstrong, a twenty-two-year-old dairyman and Wesleyan with an impressive shock of fair hair; Thomas Newing, a nineteen-year-old labourer; John O'Brien, a twenty-year-old carpenter and Roman Catholic with a scar on his arm who would go on to serve in the Boer War fifteen years later; George Vance, a twenty-four-year-old bank clerk; John Walker, a nineteen-year-old compositor who, upon arrival in Sydney, proved unfit for service and returned home to Kiama; and Robert Jervis, a twenty-seven-year-old labourer with blue eyes and light-coloured hair who was already a long way from his place of birth in the Parish of Tempelcarn in Donegal, Ireland. They all marched to the wharf behind the Kiama Brass Band, before the tear-filled eyes and aching hearts of mothers, sisters, friends and sweethearts. The whole town turned out to see them off, and none of Kiama's residents could ever remember there being a grander day. In the words of the *Kiama Independent*, 'the maiden sword of New South Wales … had been girded'.

But as grand as it was, nothing could compare with the scenes that were awaiting them in Sydney.

Two hundred thousand people lined Sydney's streets and crammed into every nook and cranny of Circular Quay to see the New South Wales Contingent (divided into infantry and artillery) depart on board the troopships SS *Iberia* and SS *Australasia,* which sailed off through Sydney Heads on 3 March 1885. The two vessels were laden with 771 men, only 40 per cent of whom were born in Australia, and on their shoulders they carried the applause, the cheers, the hopes, the dreams and the best wishes of an emerging nation. Three days into the voyage a Private F. Sessle was put ashore on Kangaroo Island, grief-stricken after learning that his wife had been killed in a boating accident on Sydney Harbour on the very day of his departure, after falling from a boat in the midst of the melee of vessels jousting to bid the contingent farewell.

'Young Australia,' wrote journalist J. M. Sanders in the *Evening News,* 'is at last fairly embarked on the stormy sea of inter-colonial strife. For the first time in her history she is to try the terrible hazards of war. As is only natural on such a momentous occasion, much patriotism, loyalty and enthusiasm has been shown.'

But not everyone shared in the enthusiasm. The national magazine *The Bulletin* was opposed to our involvement ever since the day Dalley announced it, and public meetings organised to raise funds to help with the troops' deployment were never more than only moderately attended. Enthusiasm there was, however, on the streets of Sydney that day, described by the press as the most festive occasion in the history of the young colony. There was a sprinkling of colonial naiveté too, as seen in a comment by one of the contingent's commanders, who looked forward, he said, to 'the earliest opportunity of a brush with the Arabs'. Little could he or anyone else have known that there wouldn't be any brushes. Indeed, the New South Wales Contingent would see almost no fighting in Sudan, and the nine men who would later perish were all taken by disease, mostly on the journey home.

Few accounts of the New South Wales Contingent's time in the Sudan can compare to Private Tom Gunning's memoir *Those Sudan Days,* published in 1947. Gunning's recollections provide unmatched insights into the everyday life of Australia's first expeditionary force. His memoir begins on the day they departed:

> *We were eager to be off to this mysterious Sudan, where 50,000 Arabs were embarrassing Britain ... ours was no under-cover-of-night departure; no slogans advising people to seal lips and save ships. Quite the reverse. We had passed through medical examinations; we had been bellowed at on the parade ground; we carried our old rifles – complete with saw-edged bayonets – and all this was rounded off with the glorious feeling of wearing the splendid scarlet and blue uniform. In short, we were soldiers, and Sydney shouted it from the housetops.*
>
> *One of our first shipboard jobs was to dye our brilliant white equipment and pith helmets with the only medium available: tobacco juice. This was probably the introduction of the science of camouflage into Australia's military life and a foreshadowing of the days when jungle green was to become fashionable for soldiers. A pair of special goggles was issued to combat glare and dust. When not in actual use they were usually slipped on up to the helmet, giving one the appearance of a modern speedway ride.*

Once in Sudan, Gunning lost no time in pointing out the mismatch in weaponry that favoured, to everyone's surprise, the enemy:

> *These dark gentry were exceedingly nasty customers and,*

surprising as it may seem, were equipped with better arms than the British. Each man had a range of weapons which chilled the blood of many a Guardsman. In the first place they each carried an American Remington rifle – a far more effective weapon than ours. This was supplemented by two spears, a 'throwing stick' shaped something like a boomerang, and a terrible ham-stringing 'knife-dagger' in the form of a capital J [similar, the author supposes, to an Omani Khanjar] the size of a large carving knife and razor-sharp on every edge. To this formidable kit of tools was added a shield – altogether a strange and deadly outfit, combining the old and the new.

Gunning went on to describe how the Mahdists poisoned their waterholes, which not only made the water useless but ruined the contingent's specially made water filters. The absence of filters necessitated the desalination of sea water on the troopships in Suakin Harbour and its delivery to the contingent in bags, called *jerbas*, made from animal skins – unpalatable enough vessels to have to drink from, the only saving grace of which was not knowing which particular animal the 'bag' had come from. No doubt the contingent would have preferred thinking about how best to rout the enemy and getting a few Arabs in the sights of their rifles. But the truth was it spent the bulk of its deployment working along the Suakin–Berber railway, a task however not without its own peculiar dangers. And it was the stillness of those black Sudanese nights that Gunning was at his most wary:

The natives lurked in the enveloping darkness, ready, and more than willing, to pounce on an unwary sentry with a specially selected spear. In this midnight stalking they used great stealth and patience. One procedure was to first steal some grease from the railway construction job, smear their bodies all over, then roll in the sand like a milkman's horse. Thus camouflaged, they used to lie flat on their faces and commence a tortuously slow slither-crawl towards our camp. Usually the stalker would cut a small bush, push it forward to arm's length, then inch by inch slither up to it.

Not all the natives were hostile, of course. One tribe, the Amaras, gave great service as night scouts. It was when we were camped at Otao, twenty-three miles inland, that one of their patrols discovered a Fuzzy Wuzzy who had come to the wells for water, bringing with him an old donkey and two jerbas. Without ceremony the gentle Amaras hacked off his left hand at the wrist and continued on their way without another thought of the incident. Next morning one of the mounted infantry, hearing groaning, cautiously approached through the thick mimosa scrub and found the victim, who was taken to hospital. The donkey, however, was somehow acquired by the officer's cook, who used it to carry his valise. This soldier actually brought the animal back to Australia, where it lived in luxury at a zoo, eventually expiring quietly in a paddock at Narellan, NSW.

Upon his return to Sydney, Gunning and all the men of the contingent received the Mayor of Sydney's Silver Sudan Medal, with the Sydney coat of arms below a semi-circular suspender – pierced to take a ribbon – and on the reverse circular, a letter that reads: 'Presented by the citizens of Sydney. T. Playfair, Mayor, 1885.' The medal is currently in the possession of the Australian War Memorial in Canberra. Gunning went on to serve in the Boer War as a private with the New South Wales Mounted Rifles, survived that too, and, after saving the life of a swimmer at Manly in 1908, he received the Silver Medal of the Royal Shipwreck Relief and Humane Society of NSW. When he died in 1949 Thomas Gunning bequeathed to the Australian War Memorial a framed Union

Jack he received as a gift while in London for Queen Victoria's Diamond Jubilee, a Boer War sword and scabbard, two rifles, and a bandolier he found at Paardeberg after the surrender of the Boer leader General Piet Cronje. To the Mitchell Library in Sydney he left a photograph of the New South Wales Contingent that had been presented to Queen Victoria, and a collection of books and photographs.

What we know of the conditions that the New South Wales Contingent experienced in Sudan was brought back to us by the handful of journalists who accompanied them. In one of the earliest examples of petty inter-colonial rivalry the New South Wales government decided to limit the number of journalists covering the conflict to just four, all of them members of the pro-war Sydney press, much to the disgust of reporters from Melbourne and elsewhere. The decision so angered Joseph Melvin, a war correspondent for *The Bulletin* and Melbourne's *Daily Telegraph*, that he smuggled himself aboard the *Iberia* posing as a member of the crew. (Melvin, one of the most daring and dedicated reporters of his time, had a few years earlier dragged an injured Ned Kelly away from gunfire and into a hotel in Glenrowan, interviewed him and then telegraphed their exchange to *The Argus* for the scoop of the decade.) Melvin wrote the following account of the arrival of the *Iberia* in the Red Sea port of Suakin on 29 March 1885:

> *The reception of the Australians was most enthusiastic, and every hour we have spent in Suakin has shown that the contingent is highly popular with the [British] forces in the camp. We hear in all directions expressions of the great uprush of national spirit and kindly feeling between her colonies, which has been created by this movement on the part of Australia. The appearance and physique of the contingent has been much admired. The troops are spoken of as a very suitable class of men for the work before them. The horses also have elicited the highest praise.*

It's not certain when Melvin threw off his guise, but he obviously did as he was soon working from Sudan with media accreditation and he remained comfortably ensconced with the infantry contingent until the end of the conflict. His reports, with their references to the esteem in which our men were held, and particularly the high regard shown to our horses, was a tantalising precursor of the praise for the Light Horsemen and their Walers in the First World War. Here in the Sudan, however, there would be no glory.

The infantry contingent landed in Sudan armed with Alexander Henry rifles fitted with saw-back bayonets, a greatly inferior weapon compared to the American Remingtons that their opponents possessed. The artillery contingent, who had to leave the field guns at home because they were considered too cumbersome for Sudanese conditions, were given six nine-pound Mark II field guns, all of which were brought back to Australia at the end of the conflict – payment, it was said, for the 223 horses we took there and then handed over as a parting gift to the Royal Artillery. In addition to the men of the infantry and artillery there was also a thirty-six-man ambulance corps, two chaplains, and two interpreters – a total of 771 men.

A week after their arrival the contingent was attached to the Nile Field Force of the British commander Lord Wolseley, and immediately set off on their first, and only, real engagement – an attack upon a Mahdist force under the command of Osman Digna, considered by many to be the Mahdi's ablest and most daring general. The engagement that followed, sadly for those who had come so far to fight, was something of an anti-climax. As Lieutenant William Cope noted in his diary:

The New South Wales Infantry were posted on the heights commanding the hills, and in advancing to the posts allotted to them 3 men were hit, whilst the bullets whizzed past harmlessly, one of our fellows was wounded in the shoulder. Another was shot in the foot and hopped along for some yards before he realised how seriously he was hurt. Several others were hit but all in all, the thing ended rather disappointedly, as Osman Digna retreated without showing much fight. We then burned the village, a wretched affair of grass humpies and in doing so consumed a quantity of ammunition which popped about and made things lively for a time. We then marched back to our camp, and after a short breakfast commenced our return to Suakin. As with every army since the formation of Julius Caesar's First Legion, the force was alive with rumour ... the contingent would go to India, it would go to England, it would go to Malta or Gibraltar as a garrison force, it would stay in the Sudan until their bones whitened!

But following the encounter with Osman Digna, the force would only make a series of dreary marches through the desert, past the putrid remains of slain Arabs, such as those that had been left to bake in the sun after a fight with the British in April at Baker's Zareba, described in the diary of one of the contingent's men, Arthur C. Barrett, published on the 50th anniversary of the campaign in *The Sydney Mail* on 27 February, 1935:

2 April: We camped at night on the rocks, C company (the author's company) being posted on a small hill to the right of the camp, expecting the enemy. One of our chaps raised a false alarm and fired a shot ... shots were continually exchanged. One of our men was shot, and the enemy at last became so bold that the big gun posted on the hill was fired. After spending a rather disagreeable night we were called up early in the morning (April 3) for tea (half-pint per man), and shortly afterwards marched for the enemy's village, which we reached in about an hour. But the enemy had retired and taken post on the hills, from which they opened fire on us, the bullets whistling over us harmlessly for a time.

Three of our men were wounded altogether and one Englishman shot dead. After about three hours' firing the cavalry burnt the village ... and we returned to camp, where water was served out to us. After this we started for Suakin and reached Baker's Zareba, a fortified place about halfway. Here a bloody battle had been fought a few days before, many camels and a number of dead Arabs lying about on the sand. One hole which had been dug was said to contain 80 of the Arabs. We camped for the night at the Zareba, and nothing of note occurred. Thus ended Good Friday, April 3rd, 1885, for us.

There would be a lot of sweat expended by the contingent in the heat and dust of Sudan, but barely a glimpse of the sort of glory they had been hoping for. They had even been forced to give up, at the insistence of the English generals, the wearing of their own colonial red coats lest they be confused with the 'real' red-coated soldier, the Briton. They were the apprentices to the master craftsmen. The entire Sudanese campaign in fact couldn't have been summed up better than it was in that matter-of-fact observation of Arthur Barrett: 'Nothing of note occurred.'

On 2 June 1885 the *Kiama Independent* ran a story filed by William Lambie, a correspondent for the *Sydney Morning Herald*:

I must pause here. The sun's rays are fading in the dusk away to the west over the purple mists of (the village) Hasheen. Away on the open ground outside the shipping there is a flash of fire, and three volleys in the air ring out on the evening silence. It is poor Weir's funeral. This morning the sickness finished its work, and the patient, who was worn to a skeleton when I saw him on Tuesday, passed quietly away. He had been hopeful of himself up to the day before his death, when he became delirious and never regained full consciousness. This is our first loss. The funeral was attended by Major Blanchard, Lieutenant Airey, Lieutenant Pritchard, and Private Downey, and the guards formed the firing party.

Lambie was a true giant of Australian journalism. A few weeks into the Sudan campaign he was ambushed by Arabs on camel back and shot in the right leg, becoming the first Australian war correspondent ever to be wounded in the course of his work. In February 1900 he became the first Australian journalist to be killed in the field when he was shot in the back while escaping on horseback from forty Boers near Jasfontein. It didn't have to have ended that way. When the Boer commander was told by Lambie's companion that his men had just killed a war correspondent, he was furious: 'Sir, you dress like two British officers, you ride out with a fighting party, and you try to ride off at a gallop under the very muzzles of our rifles when we tell you to surrender! You can blame no one but yourselves for this days' work.'

On 12 May, eleven days after Robert Weir's death, a gunner with the New South Wales artillery, twenty-five-year-old Edward Lewis, died of fever, himself a patient on the *Ganges* with Weir. The two men were buried side by side, under a modest mound of rock and stone on a hill outside Suakin. Later an obelisk was raised and the grave surrounded by a small iron fence. Suakin was a nothing place, a backwater, and soon lost any strategic significance it had. So when the British and Australian forces withdrew to Port Sudan, the elements began their work, eroding the marker, and in the 129 years since it was placed there Suakin has grown to become a city, spreading out across the hills that once surrounded it and obliterating any reminder that an Australian grave was ever there. My own efforts through the Australian War Memorial to try to find out what might have become of it have come to nothing. It is wishful thinking to hope the resting places of Robert Weir and Edward Lewis have remained undisturbed, but one reminder of Weir's sacrifice that is still with us can be found at the Kiama General Cemetery, Row A, Grave #51, which reads:

IN MEMORY OF ROBERT WEIR
OF THE NEW SOUTH WALES CONTINGENT
WHO DIED AT SUAKIN 1ST MAY 1885
ERECTED AS A MARK OF RESPECT BY HIS
COMRADES AND FRIENDS

George Rauchle was another of Australia's first soldiers dispatched overseas. Born in 1866 at Emu Plains, near Orange west of Sydney, he would bear witness to several wars and the rapid changes brought by industrialisation in the nineteenth and twentieth centuries. The second son of German and Irish immigrants, George watched as Cobb & Co. stagecoaches escorted by armed troopers passed through Orange on their way to the Blue Mountains railhead in the 1870s. He was there on St Patrick's Day 1877 when the rail line at last came to Orange and watched as the final spike was driven in by a local resident, Thomas Daitch. In 1951, at the age of eighty-five, George could still recall how the streets of Orange were transformed after dark when their old oil-fed lamps gave way to gaslights. 'What an adventure it was, to be taken down the town on Saturday night and see the brilliantly lighted streets and shop windows.' One day in the early 1870s George and his father attended an auction in the foyer of an Orange hotel where a large framed print of a British redcoat officer with sword drawn leading his men into battle went under the hammer. 'I never forgot that picture,' George would later say. 'As I grew older it was frequently in my mind.'

When he left school George got a job at a department

store, but soon tired of that and thought it might be interesting to become a saddler. His father thought so too, and arranged an apprenticeship with one of Orange's leading saddlers, John Paul. It began promisingly enough but ended abruptly the day George tipped a bucket of dye over the head of John Paul's daughter, who used to give him cheek whenever her father was out of the office. He then worked as a coachbuilder, but that didn't last, nor did a stint as a blacksmith, although the stone-and-iron fence that surrounds the Orange Courthouse to this very day remains as a testament to George's craftsmanship. Aged eighteen and feeling restless, George remembered the painting of the British redcoat.

> *I heard conversations in the smithy about the trouble Britain was having in the Sudan, and about the Mahdi who was causing it all. Bidding farewell to my parents I set off for the city, and the next day went to Victoria Barracks. I was duly sworn in, and promised to serve Her Most Gracious Majesty, Queen Victoria, to the best of my youthful ability. The colony was shocked when word came through that General Gordon had been killed at Khartoum. We sailed for the Sudan in March of that year. Was I thrilled!*

Up to that time just about the worst thing George Rauchle had ever experienced in his eighteen years was the day he had to walk home from school in the pouring rain. He was wet to the skin and home never felt so distant. But his father, knowing his son was out there under Orange's blackened skies, rode out on his horse and scooped him up. 'Mother peeled off my wet clothes, warmed me, and put me to bed. I will never forget that awful experience.' But worse would soon come. In just a few weeks he would be laid low for days on end by a deathly bout of seasickness while '500 miles from Aden' on his way to fight the Mahdi for queen and country:

My dear Mother,

I take up my pen with the greatest of pleasure. I have had a great seasickness, it was on me for about nine days, it was the greatest sickness that I had in all my life. For about six days I was between life and death. For five days I laid in my bunk and hardly ate anything. But now I cannot get enough to eat. We do not get the good food that they were talking about in the paper, but it is better than we got in the barracks.

You must excuse me for not keeping my promise to meet you at the Crown Hotel, for I could not get away from the ship. And when we were down we had to fall in and march back to the place where you saw me in the morning. They put us in the train and I jumped out and straight up to the Crown, but you were not there and I went straight back to the station. But the train was gone, it was ten minutes past eight but that was too late then. As for the referred pay I do not know what I will be able to do for I lost the paper that I told father that I had.

I was sorry to see that father was so much cut up about me going to the war and you too, but keep up your spirit for I will return some day, perhaps it won't be long. When you write to Melbourne get the address of your stepmother and sister so if I go to England I will be able to go and see them. But I suppose I must tell you something about the voyage. We have had no sickness aboard our ship, we only had four horses to die in the voyage. As for myself I am as happy going to war as I would be going to a tea meeting in Orange.

If you should happen to see any of my old mates in Orange you can tell Father to tell them that there was only twelve out of the town had courage enough to go to the fight for the Motherland. Give my best love to all my old mates and give my greatest love to my brother and sister, and father accept the same yourself, so good.

Bye for the present,
Geo Rauchle
Artillery
Suakin
Africa
– if any of the Orange girls ever enquire for me you can tell
them that I don't forget their names, yet.

George never got the chance to emulate the deeds of the redcoat in the painting. He was in the artillery, and the contingent's gunners saw even less action than the infantry, and they barely fired a shot!

When the contingent returned to Sydney on HMT *Arab* on 19 June 1885 the occasion was a milestone in the development of the colony. After a few days at the quarantine station on North Head they were marching through Sydney's streets in their khaki uniforms to a reception at Victoria Barracks attended by the governor and premier and where it was heartily agreed that although the dispatching of the contingent was of little significance militarily, the exercise nonetheless marked an important leap forward in colonial self-confidence.

George enlisted as a permanent soldier at the Victoria Barracks, and returned to Orange where life continued on much as it always had. In 1899 he left for South Africa to fight for Britain again, this time in the Boer War, which he survived without incurring so much as a wound. During the Great War George was deployed to Papua New Guinea but saw no fighting there and returned to Orange to work in his family's orchard at the back of the Racecourse Hotel in Towac Road. He later took a job at the Municipal Council where he became caretaker of the tennis courts in Wade Street. He retired in 1948 and spent the years that followed at his farm on Ophir Road with his brother Harry.

Bravery and a devotion to one's country ran deep in the Rauchle family. In the Great War, George's son Frederick, who was serving as a sapper with the 4th Field Company Engineers near the village of Villers-Bretonneux in northern France, performed an act of heroism that won him Belgium's highest award for bravery, the *Croix de guerre*, their equivalent of the Victoria Cross. Frederick's actions read as follows:

> *4th Field Coy, Private (Lance Corporal) Frederick Norman Rauchle, 4139 AE:*
>
> On 4th May 1918, between Fouilloy and Villers-Bretonneux, this NCO displayed the utmost contempt for a terrific bombardment by S.9 H.E. (High Explosive) shells, of recently vacated gun pits in the vicinity of which the Company is bivouacked. He rescued a badly wounded man from a wrecked dugout, and carried him away to comparative safety. It was an act of great gallantry, and a splendid availability of pluck.

Ray Rauchle is every bit as proud of his 'plucky' father Frederick as he is of his grandfather George. 'My father made the trip to England for the coronation of King George VI, and was the first colonial soldier – *ever* – to stand guard at Buckingham Palace. Here in Orange it was always George who led the town's Anzac Day marches, but when he died it was Frederick who was asked to step in to fill his father's shoes.'

George was the last survivor of the 771 men who left Sydney Harbour for Suakin on 3 March 1885. He died in his sleep, aged 96, in 1963. His death, while it closed a chapter on our nation's first military deployment, was anything but tragic. George had lived a full and rich life. He married three times, travelled the world more than he ever thought he would, and in all likelihood was somehow bulletproof, though it wasn't difficult for the men of the New South Wales Contingent to dodge the few bullets that came their way. Still, he served in three wars and survived them all without so much as a scratch.

Chapter Three
That Bent Old Man

They [the Turks] believed firmly that they were going to
sweep the English off the face of the earth and enter Cairo
in triumph. The ideas of the common soldiers on this subject
were amusing. Some of them declared that the canal was to be
filled up with the sandbags which had been prepared in great
quantities. Others held that thousands of camels would be kept
without water for many days preceding the attack; then the
thirsty animals, when released, would rush into the canal in
such numbers that the troops could march to victory over the
packed masses of drowned bodies.

– Alexander Aaronsohn, *With the Turks in Palestine*, 1916

A hundred years on and World War I seems a long way
away. While the Gallipoli landings and the Charge of
the Light Horse are the stuff of Australian legend and part
of our nation's creation myth, World War I is still mostly
remembered as a European conflict – fought in the trenches
and on the plains of Belgium and France. But the Great
War was not renamed World War I for nothing. Here was
a complex war with multiple belligerents, involving old
territorial disputes and opportunistic new ones laced with
complex political and geopolitical manoeuvring. It was a
conflict that had been brewing away for decades, and is
now recognised by historians as having little to do with

an archduke and an assassin's bullet. By the end of the nineteenth century the manufacturing dominance that Britain had enjoyed over the rest of the world since the beginning of the Industrial Revolution was in terminal decline. The sun was going down on the British Empire, and the vacuum it was leaving behind was slowly being filled by a new industrial juggernaut: Germany. Given impetus by the unification of the German state in 1870, one by one the new Reich was surpassing Britain's productive capacities: first it was steel, then machine tools, chemicals and electrical goods. But it was steel that was the driver of the new Germany, helped along by the high-phosphorous ores in Lorraine that by 1913 saw German foundries smelting twice as much pig iron as Great Britain. Fuelled by its own increasing need for raw materials, Germany also began to build a railway line that, when completed, would stretch from Berlin to Baghdad – the Berlin–Baghdad Express. The railway promised to bind Turkey and Germany together in a new economic and political alliance, an alliance that Turkey hoped would help modernise its ailing military, and that Germany hoped would provide it with a safe overland passage into British-held territories in the Far East. Admiral von Tirpitz, appointed to the position of State Secretary of the Navy in 1897, wanted to build nineteen battleships and twenty-three battle cruisers – just enough, he hoped, to make Great Britain want to avoid war in order to preserve its own superiority. He called it his 'risk theory'. But fleet sizes weren't the only things that were changing. The fuel used to power them was changing too.

Economies everywhere were becoming increasingly oil dependent, and nowhere was this more obvious than in the blue-water navies of Great Britain and Germany. Navies were switching from coal-driven to oil-driven ships, and even for countries with no known oil reserves such as Germany and Great Britain this monumental conversion was seen as a necessary gamble. It took between four and nine hours to fire up a coal-driven ship, while an oil-fuelled engine took only minutes. Where twelve men were needed to keep an oil-fuelled battleship moving, it required 500 to provide the same amount of energy to a coal-driven ship. Oil-driven ships needed one third the engine weight of a coal-driven ship, a quarter of the tonnage in fuel, could operate in a radius four times that of a coal-driven ship, and didn't leave behind them any telltale trails of dense smoke for the enemy to follow.

The benefits of an oil-fuelled navy were many and obvious, and a natural consequence of this was the securing of foreign oilfields and pipelines to keep them moving. 'We must become,' said First Lord of the Admiralty Winston Churchill in 1912, 'the owners, or at any rate the controllers at the source, of at least a proportion of the oil which we require.' The production of petroleum was uppermost in the eyes of imperial policymakers, and nothing would be allowed to interfere with its unfettered supply.

Although the Berlin–Baghdad Express would not be completed until 1940, its very construction shattered English hopes of bringing Mesopotamia peacefully under its influence. But there was another thing the railway provided that was not generally appreciated: convenient access to the oceans of oil below. When German geologists found oil deposits in Kirkuk, Mosul and elsewhere, Deutsche Bank executives moved in and negotiated mineral rights over the land on which the line would be built. And so the stage was set and the economic and strategic battlelines drawn, using steel rails and wooden bearers laid down over a desert landscape. The conflict in Mesopotamia would have an air about it that is oddly familiar to us a century later. The coming war would be all about oil.

Nobody imagined the war in Mesopotamia would drag on for as long and consume the amount of manpower and material that it did – to the point where it threatened to undermine operations on the Western Front itself. It was supposed to be a 'small' war. Sometimes called the Forgotten Campaign, the battles fought there took place in Lower Mesopotamia, the land south of Babylon stretching south towards Basra and the Gulf, home to the ancient civilisations of Assyria and Sumer, described in ancient texts as green and fertile thanks to the abundance of canals that had been cut into the desert like life-giving arteries from the banks of the Tigris and Euphrates rivers.

By the time war broke out in 1914, Mesopotamia was dirt poor after years of neglect under the Ottomans. Local Ottoman rulers had allowed the impressive system of canals to fall into disrepair, and what was once a verdant river plain had been inexorably reclaimed by creeping desert sands. What rainfall there was, which more often than not came not sparingly but in torrents, caused dry riverbeds to overflow and the water to rush off to nowhere in particular and quickly disappear. The once-mighty Tigris was now filled with silt, causing it to run shallow in the heat of summer beneath hot winds full of choking dust that blew in constantly from the Arabian Desert to the south-west and the deserts of Iran to the east. Like deserts everywhere, it proved to be a bad place to fight a war.

The British and Indian battalions of the Mesopotamian Expeditionary Force (MEF) arrived in the Persian Gulf in November 1914 with virtually no practical knowledge of the region, with no reliable maps, barely anything in the way of proper medical facilities, and were totally ill equipped to fight a war in a desert environment. Ill equipped or not, their mission was simple: to keep Britain's oil interests safe from the Turks, who were positioning themselves to threaten the Shatt al-Arab waterway, the oilfields at Abadan, and the Anglo–Persian oil pipeline. Within a month they had captured the towns of Basra and Kurna, taken over a thousand Turkish prisoners with the loss of just 65 of their own troops, and spent most of 1915 working their way slowly up the Tigris River. In September they took the strategic town of Kut just 120 miles from Baghdad and had a remarkable run of victories including Qurna, Shaiba, Amara and Nasiriyah.

The Ottoman Empire and the army that propped it up had become, in the words of historian Basil Liddell Hart, a 'Bent Old Man'. Its armies had been decimated in a disastrous military campaign in the Balkans in 1912–13 and the Great Powers – Great Britain, Germany, the Austro-Hungarian Empire, France and Czarist Russia – had been sharpening their colonial knives for years, salivating at the thought of how best to carve up its increasingly fragile dominions. Gallipoli was supposed to be the campaign that would crack open the old man's skull and finish him off. But the skull – the blood-soaked beaches and trenches of Anzac Cove that we know so well – proved impossible to smash. Evacuating from Gallipoli and the Dardenelles in north-western Turkey in December 1915, the Allies embarked on Plan B: land in Egypt and advance, snake-like, along the Sinai Peninsula from the Suez Canal and up through the Holy Land. By doing this the whole wretched empire, instead of being smashed in the head, might just be cut off at its ankles.

It had not been Britain's intention in early 1915 to occupy any of the 60,000 square kilometres of the Sinai Peninsula, but the thought of the waterway becoming a no-man's-land separating Briton from Turk and blasted to bits in the process was unacceptable, and so a defensive line was established east of it in the Sinai with headquarters at Port Said and an advance headquarters inland at Kantara (which would remain the major supply hub for all Allied forces in the Sinai until the cessation of hostilities in 1918) – a line it was hoped would be enough to deter Turkish aggression. The canal not only had to be defended, it had to be protected. It was too precious to risk being turned into a defensive hole in the ground.

The Suez Canal is one of the world's great engineering feats, linking the Mediterranean and Red seas with a lock-free sea-level waterway. It was, and still is, a strategically important thoroughfare. It always had been – even long before the canal was built. The first authenticated attempt at linking the two seas began during the reign of the Egyptian king Necho II in 610 BCE, when Necho ordered a canal be constructed from the Red Sea west to the River Nile (and so accessing the Mediterranean), a decision that cost 100,000 Egyptians their lives only to be abandoned when it was realised that the construction of a canal might assist their enemies in Persia, should they ever choose to invade. Some tomb inscriptions dating to the 6th Dynasty of the Old Kingdom around 2300 BCE suggest an attempt to dig a canal from the Red Sea to the Nile, and fresh attempts were made by almost every civilisation – Persian, Greek, Roman, Turk and Arab – that followed. Even Napoleon Bonaparte, on his Egyptian expedition of 1798, attempted to revive its construction after finding the vestiges of one of the ancient canals. He abandoned the idea after being told by his engineers that, according to their (horribly incorrect) calculations, the sea level of the Red Sea seemed to be nine metres higher than the waters of the Mediterranean. Cut a canal to join them, Napoleon was warned, and the Red Sea would simply haemorrhage into the Mediterranean and sweep away the entire Nile Delta – and who knows what else!

The canal was finally made possible by public subscriptions raised by the French businessman and developer Ferdinand de Lesseps in the 1850s. De Lesseps raised the money, established the Universal Company of the Suez Maritime Canal, and organised the raising of the 'fellahs', the Egyptian peasantry, to dig it. He refused to allow arguments about mud at its entrance preventing access, or how the sands of the Sinai would simply drift in and fill it all up, to stop him. Construction began on 25 April 1859 and the canal was opened to shipping on 17 November 1869, creating a sea-level waterway between the Mediterranean and the Red Sea and shaving thousands of kilometres off trade routes.

By its very nature, the canal has and always will contain

the potential for conflict. And so it was in good faith that Britain, Germany, France, Spain, the Austro-Hungarian Empire, Italy, Russia, the Netherlands and the Ottoman Empire all signed the Convention of Constantinople on 29 October 1888 to guarantee freedom of access to the Suez Canal regardless of whether the world was at peace or embroiled in war.

Early in 1915 Turkish forces stationed in Palestine began advancing into the Sinai on their way westwards towards the Suez Canal. This was their imperial backyard. The Ottoman Empire had held sway over the eastern Mediterranean since 1299, but by the twentieth century its influence throughout Syria and Palestine had been in a state of steady decline despite still possessing muscle enough to impose its will from Jerusalem to the Russian steppes. Except for eight years in the 1830s when a local vassal named Muhammad Ali raised a rebellion against them, the Turks had ruled Palestine without interruption for centuries. As a result it can be argued their leadership had succumbed to complacency regarding the enormity of the task that confronted them. And so it was with fading hopes of preserving their once-mighty empire that the Ottomans had entered the war in 1914 on the side of Germany and declared their anti-British sentiments early, hoping to stir up Arab resentment against British interests.

By January 1915 the British had 70,000 troops stationed west of the Suez Canal. Many in the British military doubted the wisdom of having so many men tied up in Egypt when France and Belgium were a far more immediate concern, despite the obvious and ongoing threat posed to the canal by the Ottoman Empire. An assault on the canal by Turkish forces under the command of Colonel Kress von Kressenstein of Bavaria on 3 February 1915 proved the wisdom of the build-up of troops, with British and French ships in the canal pulverising the Turkish troops with their guns and forcing the Turks into retreat just hours after they had begun their advance. Three boatloads of Turkish soldiers succeeded in crossing the canal, but were easily repulsed. In the process, von Kressenstein's Suez Expeditionary Force had stretched its supply lines to breaking point. Turkish casualties numbered 2000 killed or wounded and over 700 captured, compared to British losses of four killed and twenty wounded, with Indian losses of 25 killed and 110 wounded.

The highly entertaining and enlightening *With the Turks in Palestine*, written by a young Romanian-born Jewish author and activist named Alexander Aaronsohn, who was forced into serving with the Turkish forces, describes the optimistic mood in the streets of Palestine prior to the Turkish attack:

> *They believed firmly that they were going to sweep the English off the face of the earth and enter Cairo in triumph, and preparations for the march on Suez went on with feverish enthusiasm. The ideas of the common soldiers on this subject were amusing. Some of them declared that the Canal was to be filled up by the sandbags which had been prepared in great quantities. Others held that thousands of camels would be kept without water for many days preceding the attack; then the thirsty animals, when released, would rush into the Canal in such numbers that the troops could march to victory over the packed masses of drowned bodies.*

Aaronsohn's parents were Zionists, having emigrated to Palestine from Romania when Alexander was a child to help establish the pioneer village of Zikhron-Yaákov, near Mount Carmel. Alexander had been immersed in Zionism from an early age, and while his Jewishness didn't prevent him from being pressed into service with the Ottoman Army it did mean he was only permitted to accompany the troops as far as Beersheba in southern Palestine. Aaronsohn's opinion of the Turkish troops was respectful ('trained soldiers, splendid fighting material'), but the same could not be said for his assessment of the Palestinian Arabs. 'The Arab as a soldier,' he wrote, 'is at once stupid and cunning: fierce when victory is on his side, but unreliable when things go against him.' And go against them things certainly would, though not before there were some considerable displays of exuberance in the streets of Jaffa in the weeks leading up to the attack:

> *Parades and celebrations of all kinds in anticipation of the triumphal march into Egypt were taking place, and one day a camel, a dog, and a bull, decorated respectively with the flags of Russia, France, and England, were driven through the streets. The poor animals were horribly maltreated by the natives, who rained blows and flung filth upon them by way of giving concrete expression to their contempt for the Allies. Mr. Glazebrook, the American Consul at Jerusalem, happened to be with me in Jaffa that day; and never shall I forget the expression of pain and disgust on his face as he watched this melancholy little procession of scapegoats hurrying along the street.*

By the time von Kressenstein's army arrived back in southern Palestine they were looking much the worse for it. As Aaronsohn wrote:

> *Just what took place in the attack is known to very few. The English have not seen fit to make public the details, and there was little to be got from the demoralized soldiers who returned to Beersheba. Piece by piece, however, I gathered that the attacking party had come up to the Canal at dawn. Finding everything quiet, they set about getting across, and had even launched a pontoon, when the British, who were lying in wait, opened a terrific fire from the farther bank, backed by armoured locomotives and aeroplanes. 'It was as if the gates of Jehannum were opened and its fires turned loose upon us,' one soldier told*

me. The Turks succeeded in getting their guns into action for a very short while. One of the men-of-war in the Canal was hit; several houses in Ismaïlia suffered damage; but the invaders were soon driven away in confusion, leaving perhaps two thousand prisoners in the hands of the English. If the latter had chosen to do so, they could have annihilated the Turkish forces then and there.

Aaronsohn's description of the demoralising effect the defeat at Suez had on the Turkish troops makes for entertaining reading. At Beersheba he witnessed the defeated army trudge back from the south and saw roads littered with the corpses of camels, mules and horses. Soldiers were walking in disorganised groups, and many had deserted and would have stayed deserted had it not been for a general amnesty. And what of the local Arabs and Palestinians? Thanks – ironically perhaps – to the Allied blockade in the Mediterranean, they were short of sugar, rice, petrol and matches. Cooking fires were being started using flints, and even money was in short supply. Most of the local people had no time left for the Turks after a lifetime of occupation, and hoped the Allies would soon push into Palestine and bring an end to Ottoman rule.

Aaronsohn spoke also of his home in Beirut, the 'Paris of the East', and how the population of Lebanon was overwhelmingly sympathetic to the western powers and would have rallied behind any effort to raise them up to help throw off the Ottoman yolk. But Britain failed to appreciate the wealth of goodwill that country possessed, a failure that would cost them dearly in lives lost when, in three years' time, the Allies under Allenby would be pushing north from Jerusalem to Beirut and beyond. As Aaronsohn wrote:

I could not help wondering at the mistakes of the Allies. If they had understood the situation in Palestine and Syria, how differently this war might have eventuated!

The Lebanon and Syria would have raised a hundred thousand picked men, if the Allies had landed in Palestine. The Lebanon would have fought for its independence as heroically as did the Belgians. Even the Arab population would have welcomed the Allies as liberators. But alas!

The appointment in early 1916 of a new commander to the Mediterranean Expeditionary Force (MEF), Lieutenant-General Archibald Murray, was pivotal in changing British strategy on how best to defend the Suez Canal. Murray convinced London that rather than staying bogged down in a defensive line along its eastern banks they needed to go on the offensive, to push the Ottoman forces back across the Sinai all the way into Palestine.

Murray's strategy, though convincing, wouldn't be easy. The Sinai was a wasteland of sand, rock and desert winds, of waterholes called *hods* filled with brackish water that teased you with the promise of sweetness right up until the foul liquid touched the tongue. None of its paucity of water wells held enough fresh water to meet the needs of an army, and the pace of any advance would be entirely dependent upon the construction of both a road and a water pipeline. There were endemic hierarchical problems within Murray's own military, too. His officers had been too long in Cairo and Alexandria, and in the absence of a fighting war had succumbed to the good life. In the words of Murray's chief of staff, Major General Sir Arthur Lynden-Bell, there were 'thousands of officers hanging around hotels'. Murray ordered his officers back to their units, and began to generate what he called his 'atmosphere of war'. Meanwhile Murray's Suez plan had been granted cautious approval by the War Office, and in February 1916 he was ordered to advance to the Katia oasis, 40 km east of the canal, and construction of the much-needed road and pipeline was begun immediately by the Royal Engineers and the men of the Egyptian Labour Corps. A fight was coming for the soldiers of the Ottoman Empire.

The battles to come would be largely fought along a narrow coastal plain that had been used by armies for nearly two thousand years: an ancient caravan route from Palestine to Egypt, which started in the Syrian capital of Damascus, went south to Jerusalem, then down to Rafa and through the deserts of northern Sinai all the way to Kantara on the canal itself. More a well-worn track than a road, its path was determined not by engineers but by the location of the Sinai's precious wells, and passed over all of the scattered bones of the armies that had come before, from the Phoenicians to Napoleon.

In the past the wells dictated where the bends in the road would be, and armies went from well to well in as straight a line as they could. Now things were different. Now there would be a road. Not a road of bitumen, because the sands were too deep, but one made of sheets of two inch–squared mesh – the sort you might use to keep your chooks penned in. It would be laid three sections wide, to create a platform broad enough for men to march four abreast, and was pegged down at regular intervals into the sand. Cavalry was banned from using the road, as was artillery and any vehicle, no matter how light it might be. This was a road built for the weight of the foot soldier, and for him alone. Even so the Sinai had never seen anything like it. The railway was even more impressive. It was standard gauge (4 feet, 8.5 inches), and the first section was a 40-km section from the east bank of the canal to Katia, a small oasis town Napoleon had used in 1799 as his jumping-off point before setting out to conquer Palestine. All of the materials used, including the tracks, were supplied by Egyptian State Railways, while the locomotives and their drivers were brought out from England. 'It was curious,' wrote British machine gun company commander Major Vivian Gilbert, 'to see these engines, with their own drivers who had accompanied them to Egypt, calmly shunting and backing them in the sidings at Kantara, just as though they were in Eastleigh or Waterloo Station.'

In 1914 Australians who were motivated to enlist for service did so not through any heightened sense of patriotism or an inbred dislike of Germans, but by a unique once-in-a-lifetime chance to see distant places they otherwise would have had little chance of ever getting to. Never before and certainly not since in Australia's history had circumstances ever been so conducive to the raising of an enthusiastic volunteer army. We had no experience or national consciousness of loss on the battlefield. Of the nearly 800 men sent to the Sudan not a single one was lost to a bullet, and we fought on the periphery of the engagements in South Africa. There had been no bloody slaughters. War was an adventure for the bulletproof Australian soldier.

The various arms of our military were well aware of this wanderlust, and tailored their recruitment posters accordingly. 'Free Tour to Great Britain and Europe: The Chance of a Lifetime!' said one poster printed for the NSW Recruitment Office in 1917. These days we see these posters for what they were: shameless and misleading propaganda, damned lies and the conscious marketing of deceit.

As the war dragged on no trick, no piece of grimy psychological manipulation would be kept in the locker. After the sinking of the ocean liner *Lusitania* in May 1915 off the coast of Southern Ireland by a German U-boat with the loss of almost 1200 civilian lives, the Australian artist Norman Lindsay created a series of propaganda posters depicting Germans as monstrous, blood-soaked creatures with dripping claws who weren't content with conquering Europe and were capable of extending their reign even to our own distant shores. Caricatures like these were nothing new to Europeans. Since the mid-nineteenth century socialists had been depicted as skeletons in the European press. When Germany invaded neutral Belgium in violation of longstanding treaties the Anglo–Franco diplomat and writer William Le Queux compared the German Army to 'one vast gang of Jack-the-Rippers' at a time when visual propaganda was increasingly focusing on the so-called 'barbarism of the Hun'.

On a recent visit to my mother's nursing home in Picton, south of Sydney, I saw a whole series of World War I recruitment posters. These recruitment posters capture so vividly the values, innocence and sense of place of a hundred years ago, and were used to great effect in persuading Australian men and women to leave their families and go off to war on the other side of the world.

When we think of recruitment posters, Uncle Sam and Lord Kitchener immediately come to mind. American illustrator James Flagg's iconic poster of Uncle Sam simply told Americans, 'I want you for the US Army', resplendent as he was in patriotic stars and stripes, red, white and blue. British graphic artist Alfred Leete's powerful image of Kitchener – with his outstretched arm, accusatorily pointing forefinger and commanding moustache – was an unambiguous call to arms by an idealised father figure doing what good fathers did best: guide their children in how best to respond to life's moral challenges. But as the war progressed and casualties began to pile up it became more difficult to win over people's hearts and minds with simplistic images like the Kitchener poster, and so the message began to change. The recruitment posters of 1916 and 1917 were chillingly manipulative, filled with divisive themes designed to sow guilt and made to shame children into leaving their mothers, their fathers, brothers and sisters, and join the fight.

These were the sorts of posters before me at my mother's nursing home. One contrasted a soldier marching through a foreign field without a care in the world (or a German in sight) with another image of the same man on a deck chair back in Australia dressed in his whites and reading a book with a cricket bat, tennis racquet and bottle of wine beside him. The accusatory caption asked: 'Which picture would your father like to show his friends?' The next poster showed a young man on a bodyboard enjoying the Aussie surf above a caption that read, 'It's nice in the surf ... BUT ... what about the men in the trenches? GO AND HELP.'

In 1915 the *Sydney Mail* published a picture of a well-attended recruitment rally for Australians that had been held in London, the image of Lord Kitchener gazing down Orwellian-like from a monumentally sized poster beneath the words 'I WANT MORE MEN', and the picture encircled with photographs of fallen Australian soldiers. In the early days of the war, not even the spectre of death was enough to stem the tide of volunteers.

Newspapers throughout the colonies were trumpeting the need to defend the British Empire at all costs. 'The British fleet,' proclaimed an editorial in the *Wagga Daily Advertiser* on 4 August 1914, 'is our all in all. Its destruction means Australia's destruction, the ruin of our trade and institutions, and the surrender of our liberties. The British Empire is our family circle, and we cannot live outside it.' As people said in the street, 'If Britain goes to her Armageddon, so do we.'

One country town that enthusiastically responded to the call was Kapunda in South Australia. Its story is unique but at the same time it is the story of hundreds of towns and communities everywhere. Three hundred men and six women enlisted, of which around sixty perished in the fighting. They went into every arm of the AIF – two Light Horse regiments, five infantry battalions, various transport and supply units, artillery regiments and the Australian Flying Corps.

One Kapunda boy, Private Kenneth Richardson, a farmer who enlisted on 19 August 1914, did his best to end the tide of eager recruits when he wrote in his diary:

*War is an awful thing when you see it in its nakedness,
and when your own friends and soldier mates in the
same regiment get killed, then the full meaning of war
is recognised. No one's imagination or descriptive
and oratory powers can give one half of the terrible plight
that some men get into. When you come to see things
clearly, and in your calmer moments you begin to wonder
how any civilised nations can allow war to go on.*

In July 1916 Kenneth Richardson was shot in both eyes.
After treatment in England he was discharged from the army
in May 1917 and returned to Australia.

Recruitment posters used fear, guilt and brutish
confrontation, called into question your masculinity and
courage, and caused you to consider what your parents or
girlfriend or mates might think if you didn't rush off and
enlist. No manipulative sleight of hand that might assist in
shaming you onto a troopship was spared. They fostered
hatred (the Germans would kill your family if only given half
a chance), and invited peer groups and families to shame you
if you didn't enlist ('What would Daddy think?'). These tactics
worked – at least in the beginning before word began filtering
back that what was happening in Europe was in fact bloody
murder, before the casualty lists got too long. But many shared
the sentiments of N. G. Elsworth, an artilleryman and former
Victoria Mint official who couldn't help but feel, 'I would never
have been able to hold my head up and look any decent girl in
the face if I hadn't gone to war.' Such a sentiment was just as
well, considering many an Australian girl swore blind they'd
rather pass from this earth as old maids than go out with an
'unenlisted eligible'.

The initial response from Australians was overwhelming,
with 400,000 mobilised from a potential pool of volunteers
estimated to be somewhere between 800,000 and 830,000
men. But because the only recruitment offices were situated

in the state capitals it would be weeks before the bushmen began to appear – walking off farms and paying their own way to get to the nearest city in the hope of being recruited. Drovers rode hundreds of miles across the Queensland outback to get to Brisbane, including one whose horse failed to overcome an oppressive summer and collapsed mid-journey, forcing its rider to press on alone, trudging his way overland on little more than flour and water. Hundreds rode to railheads throughout Central Australia, and from there went on south to Adelaide. One would-be recruit walked 500 miles from Bourke in outback New South Wales to Sydney only to turn around and begin the long walk back home when his application was rejected. Another had spent days walking and hitching his way to Adelaide only to have his application denied on medical grounds. Undaunted, he made his way to Hobart – only to be rejected again – before finally enlisting in a recruitment office in Sydney.

They all came with a firm belief in their invincibility – a belief that became something of a myth in the postwar years despite the awful casualties we suffered. This idea that those who came back were somehow invincible instead of just plain lucky was expressed in the Adelaide *Mail* on 23 April 1927 in a reference to the heroism of our boys at Gallipoli:

> *Here is a crowd of men, drawn from the factory, the farm, and the counting house, bundled into khaki, allowed to run wild in Egypt for a season, and lo, they lick the flower of the Turkish army! What need, therefore, has Australia, which produces such a breed of born fighters, to worry about defence?*

Enlisting, however, was far from a sure thing. If you were under 5'6" you were too short. If your chest was below 34" in circumference, it was too small. If your teeth had holes in them, or if your feet were flat, or if you had bunions or corns, your chances shortened accordingly. Still, despite bad feet and bad teeth over 330,000 men were sent off on troopships to participate in this government-sponsored carnage, the largest migration of Australians in the history of the nation. When the dead began to pile up at Gallipoli, however, recruiting became more difficult and restrictions loosened. The minimum height was lowered to 5'2", and bishops in the Anglican Church who should have known better took it upon themselves to give recruitment a kick along by preaching that anyone who was eligible to serve and still preferred to remain civilians was nothing less than a German sympathiser.

The government also used recruitment posters to appeal to self-interest. 'We'll give you a well-paid job – six bob a day,' they said, which despite being a rather generous rate of pay for the time didn't stop our volunteers being given the disparaging nickname 'six-bob-a-day tourists'. It was, however, far above the pittance being paid to the average British conscript and was only a touch below the basic wage, a fact that caused some resentment among our low-paid allies. 'The fuckin' five-bobbers,' one historian wrote, 'brought home to the lowly Tommy, with his shilling a day, his relative poverty.' British soldiers looked on with envious eyes as our diggers played two-up or cards with their 'six little heaps of silver coins, which they seemed to handle so carelessly'. The South Africans, who were paid a miserable three shillings a day, and the Canadians, who were paid four and a couple of pence, presumably looked on too. The level of resentment between British and Australian troops that existed during the Great War, and is still not generally known, was not helped by this inequity, which persisted throughout the war and eventually expressed itself in the House of Commons in a speech by Major-General Sir Ivor Phillips in March 1917:

> *The subject of low pay is talked about every day by the soldiers ... These colonial men had 5s and 6s a day, and they drank coffee and beer and went out to buy butter,*

cheese and eggs for themselves ... What chance had my men with their 1s a day?

Despite the high number of volunteers, it is wrong to think that the nation as a whole was anywhere near as pro-war as the Anzac spirit and recent growth in 'patriotic tourism' suggests. One in every twenty-four Australians was either killed or wounded during the Great War, the highest percentage of killed and wounded of any participating nation, and the further the war ground on, the more the realisation that something horrible was happening to an entire generation of Australians began to sink in. In the 1920s and 1930s the time and energy Australians gave to Anzac Day was kept very much in check due to one simple fact: there were still a lot of people alive who *remembered*. Nowadays, it is only *remembrance*, and remembrance is a very different more abstract thing than the ability to remember. Remembrance can be easily manipulated, too. It's easy to become disconnected from the reality of what once was.

The idea of fighting 'for Britain' didn't mean a whole lot to the one in five Australians who were of Irish descent and didn't fancy fighting for a government they considered to be persecuting family and friends back home. As for our first wave of enthusiastic recruits, almost a quarter were British-born with thousands more having British parents though they themselves were born in Australia. By 1916 unemployment was rising and living standards were declining, and the promise of a paid overseas trip was appealing.

Referendums to introduce conscription in 1916 (the year of the first Anzac Day, which was initiated at least in part to further recruitment) and again in 1917 were defeated. By the end of the war it was true that 13.4 per cent of the white male population of Australia had volunteered, but that figure did little to distinguish Australia as a nation of gung-ho volunteers. In New Zealand the figure was 19.3 per cent, in Canada it was 13.4 and – hardly surprising, one must admit – 22.1 per cent in Britain. Everywhere it seemed but in the Australian media the legend of the digger was slow to gain traction. After the war Labor activists were opposed to Anzac Day being made a public holiday, and by the late 1930s even the public's interest in Anzac Day was seriously on the wane. By 1960 it had become such a polarising issue that the Anzac Day play by Alan Seymour, *One Day of the Year*, was banned from the Adelaide Festival. Make no mistake: the Southern Cross–draped love affair we have with Anzac Day today is only a recent phenomenon.

Chapter Four
Those Magnificent Men

There are old pilots and there are bold pilots. But there are no old, bold pilots.

– Harry Copland, WWI pilot, 203rd Squadron,
Canadian Royal Flying Corps

In March 1910 Harry Houdini, the world's most famous escape artist, made the first controlled powered flight in Australia when he took his Voisin box-kite biplane into the air on three separate flights over a paddock at Diggers Rest, 30 km north of Melbourne. People came up from far and wide in motor cars, buggies and on horseback to see him, and volunteered such helpful hints as 'Look out for the bloody trees!' As *Argus* columnist C. R. Pearce wrote, 'The first time I saw the biplane rise it flew for 29 seconds at a height of about 70ft or 80ft. A horse kicked with both hind legs, a cow dashed off to safer pastures, and a dog barked in delight.'

In addition to his aeroplane Houdini had also brought with him a French mechanic, Antonio Brassac, who was often overheard by curious onlookers as they were trying to glimpse the machine Houdini kept shrouded under a canvas tent, cursing Australia as 'this country of great winds' – winds that for weeks on end had kept grounded the biplane the pair had brought to Australia in the belly of a Vickers Wellesley bomber.

Even before Houdini had arrived in Australia, his aeronautical exploits were big news in the local press. His arrival in Darwin on 7 November 1909 was itself a world record for a nonstop flight, having travelled 11,526 km from Ismaïlia in Egypt. These were exhilarating times to be a pilot. Just a few months earlier, in July 1909, the French aviator (and inventor of the car headlamp) Louis Blériot became the first man to fly across the English Channel, taking off from a farm near Calais and, without the aid of a compass, landing within sight of Dover Castle 36 minutes and 30 seconds later, having flown at a speed of 72 kph and a height of 76 metres.

Military strategists the world over began getting excited at the prospect of using flying machines on the battlefield. To hasten the development of flying machines in Australia the government offered $5000 – the so-called Commonwealth Prize, a huge sum for the time – to anyone who designed and built a plane that could be adapted for military use.

The name John Duigan would probably still be familiar to many Australians if Houdini hadn't stolen his thunder. On 7 October 1910, seven months after Houdini's inaugural flight, Duigan made the first powered controlled flight of an Australian aircraft built, designed and flown by an Australian. Even though Houdini grabbed all of the headlines, Duigan's achievement is perhaps more significant. In the five countries that had achieved powered flight, the aviators concerned did so with the benefit of considerable technical assistance and resources, while all Duigan had was a few random texts he'd managed to scrounge, the engineering skills of his younger brother Reginald, and some back issues of the popular flying magazine *Aero Australia*.

Born the son of a bank manager and grazier in 1882 at Terang in Victoria's Western District, Duigan studied engineering at London's Finsbury College before returning to Australia in 1906. By 1909 he had built a 6 metre–long static glider (that bore an uncanny resemblance to the Wright Brother's Flyer) and flew it, tethered, at a height of one and a half metres. In January 1910 he began to design – from scratch – the plane that would, in October that year, make Australian aviation history.

On his farm near Bendigo in central Victoria, Duigan designed and then handmade the wheels, propeller shaft, water pump and radiator. He made his own compressed-air shock absorbers, and enlisted the Dunlop Rubber Company to supply the tyres, tubes and rubberised coverings for the wing and tail. He turned to the Brownbuilt Furniture Company to provide the undercarriage he himself had designed. The frame was made of ash, and the pilot had two control sticks: one for the front and rear elevators and one for the ailerons. The engine – a 20 hp, four cylinder, air-cooled unit – was supplied by the J. E. Tilly Engineering Company of Melbourne, but because it lacked the power Duigan thought it needed he hand-bored the crankcase and so increased its output to 25 hp.

His first attempt at flight on 16 July 1910 was more a hop than a flight, really – just over 7 metres – and it was clear the carburettor and transmission still needed some significant tweaking if a meaningful flight were to be achieved. To remedy this he fitted a new chain drive, a larger carburettor and a more robust set of exhaust valve springs.

On 7 October 1910 he took his plane from its shed and, with a little help from neighbours, wheeled it down a hill and over a creek to his 'airstrip' – a nearby s-shaped field bordered by trees that would limit any flight to no more than 800 metres. Six locals gathered to watch. History was made when Duigan flew his machine for 180 metres at a height of almost 4 metres. 'The whole time I had complete control of the machine,' he wrote in a letter to the Defence Department a few days later. 'It answered every movement of the levers perfectly. I could raise or lower her, steer in either direction and, which is far the most difficult, maintain balance sideways. Hoping that I have a chance in the Commonwealth Prize, John Duigan.'

Duigan knew the importance of being able to make the

claim that he could control his machine. Others had flown before him – indeed before Houdini and even the Wright brothers – such as the New Zealand inventor Richard Pearse who had, according to several who witnessed it, built his own flying machine in March 1903. Pearse, however, was never able to properly control it in flight and ended up crashing into a hedge.

Although he had demonstrated controlled flight Duigan never received the Commonwealth Prize – he had missed the closing date for entries. Nevertheless he was proud of his achievement. 'The machine is not a mere copy of any existing machine,' he wrote in a letter to the Defence Department on 15 August, 'but embodies many of my own ideas, combined with recognised sound practice.' Duigan went on to see service in the Great War, though not in the sands of the Middle East. Instead he was assigned to No. 3 Squadron, Australian Flying Corps and was sent to France, where he attained the rank of captain. In May 1918 while flying his R.E.8 over Villers-Bretonneux he was set upon by four German Fokker triplanes and, though wounded, shot one of his attackers down before landing his aircraft – a valorous effort for which he was awarded the military cross.

As inspiring as Bleriot, Houdini, Pearse and Duigan's feats most assuredly were, and despite the interest they and other pioneers were generating worldwide in the military application of flying machines, the Australian government had spent just $36,000 on aviation research and development in the years from 1910 to 1914. Their major investment during this time was the purchase of 734 acres of sheep paddocks at Point Cook south-west of Melbourne. Australia's first flying academy – the Central Flying School (CFS) – was established there in 1912. It began with two flying instructors – Henry Petre, a British-born former solicitor and flying instructor who was possessed, according to one acquaintance, by 'aircraft fever', and Eric Harrison, an Australian-born instructor with the Bristol Aeroplane Company, one of Britain's first aviation corporations.

It was Petre who had been given the task of motorcycling his way across hundreds of miles of Australian terrain looking for a suitable site for the new flying school. He settled on Point Cook after ruling out the only other possible site – Canberra's Duntroon area – for being too hilly. There were no hills at Point Cook, just open plains and an old lean-to. When Richard Williams, a young lieutenant with the Administration & Instruction Corps who for months had been desperately searching for a way out of what looked to be a dull career ensconced within the army bureaucracy, was selected for the CFS as a cadet he described Point Cook, with its hangars of canvas tents, as a 'ragtime show – just a grazing paddock, long grass, and that was it'.

Any flying school wanting to be taken seriously needs to have in its possession at least one aircraft, and with that in mind an order was placed with the British government for some flying machines. The CFS requested two Geoffrey de Havilland–designed B.E.2a reconnaissance biplanes, which had flown for the first time in February 1912 and set a new British altitude record of 3219 metres; two Deperduissan single-seat ground trainers (one of which would crash just days after its delivery); and one Bristol Boxkite trainer. Sadly none of these aircraft were suitable for combat (although more than 3500 B.E.2as were manufactured over the course of the war). But an air force has to begin somewhere.

The B.E.2as were delayed leaving England due to modifications and tests but eventually arrived in Sydney on the cargo ship SS *Hawkes Bay* on 3 February 1914. When their crates were opened, however, it was found that tropical mildew had rotted away much of the fabric that covered their wings and fuselage, a wholly unforeseen development that delayed the start of training while new fabrics were cut and fitted. That done, the first military flight in Australian history took place at Point Cook on 1 March 1914 when Lieutenant Eric Harrison and his student, George Merz, became airborne for five glorious minutes at a height of 30 metres in the Bristol Boxkite.

Boxkites made for excellent training aircraft despite their significant limitations. The only manoeuvre of consequence their pilots could practise was shallow turns because that was all the Boxkite's design permitted them to do. Possessing neither cockpit nor fuselage, the Boxkite's wings were attached to its tail via a timber boom, with the instructor sitting in the centre on the lower wing and his pupil right behind him, close enough to reach around the pilot's body and grab the control column, and close enough to observe how the pilot used his feet to operate the aeroplane's rudders. When the pilot felt the time was right for the students to take control, they'd switch seats midair – presumably without either of them falling overboard.

The CFS began with just four student pilots: George Merz, Richard Williams, Thomas White and David Manwell. Everything that happened there was a first. One of the two original B.E.2as became the first aeroplane the Australian military sent overseas to war when it was disassembled, crated up and shipped to New Guinea for use against the German forces around Rabaul. As it turned out, it was never taken from its crate – and was sent back to Point Cook in early 1915.

Prior to the delivery of the B.E.2as, the impatient trainees suffered from having to wait their turn flying the school's single Boxkite. And then they were forced to wait some more for calm conditions on Point Cook's open, wind-prone paddocks – a test of patience Harry Houdini would surely have sympathised with. Add to that a classroom severely lacking in theory and experience – the aircraft technicians themselves had no prior knowledge of the mechanics of flying machines and were in need of training themselves.

Tired of their slow, unresponsive Boxkite the students were desperate to get their hands on the faster, more manoeuvrable B.E.2as. In a classic catch 22, the Military Board did not consider the CFS sufficiently trained to handle them, and were slow to release them. When the B.E.2as did eventually arrive, it was decided to extend the course for two weeks to allow the trainees to get some decent flying time before graduating. And that is just what they all did. Richard Williams, his fears about being a cog in a faceless army bureaucracy forever banished, took his B.E.2a to a height of 1143 metres on a 35-minute flight over the Western District, touched down without incident – then promptly ran out of petrol while taxiing back to the hangar. Our nation at last had its first pilots, and the Australian Flying Corps (AFC), the forerunner of the Royal Australian Air Force, was born. Still, the graduates thought it a pity that although they were now qualified to fly there was no squadron for them to serve in, and no war – even a small one – in which they could fight.

So, who were these men chosen to be our first aviators? What were their backgrounds? How were they selected? Most were drawn from the middle to upper classes and were largely from non-technical backgrounds. The perception of the aviator in society was already well entrenched: he was a knightly figure – virtuous, educated, professional. Favoured were the virtues that seemed at their most prominent in the private school system, and the perceived morality of a potential recruit's civilian job was a large part of assessing their suitability as a pilot. Because of this elitist approach to recruitment the pool of potential pilots therefore would be a small one because in 1912 only 13 per cent of Australian males were enrolled in private education.

Our first aviators were not only well educated – they were young, too. The AIF's age limit was forty-five, yet two thirds of those who enlisted in the AFC were under the age of twenty-four. By 1918 if you wanted to be a pilot and were over thirty years of age your only hope of being accepted was if you were 'either exceptionally young for your age or have some special characteristics'. It helped also if you were Anglican (as were 44 per cent of the AFC's pilots) or Presbyterian (18 per cent). Labourers, Catholics and those of Irish descent may well have made excellent flyers, but they lacked the prerequisite cultural makeup.

Of those who did make the grade, 16 per cent were engineers and 14 per cent had been employed in either the transport or communications sectors. Others just got lucky. Lieutenant Reginald Fry, who had already tried and failed to enlist with the Light Horse, got into the AFC only after, by his own admission, 'stretching the facts a bit' to render himself 'a more desirable person'. Others with an established trade had a somewhat easier route. Harold Edwards had been a watchmaker, and was recruited and given the job of fitting out aircraft instrument panels. Joseph Bull was a woodworker and boat builder and had a familiarity with sails, and so was able to reinvent himself as an aircraft rigger, stretching fabrics over timber airframes. Hubert Billings had signals experience and so became a wireless operator.

The men of the AFC shared a common familial and social ancestry, but this was no bad thing. If anything it helped galvanise and mould them into a group that would, man for man, become a unit responsible for more deeds of bravery and heroism than any other unit wearing an Australian uniform. Of course they were not the working-class diggers of historian Charles Bean's mythology of the Anzacs as a democratic and egalitarian fighting force. Though they never said so explicitly, the men of the AFC would have been above all that.

The road to heroism often begins without a hint of what is to come. For Thomas White it began in North Melbourne on 26 April 1888. The son of a hardware merchant and one-time brass finisher, White became a bugler with the Citizen Military Force after family circumstances intervened to prevent him from attending the prestigious Scotch College, which would have provided him a smoother ride into the upper echelons of the armed forces. White was a gifted athlete – an excellent cyclist, sprinter and boxer and, like anyone with an adventurous streak in those early days of aviation, often found himself looking to the skies with the thought of one day becoming a pilot. In 1911 the lack of anything resembling an air force saw him join the 5th Australian Regiment and there he stayed, reasonably contented, until the day he saw the French aviator Maurice Guillaux performing loop-the-loops over the Melbourne Showgrounds in 1914. From that moment, Thomas White determined that one day he would pilot a flying machine. 'On the strength of having built a glider which never flew,' he later wrote, 'and having some technical training, possessing a motor car license, not so common in those days, and being an enthusiastic motorcyclist, I applied to join any flying corps unit that might be formed.'

Thomas White got lucky. Selected to go to Point Cook to train with the nascent AFC, he completed his training and on 1 April 1915 was made captain and adjutant of all the air force were capable of mustering – half a squadron, the soon-to-be famous Half Flight. He was then told he was going to be packed off to Mesopotamia – wherever the hell *that* was – to fight some Turks threatening British oil interests there. Well, not so much *fight* them – he later recalled being told with an encouraging pat on the back – more like 'just sort of fly over their heads, you know, photograph their positions as best you can, and try and drop these two-pound bombs on them through a hole we'll make in the floor under your feet'. The Mesopotamian deployment must have seemed like something from a *Boy's Own Annual*, a crazy figure-it-out-as-you-go approach to fighting a war instead of what it would actually be: the opening gambit in the history of Australian aviation.

The Indian government had initially supplied the bulk of resources for the Mesopotamian campaign, albeit grudgingly, as it feared that a depletion of their own forces on their Northwest Frontier could leave them vulnerable to revolt by the area's many hill tribes. And so on 8 February 1915 the Viceroy of India requested the Australian government supply trained pilots, motor transport and flying machines for the Mesopotamian campaign. The Australian government obliged, but could form only 'half a flight' – and the aircraft would have to come from Britain.

Henry Petre, an Essex-born flying instructor with experience on Deperdussin monoplanes, had come to Australia in 1911 at the request of the Australian government. By 1915 he had been promoted to the rank of captain and appointed the Half Flight's commanding officer. On 14 April, he left Melbourne for Basra by way of Bombay. On 20 April Thomas White, now in temporary command, George Merz and W. H. Treloar followed on board RMS *Morea*. And so it was that in May 1915, just weeks after the landings at Gallipoli, the first Australians from the AFC were sailing for far-off Mesopotamia. In Basra on 2 June 1915 Captain Thomas White and New Zealander Major H. C. Reilly took off on the very first airborne military action involving an Australian when they flew their French-built Maurice Farman biplane to Kurna, 96 km up the Tigris River, to observe the Turkish lines. Years later, in an eloquent recollection of life in the AFC, Thomas White described Basra's residents as 'scribes with reed pens, ink and sand' who 'squat on the ground writing love-letters at the dictation of amorous illiterates ... beneath ragged awnings that shade crate-like benches along the Basra creek'.

In the first decades of the twentieth century Mesopotamia was an unending expanse of desert with barely any towns worth speaking of, and what towns there were clung desperately to the banks of its few life-giving rivers and estuaries. Life was being lived there much as it had been lived for centuries. With little in the way of wood and stone, mud buildings dominated the local architecture. It still seemed to be a biblical land, and in this land of myth and romance would come a series of adventurous flights for White as well as a fair share of blind luck.

In early November 1915, high up in the deep blue over Ctesiphon, a small town on the Tigris River south-east of Baghdad in Lower Mesopotamia, White and his British observer and copilot, Captain Francis Yeats-Brown (nicknamed 'the Mahatma' because of his love of yoga and meditation), were on a reconnaissance flight to gauge the enemy's strengths, location and surrounding terrain. Because of the shifting nature of the shallow Tigris and the Allied force's scant knowledge of the region, British Army maps were all but useless for tactical purposes, and even reflex cameras were incapable of relating enemy positions accurately enough for them to be properly mapped.

It was supposed to be a routine flight, but became anything but routine when the engine on their Maurice Farman – a clumsy piece of equipment nicknamed 'the cow' because of its two protruding horn-like skids and the fact that it handled much like its bovine namesake – began to seriously misfire, forcing them to put down. And not within the safety of their own lines, mind you, but right before the eyes of what surely had to be the most startled mob of Turks in the entire Ottoman Army.

With the engine malfunctioning and no time for repairs before they would be descended upon by the Turkish infantry, White realised their only hope was to taxi and bump their way along the ground back in the direction of their own lines. And that is exactly what they did. With Yeats-Brown standing up behind him with his rifle at the ready in case of pursuit and screaming out directions because the raised angle of the aircraft meant White could no longer see over the cowling, the engine was throttled up and they began their spectacular getaway in an aircraft White later described as a 'museum piece of sticks and wire', a 'pusher' design with the propeller facing backwards and with wings that always struggled to generate decent lift, a perennial problem mostly due to the warm desert air.

They taxied an astonishing 25 km, much of it within sight of the enemy and coming almost to within shouting distance of Turkish lines at Kutaniyeh, where they were forced to bounce along a small ridge of sand-hills. 'The ground over which we taxied,' White later wrote, 'was broken by old canals and rough patches of cracked earth where swamps had dried up in the tropical heat, and in places camel thorn grew thickly. By careful ruddering around the worst patches, and with occasional spurts of speed from the erratically running engine the aeroplane rolled and bumped along at a rate that would not have disgraced many a motor car.' When they were within sight of their lines at Aziziyeh the engine at last decided to fire up, enabling them to fly triumphantly back into camp. Strangely, the Turks didn't mount even a half-hearted attempt at pursuit. We can only guess what they were doing as the cumbersome enemy aircraft bumped its way over uneven ground within range of their guns. Given they didn't have a flying corps of their own, they may well have simply been stupefied by the sheer spectacle of it all, the audacity of the getaway.

Everything to do with the formation of the Half Flight in late 1914 through to early 1915 was done in haste. It was trained and equipped in haste, its mechanics were sequestered from civilian life in haste, and even their uniforms were acquired, with some difficulty, only two days prior to sailing. But when called upon to go, the Half Flight was ready. Eighteen mechanics and twenty-three soldiers of other ranks were selected, and with them were four pilots, all of them officers: Captain Thomas White; Lieutenant R. Williams, who went on to become a squadron commander and wing commander in Palestine; Lieutenant D. T. Manwell; and Lieutenant George Pinnock Merz, a medical graduate and officer with the Melbourne University Rifles, a unit organised in 1910 to provide training for the university's undergraduates and selected students from Melbourne's public schools.

The Half Flight arrived in Basra on 31 May 1915 – just in time to participate in the assault on Kurna, a Turkish-held village strategically located at the marshy confluence of the Tigris and Euphrates rivers, north-west of Basra. Just five days earlier the Half Flight had taken delivery of three Maurice Farman biplanes – an aircraft that was already outdated, but at least they flew!

The advance on Kurna would have made for an odd-looking spectacle from the air. Five hundred British infantry had to *paddle* their way into combat thanks to torrential rains that saw the two rivers spill over into the surrounding plains. In they all went, in tugs and motorboats and Arab canoes called *bellums,* lashed together in pairs with a sheet of armour across the bow and a slit for a machine gun, the gunner sitting at the ready with his four mates behind him doing all the paddling! As the 1916 Australian Army handbook *Notes on Mesopotamia* later put it, the area's regular flooding was on a scale that 'made lagoons out of swamps' in a land that was 'either waterless or waterlogged'.

Kurna was easily taken. The Turks lost two gunboats, seventeen pieces of heavy artillery and 2000 soldiers were taken prisoner. The retreating army, however, weren't left alone as they headed north toward Baghdad. In hot pursuit were the indomitable Half Flight, dismaying the Turks by throwing bomb after bomb down upon them. In the days that followed a small airstrip was built at Kurna and each night the planes of the Half Flight flew back south to Basra, where situation reports were cabled to headquarters overseas and where repairs and maintenance were done in brick workshops and under iron hangers on the plane's dust-riddled air-cooled engines. Dust storms – the dreaded *shamal* – were playing merry hell with planes that were designed for use in sand-free Europe. Yet despite the fragility of the Farmans and Martinsydes, the men of our Mesopotamian Half Flight proved a resourceful bunch.

The Half Flight's three Maurice Farman biplanes were 'gifts' from the British Indian Army. All were second-hand; one was in constant need of repair, having already seen considerable service in Egypt. The planes were not equipped with machine guns, and their 70 hp Renault engines were prone to engine failure – not what you want when the countryside is rife with marauders as well as the enemy! The addition of two French-built Caudrons on 4 July, each with 80 hp engines and touted as having a faster rate of climb, improved the fleet somewhat. But like the Maurice Farmans, the Caudrons also arrived without guns, so the engineers designed their own machine-gun racks, which they fitted to the aircraft's undercarriage after the English-made mountings could not be attached to the wings of the French aircraft. As Frederic Cutlack lamented in his *The Australian Flying Corps in the Western & Eastern Theatres of War 1914–1918*:

> *The engines were a constant source of trouble and anxiety. The machines were not fitted with machine-guns; there were none of the improved types to spare from the main fighting front in France. Such bombs as were dropped upon the enemy were, for a time, 2-lb. infantry hand-bombs thrown out by hand; when 20-lb. aeroplane bombs ultimately arrived they were frequently found to have been damaged in transit. Bomb racks supplied from England would not fit, and were unserviceable; these had to be repaired locally and in some instances the only way in which the bombs could be dropped was through a hole cut out in the floor of the cockpit. In general the sole service to which these machines could be put was reconnaissance.*

The flying speed of these aeroplanes on a calm day did not exceed fifty miles an hour; at times when a strong wind blew they simply moved backwards in the face of it.

Throughout June and July 1915 the Half Flight flew regular reconnaissance missions north along the Tigris River in support of Indian ground troops advancing towards Baghdad. Barges were constructed to float aircraft up the river towards their next target – the stronghold of Kut – after an unsuccessful attempt was made to convert one of the Caudrons into a seaplane. In the meantime a series of tent hangars were erected alongside the new Kurna airfield, and days were spent overhauling engines and battling the dreaded *shamal* wind that could lay waste to a hangar as fast as it could be raised and so thoroughly shred the hangar's canvas sides that mechanics gave up pitching them and simply pegged the aircraft down on the open ground. The *shamal* could blow as hard as 80 kph – faster than the top speed of the Maurice Farmans and Martinsydes, which meant they sometimes flew backwards!

But just when it seemed reasonable to assume that their involvement in the Mesopotamian campaign was a safe and 'detached' one, high above the heads of their enemies, disaster struck. On 30 July 1915 the Half Flight's Caudrons took off at 0600 hours in the direction of the Euphrates River in an effort to drive the Turks out of an area of marshlands ahead of British and Indian forces advancing on Kut. The spectre of engine failure, however, again intervened and the Caudrons were forced to put down in enemy territory. One of the planes, piloted by Indian Army Captain H. Reilly, was helped by Arabs on the ground, which enabled him to make repairs and become airborne again. The other plane, piloted by New Zealand Lieutenant W. Burns and his Australian copilot, George Merz – who just the previous evening had volunteered to assist in Nasiriyah's chronically understaffed hospital – couldn't be restarted.

A few days after the aborted mission, Reilly took to the air to locate the downed plane. He described it as having been 'hacked to matchwood'. According to Arab eyewitnesses, Burns and Merz were chased about 8 kilometres across the desert in a running gun battle with marauding Bedouins, during which the pair tried to keep them at bay with their service revolvers, but to no avail. They died alongside one another, it was said, in a desperate last stand. And so George Merz became the first Australian airman to ever be killed in action and his death must rank as one of the loneliest in all the annals of the Anzacs. 'Though we scoured the surrounding country for miles,' Thomas White later wrote in his book *Guests of the Unspeakable*, 'we could not find the perpetrators. But wherever on the limitless desert their graves may be, the spot needs no monument and is hallowed by their heroism. In the mess hut at Basra we missed them sadly, and each wondered if, when his own turn came, he would die as nobly.'

In the wake of the loss of Burns and Merz it was decided long reconnaissance flights would be put on hold, and from July to September the Half Flight's time was spent repairing engines, maintaining their hangars, and keeping their remaining aircraft in working order. August saw two important developments: the Half Flight was attached to No. 30 Squadron of the Royal Air Force, and four Martinsyde biplanes rolled off a transport ship in Basra along with motorboats and some workshop lorries that soon proved too heavy for Lower Mesopotamia's soft sands. The Martinsydes, nicknamed 'Elephants' due to their size and lack of manoeuvrability, were a disappointing aircraft – taking forever to reach what was considered a 'workable' ceiling of 2134 m and having a maximum speed of just 80 kph.

The Allies captured Kut in late September 1915. It represented another stepping stone on the way to Baghdad, and it was around this time that the Half Flight suffered heavily from an unfortunate series of unrelated mishaps. On 25 September Petre crashed his Martinsyde, and then on 2 October crashed another before complaining to nobody in particular that 'nothing short of a croquet lawn' could guarantee them landing in one piece. The damaged seaplanes were put back on barges headed south, along with three other damaged aircraft. Nine members of the Half Flight and several British pilots were left behind in Kut and would soon face a counterattack by the Turks who besieged the town before sending its defenders on a death march to Turkey. Also in November, Thomas White and Francis Yeats-Brown took off on their ill-fated mission to Baghdad to cut the Baghdad to Constantinople telegraph, only to become POWs for the rest of the war.

Seafarers, it is common knowledge, have always been a superstitious lot. Ask any mariner and he'll tell you it's unlucky to kill an albatross, that people with red hair can bring a ship bad luck, that cats can whip up storms, and that whistling can make trade winds stronger. You never step onto a boat with your left foot first, and never ever begin a voyage on 31 December (the day Judas hanged himself) or on the first Monday in April (the day Cain killed his brother Abel). Pilots, though a much more recent invention than mariners, lost no time in creating a few superstitions of their own. The AFC never trained on Friday the 13th, and the British, Indian and Australian aircraft in Mesopotamia were numbered 1 to 12, then 12A, 14 and so on. Thomas White certainly had his fair share of luck (suffering engine failure and landing in front of the Turks at Ctesiphon could be termed unlucky), but luck on the scale he experienced in Mesopotamia, including five engine failures in a single month, always runs out eventually. Especially if you fly off on a dangerous mission on Friday the 13th.

On Friday 13 November 1915 White and Yeats-Brown set off for the outskirts of Turkish-occupied Baghdad. Their mission was to blow up the Baghdad–Constantinople telegraph line, which went north from Baghdad to Mosul (the ancient Ninevah) and across Asia Minor to the city of Scutari on the Bosphorus. The line was too tough to be cut with wire-cutters, so explosives in the form of necklaces of guncotton were loaded into their aeroplane. A virtual suicide mission, it was thought that destroying the telegraph by attaching explosives to it was the only reliable way it could be done. Arab saboteurs were considered too untrustworthy and the only other suggestion – an AFC member's idea of flying directly into them – was not met with any great level of enthusiasm. It was an important mission – important enough to risk losing an aeroplane and its crew in return for preventing the Turks from calling for reinforcements in the event of a British assault on the city. White and Yeats-Brown volunteered. In a letter to his brother Percy the night before the mission White wrote, 'Tomorrow is Friday the 13th. I have just been out on the aerodrome and tried the engine and find it alright. I am a bit superstitious, but really think that we will be successful.'

Ten kilometres west of Baghdad and 915 m in the sky, White spied not only the telegraph but a considerable amount of traffic on the roads, including a lone horseman leading more than 2000 Turkish camelry! Not one to be daunted by the problems posed by the presence of overwhelming odds he looked for a place to put his Maurice Farman down. 'I landed just over the horseman and toward the wires. I landed with some speed and as there was a light ground breeze behind me I saw that I would run into the wires, and tried to turn near the end of my run, but my lower left plane unfortunately struck a telegraph pole, knocking it down, and badly smashing the plane.'

With their plane now grounded White traded pistol shots with the approaching Arabs, who were the first to arrive ahead of their Turkish allies, as Yeats-Brown wrapped two of the necklaces of gun cotton around the base of the nearest telegraph pole. The first explosion gave a moment of respite from the advancing Arabs and the two men used the confusion to return to their aircraft and attempt an escape. As White fired up the engine the second explosion snapped the wire and the men watched in horror as it flailed about and proceeded to fall on their stricken aircraft! By this time the mob was upon them. 'I was struck on the head from behind with either a rifle butt or an adze, which made rather a nasty wound,' White later noted in his diary. They were then bundled into a *serai* and taken into the city, where they recuperated from their ordeal in a Turkish-run hospital and were treated well, allowed to send a daily cable to their families back home, and even permitted a Turkish bath.

Two weeks later, during the ill-fated Turkish defence of Baghdad when it became obvious that it was only a matter of time until the city would be lost to the British, White and Yeats-Brown were taken from the hospital north to a transit camp at Mosul and from there to the camp of Afion Kara Hissar in Turkey. The camp, in an abandoned Armenian church, was cramped to say the least. It measured just 30 m by 10 m and POWs slept on straw and improvised beds with furniture cobbled together from scraps of wood. White shared it with hundreds of captured British, Russian and French officers, including Australians captured at Gallipoli and the submariners of the famous *AE2*. (Launched in 1913, Australia's second submarine had done what no other Allied submarine had managed to do. At dawn on 25 April 1915, that first Anzac Day, the *AE2* succeeded in breaching the Turkish defences in the Dardanelles and went on to sink a Turkish destroyer. It then remained on the run for five days, until cornered and forced to surrender.)

Despite the cramped living conditions, Afion Kara Hissar must have been the site of some incredible yarns. It was during his captivity in Turkey that White recounted in his diary the arrival of the poor, wretched survivors of the Kut

March, the death march from the besieged British garrison at Kut in Mesopotamia, which fell to the Turks on 29 April 1916 after holding out for 147 days. Wasted and weak, they were marched into town, looking dazed and unable to speak, with no blankets and few clothes, trudging their way forward with dirty rags on their feet in place of shoes. Weeks later another group had arrived, and within four days twelve had died. The bodies, White wrote in his diary, 'were wrapped in dirty blood-stained sheets and were being carried to the burial ground by men who were almost too weak to walk'. White tried but was unable to find out the fate of a number of AFC mechanics who were in Kut at the time of the siege and forced to walk that dreadful march, more survivors of which would drift into the camp in the following weeks.

White eventually escaped his captors in July 1918 together with a British officer, Captain Alan Bott. After the war White said he had fled with 'a felt hat in an inside pocket of my coat, a miniature Russian dictionary, and two small bags filled with biscuits and chocolate'. (The dictionary was small indeed. I was able to conceal it entirely inside the palm of my hand when it was brought out of the archives for me during a visit to the Australian War Memorial Reading Room.) White and Bott made their escape when their train collided with another train while crossing the Kum Kafu viaduct en route to Constantinople, now Istanbul. Disguised as locals they seized their moment, eventually making their way to the docks along the Bosphorus where they stowed away in the bowels of the Ukrainian cargo ship *Batoum*. Bott recounted his escape in great and entertaining detail in his book *Eastern Nights and Flights: A Record of Oriental Adventure*, which involved running past a garrison of thirty Turkish soldiers who just 'looked stupidly' at him as he passed.

Once aboard the ship, White and Bott lived an uncomfortable and angst-ridden existence below deck for thirty-three days as the ship lay stationary at its moorings.

On six occasions Turkish police boarded the ship in their continuing search for the escapees, whose presence was kept a secret by the ship's sympathetic crew, although White and Bott were forced to hide in the vessel's ballast tanks for up to thirteen hours at a stretch. Imagine it: a cramped area completely without light, sitting all the while in a few inches of putrid water with a screwed-down manhole the only point of entry or exit. And not a clue how long they would have to stay there.

When the *Batoum* eventually got underway it sailed for three days across the Black Sea to the Soviet port of Odessa, which had recently been overrun and swept clean of its resident Bolsheviks by the Austro–German Army. White and Bott remained in Odessa for a month, courtesy of forged Soviet passports. They bought food with money they borrowed from the Dutch Consul, and were a hair's breadth away from joining the anti-Bolshevik army when news reached them of an impending armistice. So they stowed away again, this time on a Ukrainian hospital ship, and ended up in Varna in Bulgaria where they made their way to the British headquarters, and from there they returned to London via Egypt.

White arrived in London on 22 December 1918 and was subsequently awarded the Distinguished Flying Cross. While in London he met Vera, the daughter of former Australian prime minister Alfred Deakin. The two returned to Australia in 1919, where they married the following year. White went on to build a successful career first as a businessman then later as a politician, entering Federal Parliament in 1929 as the Nationalist member for the Melbourne seat of Balaclava, which he held for twenty-two years. He was elevated to the federal ministry as minister for trade and customs in the Lyons government but resigned in November 1938 after a cabinet reshuffle that he felt rewarded others less deserving than himself. In 1944 he was still serving at the Royal Australian Air Force School as an honorary group captain. Thomas

White resigned from Parliament in 1951, spent five years as Australia's High Commissioner in London and returned to live in Melbourne in 1956, where he passed away in October 1957 at the age of seventy, an old, bold pilot.

Flying was dangerous work. The enemy, fully appreciative of the importance of aerial reconnaissance, always had their guns trained on approaching aircraft – a sobering thought for pilots who had to fly as low as 300 m. Immunity from increasingly accurate shellfire was now rare, and pilots often had to perform zigzag manoeuvres to avoid being hit while either they or their copilot held a camera over the fuselage or through a hole cut into the floor – less than ideal conditions under which to fly reconnaissance or go map-making.

On one occasion over the battlefield at Ctesiphon Thomas White, not content with having put down in front of an array of bewildered Turkish infantry, descended to 300 m to pinpoint the position of an enemy gun emplacement. To get as close as possible he cut his plane's engine so it appeared he'd already been hit, which he hoped would deceive the Turks into not firing at him. The deception worked, and after gliding down over the Turkish emplacements he located his target, then fired up his engine and flew off before the enemy had time to train their guns. White's map of the Turkish positions was highly accurate thanks to a small tool he'd devised that looked like a miniature garden rake. He crossed a short wooden handle with a longer rod, off of which were a series of equally spaced pegs. When held to the forehead and made level with the eye, the pegs represented the degree of distance from the centre handle. Bearings could then be taken of other nearby landmarks, and an accurate map made.

The 22–26 November 1915 Battle of Ctesiphon proved a disaster for the British forces under the command of General Charles Townshend. Considered a trouble-free prelude to an advance on Baghdad it instead was a catastrophic defeat, with 8500 British and Indian troops killed or wounded. Already suffering from the loss of both men and aircraft, Ctesiphon also marked the end of the line for the famous Half Flight. On 7 December Petre and most of the Half Flight's mechanics were ordered back to Basra, and from there were transferred out of Mesopotamia to Egypt to join Australia's first *full* squadron: No.1 Squadron, AFC.

Throughout 1915, as the Half Flight were battling their way through Mesopotamia, Point Cook's Central Flying School was rapidly expanding. Gone were the canvas hangars and iron sheds. By the end of 1915 another twenty-four pilots had graduated, and the CFS had grown to become an impressive collection of hangars, workshops, accommodation buildings and an officers' mess, and was now more than able to respond to a British request for a full squadron to be dispatched first to Egypt, and from there to assist in the campaign in Palestine. Officially, the new squadron was known as #67 (Australian) Squadron Royal Flying Corps to avoid any confusion with the long established No.1 Squadron (British) Royal Flying Corps, one of Britain's three original Royal Flying Corps squadrons. But nobody in the AFC much liked saying #67 and queried why the number 67 and not, say, 41? So everyone just kept calling it No.1 Squadron, AFC, and tough luck if the Poms didn't like it.

On 16 March 1916 No. 1 Squadron, AFC, consisting of 195 men and twenty-eight officers, set sail from Melbourne and arrived in Egypt on 14 April, whereupon the pilots were split into two categories: those who needed further training went on to England, and those who didn't were attached to the No. 5 Wing, Royal Flying Corps and were soon flying aerial surveillance and mapping and engaging the enemy wherever possible. The British-sourced aircraft they were given, however, were every bit as frail as the Half Flight's – primitive biplanes from another era that were described by one Australian as 'toys more suitable for a flying school than for active service'. The design deficiencies were obvious and dangerous, with regular forced landings due mostly to engines that continually overheated.

The No. 1 Squadron mostly flew Bleriot Experimentals – B.E.2s. These aircraft were reviled by pilots for their rear-placed cockpit, cramped gunner's area, lack of forward firing guns and questionable reliability. But you get what you're given – although one pilot not content with what he was given was Lawrence Wackett, a young lieutenant who joined the AFC as a teenager and went on after the war to become one of the founding fathers of Australian aviation. Wackett designed a mount so he could attach a Lewis machine gun to the upper wing of his B.E.2, thus adding greatly to its offensive capability. He used it to good effect over Beersheba on 11 November 1916 when he helped fight off an attack on four B.E.2s and a Martinsyde by two German fighters. As poor as the aircraft were, the chance to fly overshadowed the aircraft's shortcomings. Even the ground mechanics wanted a piece of the action. Looking up to the sky and watching the pilots putting the planes through their paces filled the mechanics with envy. 'Air fights are a several times daily occurrence now, and it is good fun to watch 'em,' wrote engineer Thomas Baker in a letter home. 'Our latest planes are wonderful ... to see them go straight up till they stop then come down tail first, turn a few somersaults, spin around on their own axis, loop-the-loop ... oh blazes, don't I want to be an aviator!'

In June 1916 No.1 Squadron began to fly operations in its own right, independent of the British. They flew over the Sinai doing aerial reconnaissance, over the Western Desert in search of the elusive Senussi tribesmen, and by September were moving north toward the Turkish garrison at Kut. Their advance was not without incident. One Martinsyde was damaged on landing on 11 September, another crashed in high winds two days later, and three days after that a Caudron had to do an emergency landing behind enemy lines where its pilots – a Captain Atkins of the British Indian Army and the AFC's Captain John Treloar – were captured by local Arabs and given over to the Turks, who sent them to Baghdad. (Treloar had previously been evacuated from Gallipoli with enteric fever and invalided back to Australia before joining the AFC. He survived the war as a POW, and went on to help found the Australian War Memorial in Canberra.) But the mishaps did not end there. Seaplanes being floated upriver were damaged after high winds blew them into embankments and overhanging trees. Repairs were affected and several reconnaissance flights undertaken, although the photographs proved worthless, printed as they were either on out-of-date photographic paper from England or on the horrible bromide-based paper sold in Basra.

From December 1916 they flew in support of the troops as they entered Palestine, and it was during an attack on a railway line at Tell el-Hesi near Gaza that Frank McNamara landed his aircraft to assist a fellow pilot who had been shot down and, although wounded himself, scooped up his comrade from under the noses of the Turkish cavalry, helped him into his plane, and flew him to safety. For this singular act of heroism McNamara became the only Australian aviator to be awarded the Victoria Cross in the Great War. On 8 June 1917 his action was promulgated in the *London Gazette:*

> *Lt. Frank Hubert McNamara, Aus. Forces, RFC*
>
> *For most conspicuous bravery and devotion to duty during an aerial bomb attack upon a hostile construction train, when one of our pilots was forced to land behind the enemy's lines.*
>
> *Lt. McNamara, observing this pilot's predicament and the fact that hostile cavalry was approaching,*

descended to his rescue. He did this under heavy rifle fire and in spite of the fact that he himself had been severely wounded in the thigh.

He landed about 200 yards from the damaged machine, the pilot of which climbed onto Lt. McNamara's machine and an attempt was made to rise. Owing, however, to his disabled leg, Lt. McNamara was unable to keep his machine straight, and it turned over. The two officers, having extricated themselves, immediately set fire to the machine and made their way across to the damaged machine, which they succeeded in starting.

Finally Lt. McNamara, although weak from loss of blood, flew his machine back to the aerodrome, a distance of seventy miles, and thus completed his comrade's rescue.

The problem with the citation in the *London Gazette* is that it barely scratched the surface of what really happened. On the evening of 19 March 1917 eight pilots were called into a briefing and told the following morning they'd be attacking Junction Station on the Jerusalem to Beersheba rail line. McNamara, who would be flying a Martynside, was to be used in a protective role alongside the other aircraft before breaking off and dropping a new kind of bomb, a timing bomb that could be set to explode at a pre-determined height.

At dawn the next morning the aircraft swooped down over Junction Station and caught the Turks napping. The B.E.2cs dropped their bombs – six 35-pound howitzer shells per aircraft – with deadly accuracy on the ammunition dumps, with explosion after explosion ripping through the still morning air. They then broke off the attack and made way for McNamara and his experimental cargo. By then, however, the Turkish defenders were at their stations, and McNamara flew into a barrage of anti-aircraft and small-arms fire. As bullets ripped through the fabric of his wings and splintered its wooden frame he flew on, reached his target and released four bombs, all of which exploded as planned. The fifth, however, did not, exploding just metres beneath his aircraft and sending shrapnel up and through the pilot's seat into his right thigh and buttock.

As he was hit, McNamara inadvertently pressed down on the plane's rudder, putting it into a spin. Seriously wounded and losing blood, he managed to regain control of his Martinsyde and was heading for home when he saw Captain D. W. Rutherford in his B.E.2, its engine spluttering, gliding down to a forced landing – with Turkish cavalry riding out to intercept him. McNamara turned his machine around, landed, taxied up to Rutherford and told him to get on. Climbing onto the left wing (the Martinsyde was a single seater, so there was no room for a copilot!) McNamara turned his plane round, throttled up, and took off. In his own words:

> Opened up, turned around, and started to take off. Right leg pretty dud. Machine doing about 35mph on ground when started swinging to the left. Could not counter with right foot (right rudder). Swung around crashing prop lower left wing and undercarriage. Got out, bullet fired into petrol tank followed by light rifle fire from the Turks.

McNamara, with Rutherford on his wing making it difficult to keep the aircraft trimmed and in balance, crashed into a wadi. Now Rutherford's B.E.2c was their only hope of escape. As McNamara remembered, 'Started to Rutherford's BE that was not on fire yet. In landing he had ripped off a tyre, broken the centre section wires, cracked an aileron, and dropped a Lewis gun drum under the rudder bar.' McNamara removed the drum, took out his revolver and began to shoot at the advancing Turkish cavalry. Then, 'I turned the machine around to take off, opened the throttle. She stuck three times in soft ground, then lifted off just in time to escape the rush.'

Rutherford would later say that McNamara almost fainted from blood loss on the flight back.

The idea that no man should be left behind was *de rigueur* among pilots in the Great War. On 20 January 1918 Lieutenant Alfred Poole and his observer, Lieutenant Fred Hancock of No. 1 Squadron, AFC, were over the coastal town of Arsuf (scene of King Richard III's defeat of Saladin in the Third Crusade in 1191) in their Bristol fighter when they were forced down just to the rear of the Turkish lines after an unfortunate encounter with a German aircraft. The landing was not a good one: the plane came down in a wadi and then flipped onto its back, but at least the pilots walked away from the crash.

No Bristol had fallen into Turkish hands up to this point in the war and Poole wanted to keep it that way, so he punctured the fuel tank and fired his flare pistol into the fuel tank, setting it alight (flare pistols were standard issue to pilots so that not only their aircraft but also any accompanying maps, letters and documents could be set alight in the event of a forced landing). Shortly after, a Turkish patrol arrived and the men were taken prisoner. When fellow pilot Lieutenant A. R. Brown landed nearby in his own Bristol to attempt a rescue, the Turks indicated they'd shoot their prisoners if he didn't leave. He left reluctantly, and Poole and Hancock remained POWs for the duration of the war. Later that day they were sent by rail to a German command centre at Nazareth where they were interrogated on coming Allied battle plans, troop strengths, and shown German aerial photographs of camps and questioned about the number of men per tent. All in all they were treated well, fed well, given baths, and even had their flying suits deloused.

Brown's attempt at rescue wasn't the only one that went awry. When Captain Douglas Rutherford and 2nd Lieutenant Joe McElligott were forced down near Amman on 1 May 1918, Lieutenant Fred Haig and Lieutenant Ron Challinor, who had been busily dropping leaflets onto bands of Beni Sakr Arabs, landed to rescue them. On take-off, however, the additional weight forced a wheel strut to collapse and the four men were left with no choice but to surrender to the Turkish cavalry. Again, they were treated well by their captors. When Claude Vautin of No. 1 Squadron was shot down and taken prisoner near Gaza in July 1917 the pilot of the German Albatross who brought him down, Oberleutnant Gerhardt Felmy of the *Fliegerabteilung* 300, not only took Vautin on a personal tour of Jerusalem, he also flew over No.1 Squadron's airfield and dropped a photo of the two men standing side by side to show he was being well looked after. In the weeks that followed, Vautin wrote letters to his family, which were delivered by Felmy's remarkable air mail service in a singular display of chivalry and decency that begun a bizarre sequence of fraternising mail exchanges between the men of the German and Australian flying corps.

By war's end, thirty-five Australian pilots and observers had been taken prisoner. Fourteen were captured in the Middle East and twenty-one on the Western Front out of a total 410 pilots and 153 observers. All thirty-five POWs survived the war. It was a small and creditable number of prisoners, one could argue, given the hazardous nature of flying lumbering aeroplanes made of wood and canvas just hundreds of metres above gunners intent on bringing them down, and with not even the safety of a parachute to help soften the fall! Their captivity, which for many meant a lengthy period of incarceration full of uncertainty, monotony and loneliness, remains one of the untold chapters of Australia's Great War story.

As aircraft quality began to improve, Allied airmen eventually began to take control of the skies over Palestine. From mid-1917, they were flying over Turkish ground troops with virtual impunity. Aircraft were becoming faster, more agile and more reliable, moving beyond mere reconnaissance and occasional bombing runs and taking on a more offensive role. By May of 1918 the British and Australian flying corps had gained a distinct advantage over the Turks and Germans in the air, too – a fact seen in the increasing number of long-range reconnaissance flights they undertook. The Germans lost sixty pilots in the spring and summer of 1918 – forty killed and twenty wounded. Incursions into Allied airspace by German aircraft dropped from over 100 during one particular week in June to just four in three weeks during all of September.

Gone were the AFC's lumbering B.E.2s and Martinsydes; in their place were the agile Bristols. Soon they would demonstrate the destructive potential of airpower. On 21 September 1918 large numbers of Turks were reported fleeing along what was an old Roman road built into a ridge through the Wadi Fara gorge north-east of Nablus in Palestine. Two days earlier Allied mounted troops had smashed their way through the enemy's defensive lines north of Jaffa. The Ottoman Seventh Army faced being surrounded unless they found a way out. The road was filled with a crush of people, animals and vehicles all pushing their way towards the only remaining crossing point on the Jordan River still open to the retreating Turkish army. They were spotted by AFC lieutenants Stanley Nunan and Clive Conrick, who were on a dawn patrol in their Bristols. Nunan later recalled the looks of 'abject terror' on the faces of the retreating Turks as their bullets began to strafe the panicked column, while Conrick wrote in his diary:

> They had little chance of escape from my guns as we were so close to them. As I fired I saw chips of rock fly off the cliff face and red splotches suddenly appear on the Turks who would stop climbing and fall, and their bodies were strewn along the base of the cliff like a lot of dirty rags. When Nunan was climbing again to renew his attack I had a better opportunity to machine gun the troops and

transports on the road. I saw my tracer bullets hit the lead horses pulling a gun-carriage. As they reared up, they turned away from the cliff side of the road and their heads were turned back towards me, so that I could see the terror in their faces as their forefeet came down and, missing the road altogether they plunged over the cliff dragging the carriage with them. Their driver, realising what was happening, jumped back towards the road, but he was late, far too late. He seemed to just float above the gun-carriage as it rolled over and over with the horses until the transport hit the cliff face, when he was thrown far out into the valley and his body disappeared in the haze below.

After each expending 600 rounds of machine-gun fire into the scattering column the Bristols then radioed for reinforcements. The remainder of No. 1 Squadron was stationed just 20 kilometres away at Ramleh, along with three squadrons of DH9 bombers and S.E.5a fighters (around seventy aircraft) of the 40th Wing of the RAF. All were at the ready; the DH9s already had their bombs fitted. The planes took off at intervals and in small groups with orders to bomb the column 'from the head back'. No. 1 Squadron, AFC alone fired 24,000 rounds and 3 tonnes of bombs, but the overall number of aircraft – when some additional squadrons from the 5th Wing RAF joined in – numbered over a hundred and together achieved the virtual disintegration of the Ottoman Seventh Army on terrain that allowed for no movement, no cover and ultimately no hope. The next day over a thousand vehicles and almost a hundred artillery pieces were recovered by British infantry, while Allied losses in the engagement totalled two aircraft, only one of which was the result of enemy fire.

The English-born war correspondent and historian Frederic Cutlack wrote: 'the panic and the slaughter beggared all description. The long, winding, hopeless column of traffic was so broken and wrecked that the bombing machines gave up all attempts to estimate the losses under the attack, and were sickened of the slaughter.' One pilot recalled the morning as being 'a bomber's and machine-gunner's paradise' as trapped men, horses and vehicles were ripped apart despite some Turks seen waving white flags. But how can a pilot take prisoners from the air? As Antony Bluett wrote,

> When 'cease fire' was ordered the road for nine miles was literally a vast charnel-house. Guns, limbers, wagons, field kitchens, every conceivable form of vehicle … lay heaped together in a monstrous confusion; and when night fell ragged half-starved Bedouins descended upon the stricken valley, stealing from pile to pile of debris in search of loot, nor could the rifles of the guards deter them from the ghoulish task.

Writing of that day twenty years later one of the pilots who took part in the slaughter, Leslie Sutherland, who'd joined the AFC after serving in both the Light Horse and the signal service, described it as not so much war but 'cold-blooded, scientific butchery … I feel sick even now when I think of it'. But as sickening as it was it was also a tactical tour de force. The Ottoman Army that had been embedded along the eastern Mediterranean coastline had now effectively ceased to exist, and General Allenby turned his troops around and faced them towards Syria and its capital, Damascus.

The slaughter of the Ottoman Seventh Army was far removed from the romance of the flying machine duels that had lured our first pilots into wanting to fly. Contrast the terror following the action at Wadi Fara with Lieutenant Stanley Nunan's joyous account of an early dogfight he had in the skies over Palestine:

> Well it was no good sitting there and being murdered, so

we pulled our noses up and went straight into the Hun formation ... they split up all over the sky. I followed two ... Put a long burst into one from my front gun. He put his nose down vertically. I followed him down at about 200 miles an hour. My Ob [Observer] got both guns to bear ... and ripped them into him ... The Hun burst into flames and crashed in an orchard. Meanwhile his mate had been 'looking' at us from a distance. I turned on him and he took to the hills with another. I overtook them and they adopted their favourite tactics of dodging in and out of the hills and gullies ... I circled with them for 15 minutes and had the time of my life ... we put into them nearly 1000 rounds of ammunition and got so close at times that we could see the colour of their eyes ... I enjoyed it immensely as soon as I got over the first touch of stage fright.

The commander of No. 1 Squadron, Major Richard Williams, had a saying: 'If a new pilot got through his first three days without being shot down he was lucky. If he got through three weeks he was doing well. And if he got through three months he was set.' But in Williams's mind those odds shortened considerably with the delivery of the new Bristol fighters. It was the Bristol, a two-seated fighter bomber that could climb to 3000 metres in around eleven minutes and fly at 182 kph when it got there that made the slaughter at Wadi Fara possible and did more than any other aircraft to help the Allies win the air war in Palestine in 1917–18. 'Now for the first time,' Williams wrote after taking his first delivery of Bristols, 'after 17 months in the field we had aircraft with which we could deal with our enemy in the air.'

There were 2234 enlisted men and 460 officers who served in the AFC's campaigns from Belgium to Baghdad. In the later years of the war many of those men were drawn from the ranks of the Light Horse. Of all those who served, 178 were killed. Of those who enlisted 410 would go on to become pilots, beginning with the trailblazing airmen of the Half Flight and including all those who served with the Royal Flying Corps and the Royal Naval Air Service, the arm of the Royal Navy that would later merge with the Royal Flying Corps to form Britain's Royal Air Force. Of those 410 pilots, sixty-five rose to become flying aces, and between them they shot down 799 enemy aeroplanes. That's more than twelve aircraft to a man, more than twice the coveted 'five' that someone once decided would be the number of kills a pilot needed to be called an 'ace'. (The first ace was a Frenchman, Adolphe Pégoud, who was credited with downing five German aircraft in February 1915 as well as performing aviation's very first 'loop', in a Bleriot Model 11.) For many of its pilots, however, life in the AFC proved to be anything but glamorous. More than one in every four – 110 men in all – were killed either in training or in combat, yet despite the dangers the number who wanted to be a part of it all far exceeded the places available. By the end of the war it had in excess of 2200 ground crew and administrative staff helping keep the corps in the air, and plans were afoot to expand its four squadrons to fifteen by 1921, comprising almost 8000 officers and enlisted men and in excess of 270 aircraft. Then came the armistice.

Although pilot training continued as it always had at the training school at Point Cook after war's end, by 1919 most of the units of the Australian Flying Corps had been retired. A temporary Australian Air Corps was formed in 1920 to maintain the aircraft until a decision was made on whether to form a permanent air force. When the Royal Australian Air Force was formed on 31 March 1921 it and Britain's Royal Air Force were the only two air forces in the world. On 1 September 1923, upon receipt of a Royal Assent from the British government to alter the Air Defence Act, the RAAF was granted equal status to that of the Royal Australian Navy and the Australian Military Forces, and the days of the Australian Flying Corps passed into history.

If only all of the pilots and observers who served in the AFC could have come out of it unscathed in both body and mind the way Flight Lieutenant Donald Day had. As he reminisced of his flying days:

> One of the finest experiences of flying is to closely examine the large fleecy white clouds. They contain features similar to very rugged country gullies, hills etc. ... in places the gully turns sharply, too much so for a turn, and into cloud one goes; no visibility and a soft clammy feel – a most eerie experience. When flying above a cloud with sun shining, the shadow of the machines may be seen surrounded by a rainbow.

Day, formerly of the Australian Army Medical Corps, joined No. 5 (Training) Squadron late in the war and only received his pilot's wings in May 1918, too late to be deployed and fly an actual mission. Instead he sat out the war at his base in southern England. He surely would have loved his chance to test his wits against the enemy in the air, but not having had that chance did little to diminish his joy of flying. Nor should it. Having an enemy Fokker in your sights, matching wits with a man whose love of flying has an even chance of exceeding your own, should add nothing to the thrill of being a pilot in times of war. The joy of flight is its own reward, and we need be careful not to romanticise too much about the 'flying ace'. Perhaps Donald Day and all of those magnificent men simply took to the air because, in the words of the French aristocrat, poet and pilot Antoine de Saint-Exupéry, it 'released them from the tyranny of petty things'.

Chapter Five
All Pearl and Amber

You're an ugly smellful creature:
You're a blot upon the plain:
I have seen Mohamed beat you,
And it gave me little pain.
You're spiteful and you're lazy,
You'd send a white man crazy,
But I reckon you're a daisy
When the Turks come out again.

– Oliver Hogue, *The Cameliers*, 1919

Even before the Australian Imperial Force (AIF) had landed in Egypt its men had developed a reputation for larrikinism and ill discipline. In mid-1915, the troops aboard a ship docked in the Ceylonese capital of Colombo were banned from bringing beer and fruit on board. Evidence that the ban had been disregarded, however, was proving difficult to conceal as makeshift fruit stands began to appear on the upper decks, and local beer was sold from greatcoats and duffel bags at a 200 per cent mark-up! Officers and military police who tried to maintain discipline were jostled, hissed at and threatened they'd be thrown over the rails if they attempted to close the stands down.

By the time the ship reached Alexandria the 2000 troopers were thoroughly sick of being told what they could and couldn't do. When the ship's officers were given leave and the enlisted men told they would be staying aboard, all hell broke loose. One after another ropes appeared and were slung over the rails down to the pier. Everywhere men were clambering down to freedom. As Lieutenant Herbert Trangmar, a bookkeeper from Coleraine in country Victoria, remembered:

> *Armed guards were placed on the piers, but they were useless. We had been boxed up for over a month, and who could expect that the Australian boys would stand alongside a pathway to an evening's entertainment and not place a foot on it. I confess I was not far from the lead in going over the side.*

On the ground in this foreign land, the Australians might as well have still been at sea. In the final decades of the 1800s and into the early decades of the new century, almost everything the Australian government and its citizens knew or thought they knew about Egyptians came from British sources such as the widely read *Modern Egypt* (1908), a typical 'how to colonise the natives' treatise written by the 1st Earl of Cromer, Evelyn Baring Cromer. Cromer, who was consul general in Cairo from 1883 to 1907 and many say also its de facto ruler, claimed that Egypt, which was building pyramids when England was still populated by Neolithic tribes digging for flint, had somehow become fundamentally ill-equipped to govern itself in the absence of British assistance. It was therefore Cromer's mission – and the mission of all Englishmen posted there, he wrote in *Modern Egypt* – 'to save Egyptian society'. A sense of superiority was an *a priori* assumption and Cromer believed it was an Englishman's job to 'mould' Egyptians, which he called 'the rawest of raw materials', into things that could be 'really useful'. Any Australian officer who stayed in Egypt longer than his transit through the Suez Canal would have had this notion of superiority reinforced at staid British officers' clubs like the Gezira Club in Cairo, where local Egyptians were treated with a level of contempt similar to that of African-Americans on turn-of-the-century American cotton farms.

It was fatally flawed diplomats like Cromer who did all the 'hard work' in categorising Egyptians for us so we'd all know how to pigeonhole them when we stepped off our troopships. According to Cromer if an Egyptian had a green turban and walked with a 'slow gait' he was a pious Sheik. If he peered 'somewhat loweringly over a heavy moustache from the window of a passing brougham' he was a 'Turko–Egyptian Pasha', and if he was in the street carrying an armful of embroideries then 'he must be a Jew'. These racial stereotypes were firmly embedded within Australian society in the early decades of the twentieth century, and not only was our military and the senior command of the AIF partial to it, so were our federal and state governments. Yet despite Britain's long association with Egypt it was the Aussie diggers who more easily entered into the spirit of the place and talked openly, if mostly only in pantomime, with its people. We rode their beasts, we tasted their drinks and we smoked their pipes while the 'restrained Tommy', according to the war journalist Hector Dinning, 'called for English beer and for roast beef, and stuck tenaciously to his briar'.

The Australians' in-built egalitarianism stood them in good stead in the Middle East despite their predisposed tendency to consider Egypt 'the land of sin, sand, shit and syphilis'. Such impressions can sometimes take generations to pass away. As Suzanne Brugger wrote in her book *Australians in Egypt 1914–1919*:

> *Asked what he thinks of Egyptians the Australian of today is still quite likely to refer to some anecdote handed down by a father, grandfather, uncle or grand-uncle. James Aldridge's 'mischievous, tricky, night-shirted Egyptian' of the bazaars appears time and time again, stealing boots, hawking filthy postcards and demanding 'baksheesh'. Whether his image continues to affect the way in which Australians respond to Egyptians today is a matter for*

speculation; that it survives undiminished in Australian folklore seems certain.

While the majority of our Light Horsemen who were eager for a fight quickly tired of their period of preparation in Egypt, Dinning was enamoured by its colours and textures, found comfort in its landscapes and solace in its bazaars and alleyways. 'A half-day in the bazaars I would not exchange for a whole wilderness of Sphinxes,' he wrote. 'Their call is irresistible!' He even wrote gleefully of its hordes of beggars and gharry drivers that 'would put an Australian cab rank to shame'. He also ignored dietary warnings regarding Egypt's exotic foods, constantly diving into all manner of pastries and desserts sold from its roadside stalls. 'Sweets and pastry abound in excess and are curiously cheap. Toffee is sold from stands at every street corner, and the quantity you might carry off for a sixpence would be embarrassing.' For Dinning a day in Cairo was a smorgasbord of discoveries and experiences, from fragrances and spices to weavers and tent makers.

Dinning was an interesting character with a unique ability to appreciate the world around him. He acknowledged that his words on the many pleasant distractions from war might have seemed to some impertinent considering the backdrop of suffering that hung like a bloodstained curtain behind much of what he wrote. But he insisted that an astonishing transformation would one day come over our soldiers. He predicted that Egypt would, when all the shooting was done with, prove to be for many their 'first love', born out of that first innocent exposure to the colours and smells and sounds of an ancient world, and that this first love would surface, sooner or later, regardless of what damnable expressions our diggers were using to describe the place while they were there. These were all transient judgements, Dinning said, and would no doubt quickly evaporate upon returning home as former soldiers learned how to separate the horror of war from the beauty of where those wars were fought. They would romanticise it. And when they began to reminisce over Egyptian sunsets, or Cairo's spice-laden bazaars or the colours of the Sinai and began to look around for someone whose prose gave voice to their suppressed memories, Dinning determined that it would be his words that would be there for them. He would be their voice.

Dinning had fallen in love with the Middle East before he even stepped off his troopship. Its ridges of rock were streaked with colour, he said; its mountains towered above the sea and were rugged and baking hot right down to the water's transparent edge. Arabia, he wrote while still sailing up the Red Sea, seemed to be 'all pearl and amber', strung out in a golden arc over the 'grimness' of Africa. And once he disembarked and began to walk its streets, his ability to pick apart social and cultural trends was second to none, as this prophetic passage on alfresco dining and how it may one day apply to Australia makes plain:

> Alfresco cafes are ubiquitous. Their frequency and pleasantness suggest that the heat of Australia would justify their establishment there in very large numbers. Chairs and tables extend on to the footpaths, and the people of all nations lounge there in their fez caps, drinking much, talking more … you cannot sit five minutes before the vendors beset you with edibles, curios, prawns, oranges, sheep's trotters, cakes and postcards. The boys who would polish your boots are the most noisome. The military camps in the dusty desert have created an industry amongst them. A dozen will follow you a mile through the streets. If you stop, your leg is pulled in all directions, and nothing but the half-playful exercise of your cane upon the sea of ragged backs saves you from falling in.

Dinning was under a spell so powerful not even years of war could tarnish it, as this passage written in Palestine in 1917 suggests:

The Palestine autumn is very dry – thirsty for the winter rains. The ground about you is parched; crops are withered in the red earth. But this dryness in the crops gives you the beautiful brown and gold colour in the distance. The plains and hillocks of the Maritime Plain are burnished. This golden colour, upon the red earth, gains richness in the glow of the early morning that leads you to forget utterly the filth of the train and the pathos of the parched soil beside the track.

The official historian of World War I Charles Bean was instrumental in helping to establish the Anzac legend. He is remembered today for his monumental *The Official History of Australia in the War of 1914–1918*, a virtual *Iliad* which would eventually run to twelve volumes, the first six of which Bean wrote himself and the remaining six written by others under his stewardship. Bean recorded history in a very different way to Dinning. Bean was concise, precise, his text heavy with facts, logistics, strategy, of battles won and lost, all written in the wake of exacting and laborious research. At Gallipoli Bean was splashed with the blood of some poor Turk who'd been blown apart by a direct hit from an artillery shell. But Bean had no interest in ameliorating the reality of war. Dinning, meanwhile, delighted in using words to paint images of picturesque places far away from the shooting, such as a Mediterranean beach, quails and white wagtails that dash unexpectedly out of wiry tussocks, or the respite given by the shade of a lonely palm. Rather than being in opposition, each writer complements the other, and together they come as close as probably any two Australian writers did in conveying the reality and totality of war.

When Dinning left Alexandria for redeployment in France he wrote:

Egypt as a whole, despite its stinks, its filth, its crude lasciviousness, its desert sand and flies, heat and fiery dusty blasts, had charmed and amazed and compensated in a thousand ways. It was our introduction to foreign-ness and, as such, had made an arresting impression that could never be deleted. France may cause us less discomfort, and may hold a glamour and a brilliance of which Egypt knows nothing, but the impression left by France can hardly be more vivid than that of Egypt, our first-love in the world at large.

It's a pity that due to some unfathomable government oversight no representatives of the Australian press were sent to cover the coming campaign in the Sinai – an oversight that bordered on neglect and meant the general public back home – wives and fathers and mothers and brothers and sisters and friends – had little or no idea what was happening there. Letters from home were filled with comments such as 'We never hear what you're up to over there', a common refrain that had a detrimental effect upon morale. It was all too much for one young digger recuperating at the 14th Australian General Hospital when he received a pair of socks courtesy of the Red Cross with a note inside that read: 'I hope these socks go to some Australian hero in France, but not to any of the cold-footed Light Horse.' According to witnesses the unnamed trooper broke down and sobbed.

Egypt, it was thought with some justification, was the place to be if you didn't want to fight. These were the conditions of war on the Western Front; surely nothing of any consequence could possibly be going on in the waterless sands of the Sinai? Naturalist and, in the 1920s, the governor of Sinai, Major Claude Jarvis, certainly thought as much when he said: 'In France, with its incessant shelling, pouring rain and waterlogged trenches the soldier envied and in fact felt intensely hostile to his opposite number in Egypt, who in his opinion was having a "cushy" time basking in the warm sunshine and being fanned to sleep by lovely *houris*.' The commander of the Worcestershire Yeomanry, Major Lord Hampton, was a little more blunt: 'I have been told that it was at one time the vogue in England to consider the soldiers whom fate and the War Office had condemned to serve in Egypt to be only one degree better than a conscientious objector.'

Even Australians sent to Egypt – at least at the beginning of their service – weren't immune to these sentiments, either: 'Bin 'avin' a good picnic out 'ere?' yelled one newly arrived Australian in his best Cockney from the deck of his steamer on the canal to a British unit on shore. 'Awww, not too bad!' came the reply from an Englishman doing his best to imitate Australian colonial twang. 'Just bin moppin' up the Turks that cleared you orf the Gallipoli Peninshular!' Of course it wouldn't be long before these sentiments were put to rest.

If Great Britain was going to retain control of the Suez Canal it was clear the Ottoman Army was going to have to be pushed all the way out of the Sinai and back into Palestine. And if this were to happen the British and their allies would be needing three things in abundance: men, water … and camels. Camels were by far the most practicable method of transport over the soft sands that lay ahead – sands that bedevilled anything with wheels. Transport vehicles had six-inch iron rims bolted onto their tyres to add traction, while field artillery carriages had blocks of wood chained to their wheels to distribute the weight over as wide an area as possible to prevent the wheel from disappearing into the sand. For almost everything else, there was the camel. Officers were ordered to the Nile Delta to procure as many healthy camels as they could get their hands on, and eventually tens of thousands would be in service with the Egyptian Expeditionary Force – the single largest armada of camelry that had ever been assembled. After Allah had created all of the animals in the world, legend has it he then turned to man and said: 'Now try your hand.' The camel was the best we could do.

By any measure you care to use, Oliver Hogue lived a remarkable life. Born in Sydney on 29 April 1880, one of ten children, he grew to become a gifted athlete and skilled horseman who, once his formal education at Sydney's Forest Lodge Public School came to a merciful end, left home for the life he'd always yearned for – that of a bushman. Hogue purchased a bicycle and spent years riding thousands of kilometres up and down the east coast of Australia before joining *The Sydney Morning Herald* in 1907. When war broke out in Europe he enlisted as a trooper with the 6th Light Horse Regiment, and arrived in Egypt as a Second Lieutenant in December 1914. After five months at Gallipoli he contracted enteric fever and was sent to England to convalesce, was promoted to lieutenant, and became orderly officer to Brigadier Colonel Granville Ryrie. The WWI historian Charles Bean often saw the two together and wrote: 'Day after day the Brigadier tramped round ... with his enthusiastic and orderly officer, Oliver Hogue.'

In letters home to his family and in dispatches to the *Herald* he called himself Trooper Bluegum, and seemed by all accounts to be a man of rare integrity, a reporter who refused to demonise the Turks and on at least one occasion denied rumours of Turkish mutilations of their enemies. Hogue got along with those around him, 'enjoyed a good scrap', and became a published author when his letters were collected into two books in 1916: *Love Letters of an Anzac* and *Trooper Bluegum at the Dardanelles*. He enjoyed looking, he later wrote, at the way his fellow Australians 'played the game of war' and, despite the literary critic Bertram Stevens claiming his prose was not 'poetry in the serious sense of that word', it did reflect nonetheless 'the impressions of a buoyant and generous soul', and showed us a man who regarded danger as a necessary ingredient in bringing zest to life. In his disregard for danger Hogue was typical of many of those around him who tried their best to view the Gallipoli landing as a kind of tryst, playing cards and going swimming while under fire and complaining that the beaches were 'bloody poor farming country'.

At the end of his convalescence Hogue was transferred to the 6th Light Horse, which had been redeployed from Gallipoli to the Sinai, and he fought in the battle at Romani. In November 1916 he was promoted again, this time to captain – and found himself sitting on the back of a camel. Oliver Hogue – cyclist, bushman, adventurer, poet, soldier and self-proclaimed war correspondent – had been transferred to the Imperial Camel Corps (ICC), created in January of 1916 at the conclusion of the failed campaign at Gallipoli and raised in response to an uprising by the Senussi, the German and Ottoman–backed tribesmen who inhabited the oasis of the Western Desert. Hogue's time with the ICC would lead to the publication in 1919 of his book *The Cameliers*, a rollicking and at times irreverent description of the antics of this most unorthodox corps.

Comprised initially of four companies, the ICC was quickly increased to four battalions – the Australian 1st and 3rd Battalions, the British 2nd Battalion and the New Zealand 4th Battalion – under the command of Brigadier Clement Leslie Smith. Each member of the ICC did his bit to continue, whether aware of it or not (probably not), the ancient and honourable tradition of camel warfare. The Persian emperor Cyrus the Great used camels to help defeat the Lydian cavalry at the Battle of Thymbra in 547 BCE, a battle so decisively won by Cyrus that a myth began that the smell of a camel had the capacity to disorient and even to 'spook' horses, therefore making the camel an ideal beast to use against mounted cavalry. The persistent nature of the myth was one reason the Emperor Claudius sent a brigade of camels with his 40,000-strong army when it set out across the English Channel in more than 800 boats in 43 AD to conquer Britain. In India, where according to myth camels were first born out of the feet of Brahma, stone tablets, sculptural representations and friezes depict camels in early cavalry formations dating back to the ninth century.

The camel's secret weapon against the unforgiving heat of the desert is its miraculous biology. Its humps store fat (not water) that metabolises energy and allows its host to go for long periods without food or water. When they reach water, they can consume up to 46 litres in a single session. To keep the desert sand out of eyes, nose and ears their eyelashes grow in two parallel rows, their nostrils can be closed, and their ears are blessed with an abundance of fine hairs. Their leathery knees protect them from hot sand when they have to kneel, their lips are leathery too so they can munch on prickly desert plants, their hooves are split so their feet don't sink into the sand when they walk, and their internal temperature can change to help conserve water when the heat is at its worst. They can even absorb water in their blood cells.

Oliver Hogue and his fellow cameleers knew little of all this. For them life in the ICC was just an uncomplicated mix of long desert rides and occasional skirmishes with the Senussi, who were proving a troublesome disruption to British interests along the Nile Valley. The Italians and Austrians had been supplying the Senussi with arms since late 1915, including Mauser rifles, machine guns, and even light artillery pieces that had been unloaded off Austrian submarines right under the eyes of the British Mediterranean fleet. In early 1916 the Senussi began a series of winter raids that forced the British commander, General Sir Archibald Murray, to divert troops from the Sinai to engage them.

The Senussi movement was founded in the early 1800s by Muhammad ibn Ali as-Senussi, an Algerian religious leader who traced his lineage back to Fatima, daughter of the Prophet Muhammad. By the mid-1840s his followers stretched from the Algerian capital of Tunis to the shores of the Red Sea. In 1902 Muhammad Ali's grandson, Ahmed Sharif as-Senussi, was elected the movement's leader and in addition to fighting against French expansion in the Sahara in 1911 sided with Turkey in the Turko–Italian War in Cyrenaica. Then when the Turks withdrew from that campaign the Senussi, who weren't averse to a scrap, took to fighting the Italians while at the same time developing friendly relations with the Egyptians, with whom they shared a distrust of the growing Mahdist movement in the Sudan, the fundamentalist ideals of which represented a potential threat to them both. Which is why it came as a surprise to everyone, the Egyptians in particular, when in 1915 Ahmed Sharif crossed into western Egypt with a significant force of Berber, Arabs and several thousand Bedouin, egged on by the Turkish and German governments who were hoping the incursion would draw thousands of troops away from the defences along the Suez Canal.

The strength of the Senussi, who were more of a nomadic sect than a tribe, was estimated at around 20,000 men. They had an abundance of captured Italian rifles and ammunition, several artillery pieces including six mountain guns, mounted troops and camels for transport, and were led by the Turkish commander Nuri Bey, half-brother of Enver Pasha, Turkey's war minister. But it wasn't just weapons that made the Senussi dangerous. It was because of their added capacity to influence political and religious thought in Egypt that the British considered them as much a threat to the security of the Suez Canal as the Turks themselves. The Senussi campaign was triggered on 5 November 1915 when the auxilliary cruiser HMS *Tara* and the transport HMT *Moorina* were torpedoed by a German submarine off the coast from Sollum, Egypt's westernmost port. Their survivors were given over to the Senussi, and Senussi raids on Allied barracks and encampments at Sollum and Sidi Barrani followed ten days later.

On 20 November 1915 orders were given for the establishment of a Western Frontier Force (WFF). But gathering a force together when so many troops were still engaged on the Gallipoli Peninsula while keeping the Suez Canal properly garrisoned meant the WFF would by necessity have to be cobbled together with whatever troops were available. This led, from a cavalry perspective, to the formation of the 1st Composite Australian Light Horse Regiment, men drawn together from all Light Horse units currently either in training or awaiting deployment to Gallipoli as well as reinforcements from the 9th Light Horse. Despite not having the benefit of almost any training, and having little idea of how a Light Horse regiment should operate in the field, they were quickly formed into three squadrons, comprising men from the 1st, 2nd and 3rd Light Horse Brigades, their medical staff taken from the 3rd Light Horse Field Ambulance and their signallers from the 3rd Light Horse Signal Troop. Fortunately there were just enough veteran soldiers to make it all work, including Arthur Thompson of the 3rd New South Wales Mounted Rifles, who was a veteran of the Boer War (and a witness at the trial of Breaker Morant). In all, the Australian force totalled some 535 officers and men and they were sent by train from Cairo to Alexandria where they received their swords and rifle buckets, and from there they set out along the coast to Mersa Matruh, arriving there on 11 and 12 December 1915.

Add to our Light Horse a mix of three partially trained British battalions and Yeomanry regiments, the 1st Battalion of the New Zealand Rifle Brigade, a battalion of the 15th Sikhs (who would bear the brunt of the fighting before being redeployed back to India), the Notts Battery Royal Horse Artillery and the 6th Royal Scots. The campaign that followed, however, would not be characterised by large battles but rather a series of small engagements that were nevertheless a strain on the resources of the Allied forces.

It would be an odd sort of campaign, fighting an enemy that struck in small numbers, who knew the terrain and possessed a high degree of mobility. If they were to be successful in engaging them the WFF's commander, Major-General Alexander Wallace, an Indian Army officer, would have to find a way to match the nimble qualities of his adversary. First he drew a thousand of his men together, mostly from British and Australian light cavalry units, and organised for them to be trained to beat the Senussi at their own game by putting them on camels. Unfortunately what they gained in mobility they lost in firepower – without heavy machine guns or artillery they were suddenly no more heavily armed than their adversaries. The cameleers were given a reprieve, and it was decided that wheels, rather than hooves, were the answer. Taking a leaf from the French, who had used light motorised vehicles to great effect in Morocco almost a decade earlier in their own fight against desert tribesmen, Murray sequestered armoured cars from the Royal Navy, and not just any armoured cars but Rolls Royce–designed and –built armoured cars with armour plating and mounted machine guns. He also took delivery of three armoured cars that had been built in Australia at the Vulcan Engineering Works in South Melbourne. The cars belonged to the seldom-referenced, wholly obscure and quite inspiring 1st Armoured Car Section.

When hostilities broke out in 1914 a group of well-intentioned motoring enthusiasts and engineers gathered in Melbourne and thought what a good idea it would be if they could manufacture some armoured cars for the coming fight. So they found an engineering plant (the Vulcan Engineering Works) and at the same time were fortunate in being given three high-powered chassis from sympathetic benefactors – a 50 hp Daimler, a 60 hp Mercedes and a 50 hp Minerva. Wasting little time, they designed their gun mountings and drew up their specifications, sourced 3/32" steel plating from

England, and got to work putting it all together. They overlaid the plating twice, sometimes three times where necessary, and designed steel louvres to protect the cars' radiators. Turrets capable of turning through 360 degrees and housing Colt machine guns were placed on top of the cars, which, despite all of the added weight, somehow were still capable of speeds up to 100 kph. And when they were done making them the cars were given over to the Australian government, who had been pretty busy themselves recruiting and training the men who'd drive and maintain them, the men of our country's brand-new unit – the 1st Armoured Car Section. In early 1916 the unit was loaded aboard the HMAT *Katuna,* a tired old troopship that left Melbourne with its armoured cargo and had a horror eight-week crossing of the Indian Ocean that itself would be worthy of a book if the story hasn't already been told. In July the Australians joined with the armoured Rolls Royces of the Royal Naval Air Service and together, it was hoped, they would chase the Senussi across the sands of the Western Desert back where they came from.

On 15 August they were sent from Ismaïlia to Minya, a town 300 km to the south of Cairo on the Nile River. They joined the 11th and 12th British Light Armoured Car batteries in patrolling a line of blockhouses 100 km west of the oasis of Bahariya. But they wouldn't be there for long. The cars that could go at speeds of 100 kph on the streets of Melbourne went considerably slower in the desert and were proving less able than the British Rolls Royces in negotiating the difficult terrain. The Colt machine guns the Australians had attached to the chassis were working well enough, but the cars proved difficult to manoeuvre. In December they were returned to Cairo after the unrelenting demands being placed upon them saw them continually breaking down, and with repairs often impossible to effect due to a shortage of spare parts.

Then on 3 December 1916 the 1st Armoured Car Section was renamed the 1st Australian Light Car Patrol, an appropriate name change considering the sort of replacement vehicles they were about to receive: six slightly used American-made Model T Fords, with Lewis machine guns mounted to their bonnets! The care were given names, some of which were more obvious than others: Anzac, Billzac, Osatal, Silent Sue, Imshi and Bung – and the unit was redeployed to map new routes from the Dakhla oasis to the Kharga oasis, 300 km south of Minya! It was difficult to imagine any Australian troops being in a more remote and strategically insignificant corner of Egypt. But the unit survived and, contrary to expectations, somehow managed to avoid being decommissioned even when it was determined at the end of 1916 that the threat from Turkish forces in the Sinai now far outweighed anything the weakened and largely dispersed Senussi were capable of staging. So the 1st Australian Light Car Patrol were given a reprieve, were sent to the Sinai, and remained there throughout the campaign and on into Palestine in support of our Mounted Division. They choked on the dust in the Jordan Valley, patrolled the quiet roads west of Jerusalem and, in October 1918, with the war almost over, were there at rest in the midst of the final prize, Damascus.

By the end of 1916, all of the scattered oases throughout the Western Desert that the Senussi had been using as bases had been reoccupied and they were forced to retreat to their stronghold at Siwa Oasis. In an effort to capture Ahmed Sharif, Sir Archibald Murray launched an assault on Siwa in February 1917 but missed his quarry. Ahmed Sharif escaped, and in August 1918 was smuggled aboard an Austrian submarine and headed to Constantinople (present day Istanbul), where he lived out the war as a prominent member of the Pan-Islamic movement.

In World War II the Senussi had a change of heart. Oppressed by the invading Italians, whom they never tired of disliking, they threw their support behind Britain and her allies, in particular helping shot-down air crews make their way back to their front lines. The Senussi gave them food, water and shelter despite the threat of being executed by the Italians if they were found to be providing assistance to the enemy.

With the armoured cars on patrol throughout 1916 the ICC had been relieved of the task of riding through the desert in what would likely have been a series of futile pursuits of a mostly invisible enemy. Instead they had been given the equally sedentary job of patrolling oases to the south. It was dull work, and there was little of the sort of devotion shown by the cameleers to their ungainly mounts that our Light Horsemen would soon be known for in regard to their horses. Little training was provided on camel tactics and strategies, which hardly mattered given the circumstances, and what they were told came from the well-meaning but inadequate manual *Camel Corps Training 1913*, which was long on handling and how to drill a camel but bereft on how to ride one into battle. The lesson would be learned the hard way that camels, for reasons of temperament and general obstinacy, could not be disengaged from battle in the same way horses could be. The ICC would suffer significant losses during the Second Battle of Gaza in April 1917 as well as in operations against the Turkish defensive line that stretched from Gaza east to Beersheba. Then as British and dominion forces moved ever northward through Palestine into increasingly fertile landscapes the advantages the camel had over horses began to decline and the ICC would finally be disbanded in June 1918 and the Australians in it used to raise the 14th and 15th Light Horse Regiments.

The camels of the ICC would test the patience of riders time and again as they had done for centuries. Few accounts of their irascibility, however, have come down to us that match the wits-end frustration felt by the cameleer better than Antony Bluett's 1919 account of life in Egypt, *With Our Army in Palestine:*

Now the camel has all the obstinacy of a mule and, in addition, is almost impervious to pain. Flogging has little effect on him and profanity none whatever; violence is necessary. Frequently the only way to shift one of these obstinate beasts was by lighting a fire under him! Then he moved, sometimes in such a hurry that he fell over the precipice and broke his neck. I am aware that this method is not mentioned in 'Field Service Regulations', but a great many things are done on active service which do not come within the scope of that admirable volume ... You could not stop the war and wait till one recalcitrant camel was ready to allow six hundred of his fellows to pass.

On the plus side for camels, in addition to the Arabic belief that they know all the 100 names of Allah and that their urine is effective in treating ear infections, are their exceptional hearing and eyesight, dust clouds notwithstanding. On a march north from Jerusalem a camel with the 2nd Light Horse Regiment, laden with almost 100 kg of hard tack biscuits, was crossing a viaduct just prior to dawn when, blinded by the dust, it blundered its way over the edge and plunged down into the riverbed below. It was assumed the poor camel was deceased, but when the men of the 2nd Light Horse clambered down to the river they found the camel happily grazing along the riverbank.

No one who has ever spent any time around a camel would deny they're an obnoxious beast, but they weren't the only animals capable of causing handlers grief. After arriving in Mersa Matruh in late 1915, Antony Bluett described the mules' eating habits:

They ate the head-ropes that fastened them to the horse-lines, and the incensed picket spent half the night chasing them and tying them up again with what was left of the rope. Fortunately we obtained chains at a railhead, and as these were uneatable they turned their attention to the horse-blankets and ate them! Soon it was impossible to 'rug-up' at night, for there was not enough rug left. We used as pillows the nose-bags containing the following day's grain, and many a time were awakened by a half-famished mule poking an inquisitive muzzle under our heads.

Sergeant Patrick Hamilton of the 4th Light Horse Field Ambulance, who had his horse taken from him and replaced with a racing camel while in southern Palestine in 1917, soon however came to relish the camel's advantages:

In the first place, a camel needs very little attention – no grooming, one meal a day, and water every third or fourth day. Also, when not wanted, you simply tie him down by making him sit down and tying up his left front leg so he cannot get up. And there he will stay, patiently, for many hours, until needed. Secondly, you can carry almost anything you want on a camel. On a horse there is a definite limit, laid down by regulations. But on a camel I can carry extra blankets and a good supply of food. Finally, on a night march you can snooze on a camel in the roomy, four-posted, bucket-like 'saddle' over the hump, and shift your position from side to side, which you cannot do on a horse.

Camels may have been able to bear greater loads than horses, were hardier, able to cover longer distances without water and were almost as fast as their equine counterparts, but they were also wholly unattractive and smelly beasts prone to a litany of camel-specific diseases and conditions, almost all of which were disgusting. There was sarcoptic mange, which resulted in hair loss that mostly began on the head but soon spread to the more 'thin-skinned' regions such as the udder and penile sheath. Highly infectious, sarcoptic mange was easily transmitted through contact with harnesses and saddles, and transmission from camel to human was common. Once a herd has become infected, continuous re-infections were all but impossible to prevent.

Virtually every camel lived day in, day out with all manner of internal parasites including gastrointestinal parasites that resulted in frequent bouts of diarrhea and/or constipation. The wasting disease trypanosomiasis, spread by flies, killed eight out of every ten camels it infected. There was the dreaded camel pox with all its inherent crusts and pus-laden sores, viral infections including rabies and foot-and-mouth disease, and those horrible weeping wounds around their nostrils known as 'nose peg tears' caused by the use of iron nose pegs. And of course if that all weren't enough there was the ubiquitous camel spit, which wasn't really saliva at all but partially digested food returned to the mouth as cud and which gathered along their droopy lips and flicked out randomly whenever anything happened to annoy them. Which was often.

Ticks were also a perennial annoyance. 'There were big ticks, little ticks, and middle-sized ticks,' Hogue wrote in *The Cameliers*. 'Camels newly arrived from the desert were swarming with ticks,' and the job of removing them proved so distasteful that his mates coined the mock Latin phrase '*Infra dig camelorum, ora pro nobis*', meaning 'O Lord, fancy coming to this!'

The sheer numbers of camels required to carry the EEF and its supplies across the Sinai meant that there would have to be camel drivers to help tend to them, and so the Camel Transport Corps (CTC) was born. Consisting almost entirely of Egyptian labour the CTC was the visible manifestation of a broken British promise. Prior to the war Britain guaranteed Egypt that it, and it alone, would shoulder the burden of any coming conflict and that Egyptians would not be called upon for assistance in prosecuting the war. But no one of course had come even close to anticipating the numbing logistics required to fight a large-scale desert war, and the CTC soon became a vital ingredient in the fray. Their pay was mediocre and the conditions harsh, but there was no shortage of recruits and the barefooted men of the CTC in their sky-blue outer garments were soon an everyday sight for the men of the Imperial Camel Corps as they crossed the sands of the Sinai Peninsula and crept ever closer to the line they all were so eager to cross – the dividing line between Sinai and the verdant pastures of the Promised Land. But the Turks weren't just going to fall back.

On 23 April 1916 Turkish infantry overran the 1600-strong British Fifth Yeomanry Brigade at Katia, 40 km to the east of Romani, a position within striking distance of the canal that had been garrisoned to protect the railway and pipeline that were coming east from Kantara. They inflicted more than 300 casualties on a poorly led British force that fled in such haste they left behind champagne, gin, whisky, unopened letters, various pieces of antique furniture and the personal effects of five English lords. At 8.45 a patrol had spotted hundreds of Ottoman infantry and cavalry approaching, and within an hour Turkish guns were bombarding British positions.

Katia was defended only by a series of far-flung outposts spread over an ineffectual 42 km front, each too far from the other to provide any meaningful assistance. It was a poor defensive strategy and the British lost 400 men, and in response the 2nd Australian Light Horse Brigade and the New Zealand Mounted Rifles were rushed to Katia the following day, but when they arrived they found it deserted. The Turks, well satisfied with their raid, had returned east to their garrison at Bir el Abd on the old Silk Road. Over the course of the following week Murray ordered the remainder of the Anzac Mounted Division to Katia and Romani, and the towns that had a week earlier been jointly defended by just a few hundred were now home to many times that number. The only positive to come out of the debacle at Katia was that it brought to an end the strategy of establishing small defensive units in isolated outposts across broad fronts. The commander of the Anzac Mounted Division, Major General Harry Chauvel, told his men that from now on they would operate out of single, large encampments and keep an eye on the horizons via a series of coordinated patrols. It was a strategy the Allies would maintain until the very end of the Sinai campaign.

Katia turned out to be a prelude for a much larger battle to come at Romani, a battle made possible only after another heroic Turkish desert march. In July a force of 20,000 had left Palestine and crossed the desert in just six days on the scantiest of daily rations: 600 grams of biscuits, 150 grams of dates and 9 grams of tea. They brought with them two 28 kg artillery pieces, which they pulled through the sand by hand after the mules that were pulling them dropped to the ground from thirst and exhaustion. There were no tents taken on the march (everyone slept under the stars), and even the officers had to suffer a baggage allowance of just 5 kg. Like almost the entire Ottoman Army in the Great War they were poorly equipped, poorly fed and poorly supplied, having to fight under circumstances the Allied forces who opposed them never had to endure.

Ever since the war began the Ottoman armies, and in particular its foot soldiers, had disadvantage as their constant companion. Almost always they were outnumbered. A shortage of accurate maps saw Turkish officers tearing maps out of guidebooks. Their officers rarely received any meaningful leave (not to mention their NCOs and infantry, for whom leave was merely a concept), and the infantry almost never received mail from home, a privation they had long been accustomed to with their mail system only ever having operated with any real efficiency in the Balkans campaign. On their final approach to Romani, for instance, Turkish infantrymen laboriously laid wooden planks over miles and miles of soft, sandy desert so they could drag their artillery pieces with them, inch by exhausting inch, and were then forced into a march across the final 16 kilometres before being ordered into a spirited assault against a superior, well-entrenched and well-fed enemy!

The Turks arrived at Romani late on 3 August 1916 with barely any mounted troops, wearied after their long march, and with inferior artillery. Nevertheless they began to close in around Katia and Romani, and this time the intention of the army's commander, Kress von Kressenstein, was not to hit and run, but to establish a fortified position from which he could, with his big guns, move forward and disrupt and if possible prevent the passage of ships through the canal. Back in Palestine Turkish officials had the battle won before it had even been fought. Djemal Pasha, the commander of the Ottoman forces issued a telegram proclaiming the defeat of the British forces at Romani before a shot had even been fired. A subsequent telegram, sent after news of Turkish losses began to filter in, claimed the canal had been breached, British warships sunk, and the EEF routed and in a chaotic retreat. Turkish losses were 'five men and two camels' (the camels, it went on to say, were later retrieved). But then the most accursed luck came out of the desert! A terrible sandstorm had blown in, and 'the glorious army took it as the wish of Allah not to continue the attack, and has therefore withdrawn in triumph'. Of course what had actually happened at Romani and what was happening in Djemal Pasha's fertile imagination were two very different things.

Only the 1st Light Horse Brigade was in position early on 4 August to repel the initial Turkish assault, and it was quickly forced to fall back. But as the day wore on reinforcements arrived and the position stabilised. 'Allah finish Australia! Allah finish Australia!' was the cry some recall hearing at Romani that was, in the words of Oliver Hogue 'a cry that tickled the Anzacs immensely'. Hogue was there, in the front line at Romani, when the Turks came at them like 'a spear thrust right at the heart of our position. Abdul,' he wrote, 'had staked his all on one desperate charge.' But in the maze of sand dunes that surround Romani the heavily laden Turks floundered. They did manage to take a few strategic hills – notably Mount Meredith, Mount Royston and Wellington Ridge – and even fought their way into areas in the south of Romani, but that was as far as they would get. When the British, Australian and New Zealand forces launched their counterattack the Turks – who had lost over 2000 men in the initial assault – fled the battle on foot. The New Zealand Mounted Rifles took 500 prisoners in the vicinity of Mount Royston alone, with Oliver Hogue describing their brutal assault upon the hapless Turks: 'With a blood-curdling yell the Maorilanders charged with the bayonet, and cut their way clean through the attacking column, cleaving it in two.'

As far as retreats go the Turks couldn't have wished for better. They were adept at moving quickly over sand, so much so that even our mounted troops were unable to catch them. As one soldier with the British Yeomanry wrote: 'He fought like a man and a gentleman, and though we chased him out of it he is by no means routed into rabble, and when we go and dig him out, I think we shall find him as game as ever.' Five thousand Turkish prisoners were captured at Romani including a number of German officers, one of whom was asked: 'Say, old Hun, what do you think of the Australians now?' The officer replied: 'They are splendid fighters. Still, I do not think they are any better than they think they are.'

In his account of the battle in his book *Desert Column*, Trooper Ion Idriess wrote of how the Anzacs, who took the brunt of the attack, fought and took 105 killed and 30 wounded that day, more than 50 per cent of the EEF's overall casualties despite being only a small percentage of the Allied force. Nevertheless their sacrifice had saved the day:

From palm to palm, from mound to mound, we fought

*forward, sweat creasing rivulets of sand down our faces,
matting the hair on bared chests ... Over every bare patch
the Turks had machine guns trained ... the men ... simply
had to rush through a continuous stream of bullets ... We
fired back, split up into many little groups ... We'd jab our
bayonets through the bushes, and the Turks would stab
back – we'd burst in around the bushes and glimpse the
Turks' gasping mouths as they hopped back behind the
next mound.*

At Romani a trooper in the 6th Light Horse had three
bullets pass through his body courtesy of Turkish snipers.
Unable to crawl to safety and with no stretcher-bearers to
spare, six men from his regiment crossed a hundred yards of
coverless terrain to get to him, and that heroic act only done
thanks to the grace of the Turkish gunners. When the wounded
man was reached his rescuers took off their tunics, wrapped
them around their rifles, and placed their weapons under the
wounded man's body. Lifting him up into a crouching position,
with one digger supporting his head and another his legs, they
began to make their way back to their lines. At any moment
a burst of gunfire could have ended it for all of them, but still
they continued. The men were gasping, and some were too old
for that sort of thing but still they carried on, the setting sun
making them a difficult target for an enemy who in any case
clearly had no stomach for that sort of slaughter.

At last, with darkness descending, the group arrived at
a horse line. 'I can hang on if you put me in the saddle,' the
wounded man told them. So they placed him on a horse – it
was the man's own horse he'd brought with him from his farm
in Australia – and with one of his six rescuers riding beside
him, they disappeared from view.

Whether Australians had fought or not at Romani
remained a mystery to the folks back home. Romani had been
a great victory, but a victory won by the British in which some

Australians and New Zealanders happened to take part. Not until 1917 did a paragraph appear in the Sydney *Bulletin* with the horrifying statistic: 87 per cent casualty rate. The British cables quoted in the Australian press used phrases like 'our mounted troops' or 'the victorious Desert Column'. And at the Second Battle of Gaza that was to come, when the Imperial Camel Corps made up of Australians became the only unit to reach its objective in that failed attack, British cables spoke only of how 'the Camel Corps did good work carrying water for the Light Horse'.

British propaganda aside, Romani settled any pretensions the Turks had regarding Egypt and of any credible threat the Ottoman Empire might pose to the Suez Canal. It restored Egypt's territorial integrity, and was the first real victory of the Allied war effort after a string of losses in France and at Kut in Mesopotamia. And it was at Romani that our Light Horsemen first began to realise just what their horses were capable of – travelling every day through sand so deep it reached up to their fetlocks, carrying up to 100 kg on their backs and enduring days without water – and all of this at the height of a Sinai summer! After the battle the enemy fell back to Bir el Abd, then further east again to El Arish. When a combined British and Anzac force arrived at El Arish on 20 December 1916, however, they found it abandoned, its garrison having fallen back to Magdhaba, some 50 km to the southeast.

The Sinai campaign proved to be a very different war to that being fought in the trenches of the Western Front. In the Sinai the front was fluid, scattered, moving quickly here and there with night rides catching enemies unawares and where much of the fighting was in the open or in small redoubts. In France and Belgium the armies were largely stagnant, with fronts that barely moved or when they did twitched murderously back and forth over the same pockmarked landscape of bodies and mud. In Sinai there were sand dunes, trenches, open fighting, mountains and mountain passes, at least five distinct 'theatres' if you like: the initial fight in 1916, a transitional period in 1917 in trenches along the Palestinian border, Gaza–Beersheba from March to October 1917, the campaign in the Judean Hills fighting hilltop to hilltop from late 1917 to January 1918, and the Jordan Valley to Jaffa line and eventual breakout in 1918. Our own diggers' recollections of what it was like to fight in Sinai and Palestine depended upon which of these five very different campaigns, or combinations thereof, they participated in. If you were hit by a bullet, though, it didn't matter the aspect or circumstances of the fight.

The weather in the Sinai routinely went from blisteringly hot during the day to, in the words of T. E. Lawrence (of Arabia), a 'winter cold with the unbridled cold of a country over which the wind can rage in unchecked fury'. It was a shockingly empty place, with few towns of any meaningful size, no roads and few crops. Even the Bedouin tribes that had lived there for centuries had enough supplies only for themselves with none to spare for passing regiments. The need for water was mentioned in every communiqué. The Sweet Water Canal – a man-made canal from Port Said in the north to Suez in the south completed in 1863 to bring drinking water to the canal zone – was fine for those troops stationed along the Suez, but armies move fast in the desert and what wells of sweet water there were as the desert columns moved east could not hope to provide enough of the precious liquid for an entire army. Hundreds of engineers frantically constructed aqueducts to take water to soldiers who were always several steps ahead of them, with donkeys and camels sequestered to take it to the front lines in water bags. 'I can honestly say,' said Corporal Roy Dunk of the 3rd Light Horse 'that, except on special occasions, I was thirsty for the whole nine months we were crossing the Sinai.'

Despite the victories in the Sinai the British strategy remained fundamentally defensive, mired in the original thinking of the EEF which was to create a defensive line at El Arish, 24 km west of the border with Ottoman-controlled Palestine and, once there, all that would be needed was garrison duty and patrolling along quiet lines of trenches. The canal had been saved; there was no need to push on. The election of David Lloyd George in December 1916, however, would change all that. Lloyd George wanted to push on into Palestine, and knock the Hun's ally clear out of the war.

In his typical light-hearted fashion Oliver Hogue remembered the Battle of Magdhaba on 23 December 1916 as 'one of the most brilliant and picturesque little battles in the whole war'.

> *No student of war would believe that a small body of dismounted cavalry and camelry, armed only with rifle and bayonet, could charge across open country and capture a strong natural fortress, heavily entrenched, defended by a resolute soldiery scarcely inferior in strength and armed with artillery, machine guns and bombs. And this on the top of a 20-mile night march over unknown country. Yet that is exactly what the Anzacs did.*

Unlike the many stalemates and pointless horrors that had characterised so much of the fighting in Europe, the Battle of Magdhaba was 'a fair dinkum scrap', fought in the open and fought with intent. It wasn't trench warfare, it didn't drag on for days, weeks or months, and you knew who the victor was when it was done.

In 1925 the great Australian war artist Harold Septimus Power painted *Camel Corps at Magdhaba* in which he depicts, with a hypnotic blend of muted blues and yellows that capture the beauty of the desert in its early-morning light, the men of the ICC as they prepare for the assault on the Turkish positions after a night march of more than 80 km, a march that would have been a walk in the park for the sturdy Turk but which left the men of the EEF feeling decidedly wonky. As Antony Bluett wrote:

> *Our horses and men were deadly tired after their long march, and the watering problem was acute. There was literally no water between El Arish and Magdhaba, and the wells at the latter were in the hands of the Turks. However, the Imperial Camel Corps, the Anzacs, and the Royal Horse Artillery, entirely oblivious to everything but their objective, captured the whole series of redoubts and the survivors of the garrison, who fought on till they were completely surrounded.*

Bluett knew how to put things in perspective. With water in such limited supply it was the opportunity to bathe in the sea, to properly wash and cleanse one's entire body and to feel, at least for a while, human again, that had the potential to all but obliterate the unsavoury memories of privation and combat. At El Arish he saw men shed their clothes for the first time in ten days and plunge themselves into the warm waters of the Mediterranean. It was, he wrote, an act approaching 'unwonted luxury', and despite all of the leave that was to come in Palestine nothing would ever approach the joy of bathing in the coastal waters of the Sinai. 'It is ludicrous to note,' he wrote, 'the number of places about which everything was obliterated from the memory, save the fact that one had a bath there.'

The Desert Mounted Column that had fought at Magdhaba departed El Arish at four in the afternoon on 8 January and marched through a moonlit night, with just a few hours' rest, and by dawn came upon Turkish defenders just a few miles from Rafa. The last remaining Turkish stronghold along the eastern frontier, Rafa would be the third major battle of the Sinai campaign and the EEF's victory there would, at last, deliver the peninsula wholly into the hands of the Allies. Rafa was nothing to look at, just an insignificant village. Nearby, the keep of a medieval castle on a hill called el-Magruntein was surrounded by a flat open plain filled with all of the usual Turkish trenches. But it had another feature that many a Tommy and Light Horseman had almost forgotten existed – green grass. The first real pasture the EEF and, more particularly, their horses had seen since leaving the Nile Delta.

The Battle of Rafa on 9 January 1917 saw the 1st and 3rd Australian Light Horse Brigades, the New Zealand Light Horse Brigade, three battalions of the ICC and the British 5th Yeomanry Brigade under the command of Lieutenant General Philip Chetwode encircle 2000 embattled Turks. The New Zealanders were to the north, the Australians on the east and north-east, and the British to the west. Rafa was so close to the border with Palestine that the New Zealanders had to cross over into the Holy Land in order to reach their positions, but it's a blessing they did. In the face of overwhelming machine-gun fire from the Turkish trenches, Chauvel and Chetwode gave orders to break off the attack, and if it wasn't for Hogue's 'Maorilanders', they would have done just that.

When the order was given to withdraw, the New Zealanders, who were the furthest of all the units from headquarters and later would claim that no such order was ever received, were in the midst of a bold and decisive charge towards the Turkish positions, clambering up a 700-metre slope, their bayonets bared. It was a Charge of the Light Brigade without the horses, a charge so audacious that when the nearby cameleers saw what was happening they – Oliver Hogue among them – were so inspired by what they saw they went and made a successful charge of their own! The Turkish lines broke and hundreds began a retreat to the north-east toward some 2500 Turkish reinforcements who were on their way to relieve them. Seeing their own troops busily retreating towards them and thinking that the battle had been lost, the reinforcements turned back. When news of this reached

Chauvel, courtesy of aerial reconnaissance, he was overjoyed. It should be remembered, however, that while the charge of the New Zealanders and the cameleers was without doubt the pivotal moment in the attack, neither charge would have been possible if the defenders hadn't first been forced back into their trenches by a sustained barrage from British artillery. Nevertheless the Turks at Rafa had surrendered in droves, no reinforcements would be forthcoming, and the last battle of the Sinai campaign had been fought and won by the Allies.

Rafa under the EEF was transformed from a sleepy oasis into a swelling sea of men and material who gathered there for the coming drive into Palestine. Day after day brigades of mounted troops, artillery and infantry poured in on the newly laid railway, which had at last caught up with the advancing front, thanks to the tireless and mighty efforts of the indomitable Egyptian Labour Corps, a phalanx of Egyptian labourers that not only built railroads and laid water pipes but also managed sanitation, loaded lorries, manned wharves, and laid metalled and wire-netting roads over desert sands. They worked in animal hospitals, and were even sent to aid T. E. Lawrence in organising his Arab revolt. But it was for the laying of Sinai's railroads that they would best be remembered, positioning sleepers and bolting on the rails at the rate of 24 km a month. By the end of 1916 some 13,000 Egyptians were working alongside the troops of the EEF, and by early 1917 it seemed like a railway line was appearing from behind every sand dune. According to some accounts it wasn't uncommon to think you'd bivouacked in some godforsaken corner of the desert only to be woken from a deep sleep by the shrill, piercing whistle of a steaming locomotive.

At this point something needs to be said about that accessory without which our mounted troops would not have been mounted: the horse. Cavalry horses in Egypt, Sinai and

Palestine had a lot asked of them in the Great War. First they had to carry those two indispensable trappings of every riding horse, whether at war or at home: the saddle and harness. Most of the saddles used by Australia were a British design called the 'swivel tree saddle', so called because of the two hinged wooden boards attached to the saddle's frame that allowed it to be adjusted to fit horses of varying girths. The saddle, which was placed over a standard-issue blanket, sat on two padded felt strips that ran parallel along either side of the horse's spine, designed to place as little pressure as possible on its back. The saddle's shoulder blades were designed to be unfettered in their movement, and the saddle needed to be level, not inclining to the front or to the back, with its side bars standing off of the horse's ribs. They were designed to carry an array of stores and equipment. At the front hung the rider's greatcoat, and alongside it a waterproof groundsheet. Behind that were packed a mess tin, a billy can, plates, utensils and a blanket. Weapons included scabbards and various kinds of swords. There was the horse's nosebag and an additional bag containing replacement horseshoes and a supply of nails. Bandoliers – pocketed belts of ammunition – hung about the horse's neck along with extra bags of grain our diggers called 'sandbags'.

Then there was the harness, the proper maintenance of which was spelled out line by copious line in the Light Horse Association's *Rider's Training Manual*. Its leathers, including straps and reins, needed to be long enough to curl around the rider's forefinger without cracking or showing any sign of perishing. All stitching that came into direct contact with the horse's skin needed to be free of knots. Stirrup straps required occasional adjusting so as not to give a buckle time to wear away a hole in the leather. Both harness and saddle, and especially internal surfaces prone to horse sweat such as breast collars and girths should, if time permitted, be soaped every day and dubbin rubbed in to effect a shine. Girths also should be well greased, and all iron components cleaned and lubricated with an oil-filled rag.

There was also all the 'incidental' hardware – head collars, bridles, nose bands, mouthpieces, cheek and jowl pieces and brow bands and other odds and ends designed to guard against pinched lips and tongues. It wasn't uncommon for our poor Walers, for days at a time and often over unfamiliar ground, to carry loads in excess of 150 kg, and it was a joke among the Light Horsemen that once you were fully loaded and in your saddle you were hemmed in by such a preponderance of equipment that unless you were hit square in the chest by an artillery shell, it was impossible to dismount.

The tales of what our Light Horsemen were able to do in the saddle are legendary, but at the time their prowess was not so obvious. Antony Bluett of Britain's Honourable Artillery Company put it this way:

> *The popular idea, I believe, is that all Australians are born in the saddle and that they dash about doing wonderful things with a lariat before they are out of long clothes. This is ludicrously wide of the mark. The percentage of Australians who can ride at all is less than that in England; and very few of even the good horsemen are comfortable for some time on an ordinary English trotting horse. Their own horses have only two gaits: the lope and the gallop.*
>
> *The highest percentage of good riders was to be found in the men from Queensland; even the men from the other states said that, though they would die rather than admit that any other good thing could possibly come from a rival state. As fighting men there was nothing to choose between them.*

Bluett found the Australians to be a difficult mob to get to know. 'Once their confidence was gained,' he wrote in *With Our Troops in Palestine*, 'the Australians were very stout allies.

But they were drawn more to the Scottish than to any other British troops. Perhaps it was the Scot's clannishness that attracted them.'

Another observation by Bluett on the peculiarities of Australians is, well, just too precious not to be given mention:

> *A good story went the rounds. The Turks, holding a certain advanced section of the line, sent a messenger under the white flag across no-man's-land to our trenches to ask the nationality of the troops holding them. If it was English, the messenger said, his comrades were prepared to surrender. As it chanced, a battalion of men from the Home Counties was in possession of the trenches, and the messenger returned with information to that effect. Within ten minutes the whole party of Turks were in our lines! Later they were asked why they had been so anxious for their captors to be English; the reply was that they had been told that the Australians were cannibals, and habitually ate their prisoners.*

A small digression. In April and May of 1916, before Romani and Katia, when some of our infantry were being taken out of Egypt for redeployment in France, more than a few Light Horsemen anxious for a fight and feeling that Germans in Europe would provide better opposition than Ottomans in the desert stowed away in the flotilla of Marseilles-bound troopships. Of those who made it through to the Western Front most were done a favour and arrested by the Military Police and returned, dejected, to Alexandria. One such returnee was Francis Curran of the 7th Light Horse, who was tossed back on a troopship in Marseilles and was still under arrest for desertion when the Turks swept in at Romani in August. During the fight Curran broke free of his confinement – such was his aversion at having to miss out on a scrap – grabbed the nearest stretcher (his rifle had been requisitioned), and brought in off the battlefield amid a barrage of Turkish fire no less than fourteen wounded Australians. Curran, a postman, footballer, avid boxer and competent horseman from the New South Wales country town of Tenterfield, was an honest-to-goodness Australian hero.

Francis Curran enlisted in the AIF on 23 January 1915 and was assigned to the 7th Light Horse Regiment. He embarked at Sydney for Egypt on HMAT *Argyllshire* on 9 April and, from the moment he arrived in Egypt, wanted to be with the infantry. Galled at having to wait until May to join the Anzacs at Gallipoli, Curran hurled himself into the fray as a 'bomb thrower' in the trenches at Lone Pine – literally tossing bombs into enemy positions. Those who saw him engaging the enemy in what became known as 'bombing duels' were so impressed they wrote of this fearless Francis Curran in their letters home, some going so far as to call him 'the bravest man in the 7th if not the entire campaign'. There are accounts of Curran catching Turkish bombs (the Turkish grenades were just the right size for catching, about the size of a cricket ball, though with only a few seconds on their fuses) and tossing them right back at their tossers! Grenades that got through that he wasn't able to throw back he smothered under sandbags. Curran received the Distinguished Conduct Medal for his heroics at Lone Pine, the first DCM awarded to a member of the 7th Light Horse, though it wouldn't be the last.

But it was Curran's heroism as a stretcher-bearer at Romani on 5 August 1916 that saw his luck finally run out. On his fifteenth journey out into the blistering heat of no-man's-land coming to the aid of a fallen comrade he was felled by a single bullet through the heart. In Egypt you can visit the resting place of Corporal Frank Curran, DSO at Row B, Grave #22 at the Kantara War Memorial Cemetery, a short stroll from the banks of the Suez Canal.

The 6th Light Horse Regiment was full of sergeants when it first arrived in Egypt. By the time their ship had anchored in Alexandria after their evacuation from Gallipoli, almost half the men had promoted themselves by using indelible pencils to produce credible facsimiles of sergeant's strips on their hats and sleeves. One evening in March 1917 the regiment, encamped just out of El Arish, had saddled up for their last ride in the Sinai and were either about to cross over, or had only just crossed over – nobody really knew for sure – into Palestine. The significance of the occasion wasn't lost upon the increasingly savvy, world-weary men like George Berrie, his good mate Snow, and the rest of the 6th Light Horse, and in keeping with their newfound world-weariness a heated debate arose as to whether Sinai was a part of Africa or Arabia. Surely it belonged to Africa, as it clearly belonged to Egypt, and Egypt was a part of Africa? Or is the canal itself the actual dividing line? But then how can a man-made trench be a continental divide? Surely any boundary had to be natural? The debate went on for some time, and during it poor Snow had forgotten the 'no smoking' rule. Worse than that, he had also forgotten that a regimental colonel was riding just a few paces behind him. After a few draws the smoke was detected, Snow's name taken down (again), and the fine he was ordered to pay was a hefty seventeen and sixpence! From that moment on, the men of the 6th Light Horse all agreed on one thing at least: that a packet of Onslow cigarettes were without doubt the most outrageously expensive brand of cigarettes in the entire Middle East.

Chapter Six
The Dinkums and the Fighting Fourth

*The two most dangerous diseases prevalent among tourists in
Egypt are typhoid and dysentery caused by microbes which
live in the human intestines. In our country and in England,
where as a rule men's habits are clean and the sewage system
elaborately careful, there is very little chance of anything from
the interior of the human intestine getting to our food and so
infecting us. Our whole sanitary system is designed specially
to prevent this. But in countries like Egypt ... the chance occurs
every day.*

  – Charles Bean, *What to Know in Egypt: A Guide for Australian
  Soldiers*

The SS *Kyarra* was never meant to be a hospital ship.
Built in Scotland for the Australian United Steam
Navigation Company and launched on the River Clyde in
1903, it was created to be a coastal steamer and plied the
route between Fremantle and Sydney for ten years carrying
passengers and cargo before being requisitioned by the
Australian government on 6 November 1914, refitted, and
used to transport our very first medical units overseas to
patch up, they were told, our diggers on the Western Front.
The military had tried to secure a larger, more practical
vessel for the voyage, but their efforts came to naught and
the *Kyarra* was, in the end, the best they could manage.
It sailed from Melbourne on 5 December with eighty-three
medical officers, 160 nurses and around 500 enlisted men
and administrators of the Australian Army Medical Corps

(AAMC), the equivalent of two complete general hospitals, every last one of whom was under the impression they were heading to France. After all, that's where they'd been told they were going. That's where all the fighting was.

And what a voyage! More than 750 members of the First and Second Australian General Hospital, the First and Second Stationary Hospital, and the First Casualty Station were aboard, each being tossed about like corks on the waves in a puny 7000-ton steamer! Living conditions were overcrowded too, and unsanitary to boot. The engines were either on the verge of breaking down or needed running repairs, and its speed never seemed to get beyond that needed to cut a laborious path through the waves hitting its bow. The food was poor too – *so* poor in fact that an outbreak of food poisoning swept through the ship and laid low twenty-two officers and several nurses. There was no fruit, either fresh or tinned, and the only thing to drink was water mixed with limes. Bronchitis, tonsillitis, a maladorous eye disease no one could identify – even influenza – all came and went. But life on board went on regardless. Nurses trained their orderlies, officers were drilled, and everyone was still expected to attend evening lectures, albeit lit by electric lantern lights. By the time the corps arrived in Alexandria it was a miracle no one was crushed to death in the rush to disembark.

From Alexandria they were quickly dispersed across Egypt: the First Casualty Station to Port Said; the Second Australian General Hospital to Mena House, a historic hotel by the Giza plateau; the Second Stationary Hospital went to Mena Camp to establish a Venereal and Infectious Diseases camp; and the First Stationary Hospital to a military camp at Maadi, south of Cairo. The First Australian General Hospital set up in Cairo's magnificent Heliopolis Palace Hotel. Built in just two years from 1908 to 1910, it was Africa's largest, most opulent hotel. The rank and file were housed in the basement, the first and second floors became administrative offices and officers' quarters, the third floor housed the nurses, and – at least initially – patients were put in the restaurant and its public spaces, such as the Rotunda and Great Hall. Its rooms were lofty, its windows panoramic, and its doors opened to its first patients on 25 January 1915.

When Lance Corporal William Dalton Lycett of the 4th Field Ambulance arrived at the First Australian General Hospital on 5 February 1915 after disembarking at Alexandria he thought it 'a fine looking place', and decided he'd take a donkey ride to celebrate just being there. He paid the donkey's owner one piastre, around two and a half pence. The next day he applied for and got a pass to go into Cairo with some friends, and paid half a piastre for a seat in an electric car from Heliopolis Station. Cairo too, he wrote in his diary, was 'a fine looking place'. For tea he had ham and eggs and stuffed tomatoes (eight piastres), took a carriage ride through the city's dusty streets (ten piastres), saw a movie (six piastres), and arrived back at camp safe and well at 22.00. William Lycett had had a fine day.

The care available to our diggers in the hospitals and clearing stations of Egypt and Palestine in the Great War, as basic as they were, stand in stark contrast to what was available during the Mesopotamian campaign in the ancient lands south of Baghdad.

In Mesopotamia there was an acute shortage of doctors, nurses and medicines of all kinds. Almost half of all who were dispatched there developed sandfly fever, colitis or dysentery, and one in five had either tuberculosis or malaria in their bloodstream by the time they returned home. Then there were the *ukhts*, the so-called 'Baghdad sores' – a sloughing ulcer that began innocuously enough as a small, red pimple, then grew until it measured the size of a 50-cent piece. Inflicted by a parasite courtesy of a sandfly bite, an *ukht* usually made its home on the face, hands or ankles and would often still be there twelve months after the initial infection. The locals suffered them too, and it wasn't hard to trace their spread among the populace thanks to the disfiguring scars the sores left on their faces.

If they'd been privy to the statistics, our diggers holding the line against Rommel in the trenches around Tobruk in 1941 wouldn't have spent much time worrying about the prospect of being wounded. In the Western Desert there was nothing like the overwhelming number of battlefield casualties being suffered in Europe, with most of the wounds being superficial, though a precise reason why this should be so is hard to pin down. Of the more than 350 casualties treated by Australia's 2/1st Casualty Clearing Station at Mersa Matruh, for example, just three had penetrating abdominal wounds, six thoracic wounds and three head injuries; the remainder were wounds or fractures in either the arms or legs. Minor injuries by many standards maybe, but that didn't prevent diggers often being in severe distress upon arrival at dressing stations and hospitals after often long journeys on miserable, rutted roads that were nightmare trips for anyone with a fracture that had to be kept stable. Most surgical cases arrived at one of the several Australian base hospitals within six hours of being wounded, with lower limb wounds the most common. North Africa was, after all, a war of mines and booby traps.

Fortunately by World War II medical officers were trained in how to provide blood transfusions. There had been gargantuan strides in the area of blood transfusions in the interwar years thanks in no small part to the pioneering work of the African–American surgeon Charles Drew. In 1940 Drew, who was born into a middle-class family in the Washington, D. C. neighbourhood of Foggy Bottom, established a prototype program at New York's Presbyterian Hospital for the storage, testing, preservation and transportation of blood plasma. Drew's research into fluid balance, diagnosis of shock victims, transfusions, and precisely how to 'bank' blood with the help of anti-coagulants, even what was the best shape for storage containers, was groundbreaking. The thousands of lives saved in World War II through the safe and effective transfusion of blood plasma would not have been possible without him.

Between April and September 1941 there were eighty-seven major amputations done in Tobruk, the majority of those performed immediately upon the soldier being retrieved. Perforated eardrums were common due to shell blasts and were sometimes so large they could not be healed. Magnets were distributed to medical units to remove metallic fragments from eyes, but as most shrapnel was non-magnetic they were of little or no use. More than 300 prescriptions for glasses were ordered from Egypt during the siege, but only sixty-seven pairs ever turned up. Dysentery was an ever-present concern, but due to the diligence of hygiene services never manifested itself as anything more than a threat. Fevers were common, as were persistent and unusually virulent frontal headaches. But mostly it was diarrhea – 1106 reported cases from April to October 1941. Add to that relapsing fever – an infection spread by ticks, which became increasingly commonplace as the siege dragged on and was difficult to control because proper diagnosis was not always possible.

April began quietly for William Lycett. There were some April Fool's Day pranks and soccer matches at the Heliopolis Sporting Ground. Patients were few as there was little real fighting going on, just three one night, five the next, two the night after that. Then on 12 April, everything changed. Lycett's unit received orders to go to Alexandria and board the troopship *Californian* – apparently there was an operation about to begin somewhere in the Dardanelles. After meandering its way north through the Mediterranean and through the islands of the Aegean, the *Californian* finally arrived at its destination on 25 April 1915, dropping anchor about a mile off the Gallipoli Peninsula. 'Fleet is bombarding the coast all along,' Lycett wrote that night in his diary. 'Some Australian troops landed at this point this morning and have been fighting all day. The sound of rifles has not ceased, same with ships guns till about 8pm. Hydroplanes and an observation balloon have been up all day. No firing going on at present. The sight of a lifetime.' After three days spent on the decks of his ship witnessing the bloody baptism of a nation, William Lycett was ordered to scramble over the side and into a waiting trawler. His unit was going ashore, and there they would stay until 15 September – 144 days.

In that time he would witness an unexploded shell fall into a soldier's grave as he was being buried, dress and redress wounds, and treat men whose faces were blackened by the powder the Turks used in their shells. During ceasefires he collected his dead while Turks collected theirs just yards away. He saw men as they were shot through the heart, the eye, the brain. He saw battleships bombard wheat fields and set them ablaze. By 4 June, fifty from his corps had been killed, and no reinforcements came. On 10 June he ate fresh rissoles for breakfast, and watched as a sand bag he'd been sitting on just seconds earlier was cut to shreds by the shrapnel from an exploding shell. He saw his mate Neville Anderson killed when the shockwave of a shell smashed the base of his skull. By August his hospital tent looked like a sieve, it was so full of bullet holes. But William Lycett survived and on 15 September 1915 he and the 4th Field Ambulance were relieved and on their way to the Greek island of Lemnos, where for three months he played rugby and cricket and wrote letters home and went for walks in peaceful valleys and sang in a male voice choir. On 29 December his troopship dropped anchor inside the breakwater at Alexandria. William Lycett had survived the horrors of Gallipoli. He left the 4th Field Ambulance and went to France to save lives in the stinking gluey mud of the Western Front. He would survive that too, returning to Egypt in December 1919 on his way home to Australia.

Almost from the day it was set up, the First Australian General Hospital in Cairo began to expand. The nearby Luna Park fun park and Racecourse Casino were soon swallowed up and fenced off to become an open-air hospital and infectious disease camp. Luna Park in particular became a testimony to the efficacy of an open-air hospital in dry climate, recording just one death from more than 5550 patients admitted from April to November in 1915. Despite the efficiency with which the entire network of primary, auxiliary and convalescent hospitals were established, however, it wouldn't be long until every last man and woman from the *Kyarra* was soon in agreement with historian Charles Bean's conclusion that there were many things in Egypt besides bullets and shrapnel capable of laying a man low.

There were so many casualties from the Dardanelles that soon there weren't enough iron beds in all of Egypt to meet demand. The solution was to make beds from palm wood, the only timber available in any meaningful quantity in a land devoid of forests and used in beds there since the third millennium BCE.

Luna Park's capacity was increased to 1650 beds, and a train line – the Heliopolis Siding – was laid from central Cairo near to the Heliopolis Palace Hotel. When 16,000 wounded diggers arrived in the first ten days of May, the Gezira Palace Hotel was hastily converted into an auxiliary hospital, as were various commercial buildings throughout the city. On 5 May the beautiful Al Hayat Hotel in Helouan south of Cairo on the Nile River was emptied of furniture and fitted out with palm beds. Even a school in Alexandria became a convalescent hospital for 500 patients. In all, 10,600 beds had been cobbled together, almost all of it the work of those first few hundred volunteers from the AAMC who came to Egypt on the overcrowded coastal steamer, SS *Kyarra*. What they had achieved was nothing short of heroic.

When it became apparent that the fighting at Gallipoli wasn't going to be over any time soon it was decided to expand and further equip these auxiliary and convalescent hospitals for the many wounded to come. A lake at Luna Park was drained and turned into a patient dining room, and a barber shop and canteen were added. Iron beds eventually replaced the palm beds, and there were ample bathrooms and latrines. Even its tennis courts were covered over and given louvred roofs. Those for whom it was thought a seaside climate or a spell of saltwater bathing might aid their recovery were sent to the Ras el Tin Convalescent Hospital in Alexandria. Everyone received hot chocolate and lime juice, biscuits, pyjamas, shirts, handkerchiefs, cigarettes, soap, cutlery, socks, drinking mugs – even a pair of slippers – chocolate, writing paper, envelopes and nail brushes too! It was enough to take the sting out of getting wounded.

It's difficult to imagine how many men from the Dardanelles campaign would have needlessly died of untreated wounds and infections if these preparations hadn't been made. It was a baptism of fire for the AAMC, and put an end to any lingering doubts its doctors, nurses and administrative staff may have had as they descended gangplanks in Alexandria on 14 January, that being in Egypt rather than Europe meant they wouldn't have their hands full. The evacuation from the Dardenelles and Gallipoli meant that a quarter of a million Turks were now freed from having to defend their home soil, and were being redeployed to the Holy Land to prop up their empire in the east.

In a letter to Major General W. Bridges, Major General W.

Birdwood conveyed some of his concerns about the temptations of Cairo:

> *We have been given some breathing time here [in Cairo] by Lord Kitchener for one object, and one object only – to do our best to fit ourselves to join in the struggle to the best advantage of our country. I honestly do not think that all of our men realise that this is the case. Cairo is full of temptations, and a few of the men seem to think they have come here for a huge picnic; they have money and wish to get rid of it. The worst of it is that Cairo is full of some, probably, of the most unscrupulous people in the world, who are only too anxious to do all they can to entice our boys into the worst of places, and possibly drug them there, only to turn them out again in a short time to bring disgrace on the rest of us.*

There are no official figures about the extent of venereal disease among Commonwealth forces in Egypt during the Great War. The New Zealand Medical Corps guessed there could have been more than 16,000 cases, but behind closed door vastly greater numbers were touted. One estimate put infectious rates of New Zealanders at 7600 per year, and the Kiwis represented only a minuscule percentage of the Allied contingent. The rates of infection for Australians were particularly high – so high in fact that a special military order was issued on 1 February 1915: 'No pay will be issued while abroad for any period of absence from duty on account of venereal disease.' And not only would a soldier's *own* allotted pay be withheld, but the pay they were signing over to their families was also forfeited, and would have to be made up *first* in the wake of their recovery and return to service before they could begin to receive their own wages. Forfeiting wages sent home meant that families learnt of their loved one's infidelities, the concealment of which was a crime under Section II of the *Army Act*, and it was hoped this might shame the troops into good behaviour. But it was no easy thing winning over the hearts and minds of men on leave when faced with the temptations of Cairo's glut of so-called 'amateur prostitutes'.

One venereal disease hospital at Abbassia was almost always full, and in early 1915 some 450 Australians were sent to Malta for treatment because there just weren't enough beds and staff to look after them. From February to September 1915, 1344 diggers were returned to Australia for treatment. Another order was issued, this time forbidding alcohol to be served to soldiers on leave after 2200 hours, and a curfew placed on those on leave in Cairo. Medical officers and staff began speaking in dramatic terms of how they must 'prevent the spread of VD and the downfall of the Empire'. It was suggested that armed guards be placed around the known prostitute quarters of Cairo, but that idea was abandoned when it was feared such action could force the women in question out of the city and closer to the camps.

From March 1917 the introduction of prophylactics combined with early intervention treatment reduced the number of venereal disease cases by a third, though the last six months of 1918 saw figures return almost to their peak. In the nineteen months until December 1918, 235,277 AIF soldiers serving in Europe and the Middle East went on leave, and more than 142,000 prophylactic 'outfits' were handed out. More than 12,000 presented themselves for treatment overseas, and of those who returned to Australia and received treatment, 70 per cent were aged between twenty and thirty. Eighty-five per cent of all those who presented with symptoms were single.

One positive approach to the VD dilemma, wrote James Barrett, a consulting oculist with the AAMC, was the establishment of soldiers' clubs, made possible with the assistance of the YMCA and the British Red Cross Society, which provided an alternative outlet for men with too much time on their hands:

> *The soldier on leave, tramping about the streets of Alexandria, gets leg-weary and falls an easy victim to the wiles of the various agents abroad. He now can visit his own club, where the entry is free to all men in uniform. He there receives war telegrams, stationery, cheap and excellent meals, and enjoys various forms of entertainment. He meets his friends, and can spend the time under the most pleasant conditions. The building already requires extension, as the pressure on the accommodation is so great. Similar action was taken in Cairo, where after many unsuccessful attempts the Rink Theatre in the beautiful Esbekieh gardens was obtained, owing to the sympathetic help given by His Excellency Sir Henry MacMahon and other authorities. This open-air theatre is a little over an acre in extent, and is a valuable property. It had been leased to a restaurant keeper in the vicinity. Arrangements were made for the supply of light refreshments at bed-rock prices in the theatre, and other meals at low prices at the restaurant which is about fifty yards away. In addition a soldiers' club, managed by ladies, is equidistant, and at this comfortable resort refreshments are supplied in quiet rooms at low rates.*

The soldiers' club managed by ladies that Barrett referred to was begun by Alice Isabel Chisholm. She was the wife of a wealthy New South Wales pastoralist who, upon hearing the news that her son had been wounded at Gallipoli and was recuperating in Cairo, set sail for Egypt to be by his side. When she arrived in Cairo she was appalled by the dearth of amenities for soldiers, so she set about establishing a 'canteen' in the outer suburbs of Cairo, not far from the doctors and nurses of the First and Second Australian General Hospitals who were working out of the Heliopolis Palace Hotel. Her son recovered from his injuries and rejoined his regiment, but fifty-nine-year-old Alice Chisholm did not go home. During a lull in the wake of the battles at Romani and Katia Lieutenant General Harry Chauvel, concerned that his idle troops might create more adverse publicity if left to their own devices, asked Alice if she'd set up a soldiers' club in Port Said. She agreed, and when that was done she set up a third canteen at Kantara, a railway junction on the Suez Canal, with the help of a friend she'd met in a Cairo hospital, Verania McPhillamy.

Verania McPhillamy had recently lost her sweetheart, Ronald 'Ronnie' MacDonald, a trooper with the 1st Light Horse Regiment. The two had met in Sydney in April 1914 at a dance at the Royal Easter Show, and Ronnie had visited her when she was recovering in Sydney's Lister Private Hospital after having her appendix removed. The two soon fell in love, and waved each other goodbye at the docks at Woolloomooloo when MacDonald left for Egypt aboard the troopship *Star of Victoria*, taking with him three keepsakes his sweetheart had given him for his journey: a pen, a set of binoculars and a tiny sliver of blue ribbon.

MacDonald was sent to Gallipoli and survived, but prior to going there had spent five months in Cairo and, like many diggers there, had fallen in with prostitutes. When Verania McPhillamy arrived in Egypt to nurse the Gallipoli wounded as a volunteer nurse in January 1916 she learned of her sweetheart's experiences. Though heartbroken, she stayed in touch with him through letters that were filled with pain but hinted at the possibility of reconciliation. Ronnie's letters, written with the pen Verania had given him, were filled with guilt and tinged by the horrors of war:

> *Very close to Hades. You feel that you never want to see me again, let alone write. You can't feel any worse about me than I do about myself. I'm going for the infantry or any old thing the first chance I get. One crowded hour in*

France will beat this rotten job. Have never known the heat the way it is today – all my candles have melted together.

Ronnie's pleas to Verania to restore their relationship seem not to have been in vain. The letters continued, and in June 1916 she sent him some tobacco as a birthday gift. On 8 August he scribbled a hurried letter to her prior to leading an advanced guard towards a Turkish stronghold at Bir el Abd, about 30 kilometres out of Romani. Fearing he may not be able to write to her for some time if the fight bogged down, he ended the letter with 'Goodbye till then, my dear little girl'. Later that day, Ronnie and two Light Horsemen entered a sandy valley near to the enemy stronghold and were killed by snipers hidden in the dunes. Before their bodies could be retrieved they were stripped of anything of value by a group of prowling Bedouins.

The Kantara canteen had grown from a marquee pitched in the sand in the early months of 1916 into an orderly collection of timber buildings, with the nurses aided in their daily tasks thanks to the requisitioning of a few soldiers who helped dispense tea and also cooked and served meals. Officially it was called the Empire Soldiers' Club. Unofficially it was simply 'Mother Chisholm's'. And it never closed. Oliver Hogue described the canteen at Port Said as a 'refreshing oasis', where a soldier could have a shower, get some rest and receive 'a cheery Australian welcome'. The canteens all grew in size to cater for the ever-increasing numbers of soldiers, and profits were used to keep prices down and improve accommodation. By the end of the war the canteens had served and lifted the flagging spirits of thousands of Australian and Allied servicemen. Refreshments were constantly given out to passing hospital trains, and no one was ever refused a meal of iced tongue and salad, ingredients made possible when Verania

McPhillamy, on a trip to the Cairo markets, found herself in the midst of a negotiating frenzy with merchants and ended the day cornering the tinned tongue market!

McPhillamy was the daughter of a wealthy grazier and racehorse breeder from Forbes in western New South Wales. Her romance with Ronnie MacDonald was her primary motivation for volunteering in Egypt but she stayed until the war's end in 1918, when she went to Jerusalem and opened her 'home away from home' – a resting place for weary diggers in the house of a wealthy German, which she furnished with chairs, curtains and a piano.

On her way home to Australia after the war, McPhillamy met her husband-to-be, Lieutenant Colonel Clive Single of the 4th Light Horse Field Ambulance. The two were married at Warroo near Parkes in New South Wales on 21 June 1920. They had four children, all of whom pursued a university education, something Verania had always wanted for herself but never achieved. Verania Single died in Sydney on 3 February 1961.

Alice Chisholm was made an Officer of the Order of the British Empire in 1918, and Dame Commander of the Order of the British Empire on 3 March 1920. She was sixty-one years old when she became the subject of one of the very few pencil portraits composed by the prolific Australian war artist George Lambert, who sketched her in March 1918 during a visit to her canteen in Kantara. Lambert made no attempt to hide her tired lines or soulful eyes in a portrait full of grace and devotion to duty. 'Here,' Lambert would later reminisce, 'one could halt and have a bath and good food. It had a touch of home, so pleasant, so grateful. When I asked her for a sitting she modestly protested that she was not important enough. I got her to sit in a strong light; she had an interesting, careworn face, and a very charming personality, and her portrait was one of the best of my carefully made drawings.'

In August 1919 the *Goulburn Evening Penny Post* wrote of her: 'Every digger who passed through Egypt will agree that Mrs Alice Chisholm is entitled to be reckoned one of the "Dinkums". She was no fair weather war worker, but one who for four and a half years shared many of the troubles and trials of the desert campaign.' Alice Chisholm was ninety-seven years old when she died at her home in West Pennant Hills, Sydney, of a stroke in May 1954.

The Australian Army Nursing Service (AANS) was established in 1903 as an adjunct to the Australian Army Medical Corps, and during the Great War more than 2000 of its nurses volunteered for active service, working alongside a thousand other Australian nurses from organisations such as the Red Cross. They worked in trains, in clearing stations, tents, troopships, hospital ships and, of course, hospitals, from India to Belgium. Eight would be given the Military Medal for bravery, the highest Imperial award of them all. Twenty-five would lose their lives.

Of all of the women who volunteered to serve as nurses and who suffered the tribulations of the Great War, few garnered the sort of controversy that surrounded Ettie Rout. Born in Tasmania but brought up in New Zealand, Rout worked as a shorthand writer in the Supreme Court after finishing school. It was a role that provided her plenty of insights into all of the social issues of her day. By 1904 she had her own business and was finding work as a reporter as well as developing an interest in cycling and vegetarianism. She had a liking for wearing men's boots and short skirts, and when war broke out she helped establish the New Zealand Volunteer Sisterhood, which provided catering and hospital services for New Zealand soldiers stationed in Egypt.

Ettie Rout believed passionately in socialism, equal pay for women and universal healthcare – the last of which was just as well because when she arrived in Egypt in February 1916 she found herself up to her bootlaces in venereal disease.

Tackling the problem head-on, she quickly made herself unpopular with the New Zealand Medical Corps and various women's groups who accused her of attempting to 'make vice safe' after recommending the distribution of prophylactic kits to servicemen. She also wanted to establish regular inspections of selected Cairo brothels. Rout went to London to argue her case and even created her very own prophylactic kit, which the New Zealand Expeditionary Force began to use towards the end of 1917, an initiative for which she received no acknowledgement for having pioneered. With the *War Regulations Act*, the New Zealand government even had her banned from being published in the nation's newspapers.

The Great War was revolutionising the approach to surgery and medicine, if only because of the massive number of medical emergencies it was generating. Experimentation in surgical techniques, made necessary due to overwhelming workloads, were occurring daily and the role of nurses needed to adapt too. Nurses all of a sudden needed to learn techniques such as fluid resuscitation, the warming of patients, new methods of blood transfusions and the treatment of septic wounds. Some even found themselves using scalpels for the first time in their lives. Women were volunteering for nursing duties in increasing numbers, and not only nurses but female surgeons too. Sadly, the reception they received reflected the misogynistic attitudes of the time.

Female surgeons such as English-born Dr Lilian Cooper, the first female doctor registered in Queensland, and New Zealand–born Dr Agnes Bennett of Neutral Bay in Sydney both volunteered for service but were turned away by recruiting officers because they were women. Agnes Bennett was born in 1872 and left Australia in 1895 to study medicine at the University of Edinburgh. Returning to Sydney in 1901 she set up a private practice in Sydney's Darlinghurst, but such was the level of prejudice against women doctors that she was forced to abandon her practice and take a lesser position at a psychiatric institution. Dissatisfied, she took over the practice of a female doctor in Wellington in New Zealand in 1905 and in 1908 was appointed to the position of Chief Medical Officer at Wellington's St Helen's Maternity Hospital. A consummate defender of women's rights, Bennett completed her MD at Edinburgh in 1911, and in 1915 became the first commissioned female officer in the British Army. Given the rank of captain, she enlisted for overseas service with the non-government Scottish Women's Hospitals (SWH), and was sent to Cairo in 1916 where she worked as a medical officer in its war hospitals before going on to serve in Serbia and northern Greece.

Agnes Bennett was a typical example of Australia's small but growing number of female doctors and surgeons who, because of prevailing government policies, at the time were simply not permitted to enlist and serve with Australian units. Consequently many ended up attending to the needs of soldiers with organisations from other nations, and thus have never been properly recognised in Australia. The list is a long and impressive one. Dr Phoebe Chapple left Adelaide to serve with Britain's Royal Army Medical Corps and was the first female doctor to be awarded the Military Medal. Dr Elisabeth Hamilton-Browne from Sydney was sent to Egypt and then to France, where she was in charge of 500 American clerks as well as working as an assistant surgeon with the Royal Army Medical Corps. Elsie Dalyell was a pathologist and bacteriologist who helped battle the typhus epidemic in Skopje in 1915. Dr Katie Ardill was refused permission to enlist with the Australian Expeditionary Force and so she joined the British Expeditionary Force and became one of its first doctors of either sex to be given field services. Dr Lucy Gullett paid her own way to London in 1915 to join the French Red Cross in Lyons. Head to head it is a list as impressive as any comparable grouping of male doctors, and a sorry commentary on the blinkered nature of recruiting in Australia. And if you were neither a doctor nor a nurse but had a willingness to help and happened to be female? Forget it. Not even if you owned your own ambulance.

Olive King owned her own ambulance. It isn't clear how or precisely why she got it, but get one she did. Despite being the daughter of a privileged Sydney family, Olive King spat out her silver spoon early in life and was as adventurous as the wildest jackaroo. As a teenager she climbed Mexico's 5426-metre Mt Popocatépetl with a group of like-minded male friends, and by the time she was eighteen had developed a keen interest in languages, travel, motor mechanics and rally driving.

Olive King was living in England when war broke out in 1914 and she immediately went to enlist. She even brought her ambulance with her to the recruitment office. But like Agnes Bennett and so many others, she too was rejected and, undaunted and possessing the same never-say-die spirit as her fellow female pioneers she also joined the SWH, despite resenting its puritanical slogan of 'No lipstick, no rouge, no high heels, no jewellery and no dancing in uniform'. Nevertheless, Olive King gritted her teeth, packed up her ambulance, and took it with her to Belgium. Then she drove it through France. And Greece and Serbia as well. Along the way she accumulated no less than five service medals for valour. If you were a nurse in 1915 there were proper avenues to service. But one can only wonder to what degree Australian officialdom hindered the management of our diggers' wellbeing by refusing to take seriously the reservoir of talent and determination that resided in Australia's female doctors and surgeons.

Agnes Bennett may have spent only a short period in North Africa, and Olive King none at all, but their commitment was typical of the many courageous women who did. The Great War opened, according to author Susanna De Vries in her book *Heroic Australian Women in War,* 'the door to the Doll's

House'. Almost immediately after war was declared women began walking away in their thousands from their traditional roles in light industry and as homemakers to become nurses or nurse's aids, lorry drivers, telephonists and secretaries.

Many wrote eloquently of their experiences, and in doing so added immeasurably to Australia's military tome. Sister May Tilton, who joined the AANS in August 1915, wrote that 'saying goodbye to our patients was like parting from brothers'. Sister Nellie Pike wrote of the diet she fed our returning soldiers from Gallipoli while stationed on the Mediterranean island of Lemnos: 'We kept our patients alive with soup made from dried cubes and cooked over an open outdoor fire in a dixie and with bully beef, army biscuits, salty bacon, badly cooked porridge, prunes, rice and straw. The straw was not an issue; it just got in during the cooking process.' Jane Lempriere described how soldiers would come out of their chloroformed states after an operation and 'call for their ward sister like a lot of children calling for mother'.

Alice King was born in Melbourne, trained as a nurse at the Alfred Hospital, and enlisted in the AIF in November 1914 after a boating accident in Perth claimed the lives of her husband and two young sons. She left for Egypt on the SS *Kyarra*, and worked in Egypt with the 1st Australian General Hospital, tending to the first waves of wounded from Gallipoli before being transferred to France in 1916. At 10.25 pm on 22 July 1917 she and three other nurses were caught in a bombing raid at Trois Arbres on the Western Front while working in a casualty clearing station. Casualty clearing stations were the closest medical facilities to the front lines and were often a target for enemy artillery and aircraft as they were generally sited close to ammunition dumps, railway lines and other strategic targets. That night German planes dropped a number of bombs on the station as Alice King was following an orderly along some duckboards towards the pneumonia ward. She was holding a lamp to help her find her way when the first bomb hit just metres from her, making a crater a metre and a half deep. With her lamp blown from her hands, she fell into the bomb crater. 'I shall never forget,' she later wrote, 'the awful climb on hands and feet out of that hole ... filled with greasy clay and blood.' Struggling back into what remained of the ward she found a delirious patient on the floor and tried to lift him back into his bed. It was then that she found one of the legs of the orderly:

> I had my right arm under a leg which I thought was his but when I lifted it I found to my horror that it was a loose leg with a boot and a puttee on it. One of the orderly's legs had been blown off and had landed on the patient's bed. The next day they found his trunk up a tree.

On a troopship home in January 1919 Alice King would meet her future husband, Dr Sydney Appleford, and the two settled down to a quiet, happy life in the town of Lang Lang in south-eastern Victoria, where they had four children. As best as anyone can remember, Alice King never talked about the things she saw in the war. The other three nurses who were on duty at Trois Arbres that night – Dorothy Cawood, Mary Jane Derrer and Clare Deacon – never wrote of their experiences. All survived the war, and were the first Australian nurses ever to be awarded the Military Medal. Dorothy Cawood was diffident about the honour, writing to her parents: 'Do not blame me for this. It is Fritz's fault. He will do these dastardly tricks.'

When Hector Dinning was in France he saw firsthand how the nurses tended to the torrents of wounded that came their way and was overwhelmed by what he saw as nothing less than stoic, grinding and largely unrecognised heroism:

> Anything one might say about nursing sisters in France must seem inadequate. The wounded Tommy who has fallen into their hands is making their qualities known.

They work harder than any M.O., and M.O.s are hard-worked. Indeed, I defy a man to bear indefinitely the kind of work they do indefinitely – its nervous strain and its long hours. The M.O.s do their examinations and their dressings and pass on, they are the merest visitors. The sisters stay on and fight for the man without cessation, and then see him die. And their work will leave its mark upon them forever. They have not a man's faculty for detachment.

Women like Agnes Bennett, Alice Chisholm, May Tilton and Alice King were plunged into the deep end of front line nursing, but they emerged quickly to treat all manner of injury and disease they had little or no knowledge of. When the Great War was done, almost 2300 Sisters of the Australian Army Nursing Service had served in our overseas campaigns. Twenty-five died and over 380 were decorated for courage under fire.

Egypt was a bacterial petri dish in the early years of the twentieth century. In 1913 the US-based Rockefeller Foundation conducted a survey in Upper and Lower Egypt and found that 60 per cent of the population was infected by hookworm, malaria and a variety of parasitic diseases. The place was awash with all manner of diseases that were virtually unknown in Australia, including the virus bilharzia. Colloquially known as 'Bill Harris', it was spread via a parasitic worm that lives in the waters of the Nile and can penetrate your skin in no time if you so much as wade along the river's edge. The worm, once inside you, then grows inside blood vessels and produces eggs, some of which travel to the intestines and bladder and then on into the stool or urine. Symptoms include rashes, itchy skin, fever, chills and muscle aches. Repeated infections resulted in damage not only to the intestines and bladder but also the liver and lungs. Once this was understood, orders were given that no river water could be touched without first being treated. At Kantara an elaborate system of pumps was built to draw the water in from the Sweet Water Canal, mix it with aluminium, then pump it into settling tanks and through a series of filters before it was sent *underneath* the Suez Canal to its eastern banks to be stored in purpose-built reservoirs before being chlorinated and finally pumped further east to the men in the field.

Sometimes soldiers would be unfortunate enough to be in the wrong place at the wrong time, collect infection after infection, and catch all manner of diseases. William Japhet Smith, a butcher from Echunga in South Australia who joined the 9th Light Horse in January 1916, was as fit and healthy as any volunteer could be until the day he set foot in Egypt, when he began to be plagued with ill health. First he contracted mumps, then myalgia – acute muscle pain caused by the over-stretching of muscle groups – which then developed into chronic rheumatism and resulted in the wasting away of his right leg. No longer able to perform his duties as a sapper, Smith was transferred to a signal squadron, but continued to fall ill and spent several extended periods in hospitals in Palestine. Doggedly fighting his way from one illness to the next he managed to stay with his unit as it advanced towards Damascus, where he finally died – a victim of malignant malaria – in October 1918, just weeks before the signing of the armistice in the forests of Compiègne.

The term 'field ambulance' is a British invention used to describe a mobile medical unit equipped to provide first aid to soldiers often while still in sight of the front lines – and very often on them. Most field ambulances were composed of men from a single state, but the AIF's 4th Light Horse Field Ambulance was made up of men from *every* state – and also required that all who served in it must have a minimum twelve months of desert experience. The unit was commanded by Colonel Robert Fowler, a medical practitioner from the Melbourne suburb of Toorak. One of the men under Fowler's command was Patrick Macfarlan Hamilton, who kept a meticulous diary of his time at war – providing readers and historians with a lucid insight into day-to-day life with a field ambulance unit.

Field ambulance units were composed of three sections: bearers, drivers and the tent division. Thirty-two mounted stretcher-bearers did the hard and often dangerous work of collecting and carrying the wounded, the drivers drove the ambulances, called sand carts, and were responsible for caring for the ambulance and its horses, while the tent division was responsible for the care of the wounded in dressing stations until they were sufficiently recovered to be evacuated.

A ride in a sand cart wasn't comfortable, but it was smoother than a cacolet, a sort of stretcher-bed set within an iron rail that hung either side of the camel with a hood above it to keep off the sun. The cacolet occupant was held aloft in specially designed saddles that, though functional, tended to accentuate the natural rhythm of the camel – a continuous jolting akin to some fiendish torture device, the conscious equivalent of a bad dream.

Everywhere our mounted troops went – Romani, Magdhaba, El Arish, Gaza and the Jordan Valley – field ambulance units went with them to collect their dead and patch up their wounded. And because the key ingredient in the Light Horse's effectiveness was speed, the field ambulance mobile sections had to be just as quick into battle, sometimes with only a minute's notice and with not so much as a pistol in their defence. Morever, a field ambulance officer's priority was not avoiding being in the rangefinders of the enemy but trying to ignore the fact they might get their heads blown off while trying to retrieve the wounded. The only consolation was that in war there is nowhere that is truly safe. On 4 May, a week and a half after the withdrawal from Gaza, the 3rd Light Horse Field Ambulance Hospital was bombed by German aircraft on a moonlit night, killing sergeants William Dyer and William Wallace and three patients, and injuring two dental staff. This was the lot of every field ambulance unit. In the wake of the Second Battle of Gaza in April 1917, Hamilton wrote in his diary:

> About 6 am fighting started after a very heavy artillery bombardment. Our lads advanced in open order, and we moved up the wadi for a couple of miles and waited. Then the Turks fell back. The ambulance moved out into the open, and we started to collect wounded with plenty of shells exploding all around. Harold Major [a wool classer from Melbourne who would become Hamilton's lifelong friend] and three other bearers with myself went out on the left flank collecting wounded, filling about five [sand] carts. The wounded were all scattered over a wide, open area, with no cover. Then we ran into a hot corner, with rifle and machine gun fire all around us. Bullets everywhere and we had to run for cover in the wadi. Harold nearly hit by a high explosive shell. A marvellous escape! A tank in flames, in between two cross fires. We went out again, and cleared the wounded.

And on it went. Later that day Hamilton's unit ran out of stretchers, such were the number of wounded. They improvised new ones by tying discarded rifles together with bandoliers, thereby fashioning a crude but effective stretcher. With help from retreating troopers, they carried their mates to safety almost a kilometre to a wadi in the rear. But as Hamilton later wrote, 'I am quite certain that the Turks let us get away. They could see clearly what was happening and could easily have mown down by machine gun fire our little, straggling, slow moving band.' That day at Gaza was, Hamilton wrote, 'the baptism of fire for the 4th LH Field Ambulance'.

In May 1917 Hamilton was again promoted, this time to Sergeant in charge of Bearers. He reached this position in the Light Horse Field Ambulance the same way all of those serving alongside him did: by being a determined and frequent 'volunteerer'. First you join the military by volunteering to serve with the AIF, then you volunteer again for the various service arms – engineers, artillery, medical corps, whatever. Those, like Hamilton, who chose the Army Medical Corps could then elect to serve for instance in a hospital or field ambulance. Once there, if you had any horsemanship about you, you could put your hand up for the Light Horse Field Ambulance, and from there become a stretcher-bearer, a driver or an orderly. The result of this filtering process was that these were no ragtag units. No one who served in the Light Horse Field Ambulance was there by accident. The thirty-two stretcher-bearers in Hamilton's unit – men of whom now little is known, men like Norm Challis and Tom Nash, Curly Smith and Bert Austin, Bluey Soutter and Bill Gadsby – all joined the AIF because they wanted to *save* lives, not take them, and from that reservoir of decency developed bonds of mateship that were as deep and as true as those of the most battle-hardened troopers.

In September 1917, while camped at Tel el Farah about 18 miles south of Gaza, Hamilton was transferred to the Tent Division as medical sergeant in charge at about the same time the Tent Division received its first allocation of camels, 'probably the most uncomfortable form of wounded transport ever devised', Hamilton would later write in his diary. Comfortable or not, on 27 October, with medical orderlies riding donkeys, mules pulling supply wagons and the Tent Division on its camels, the menagerie that was the 4th Light Horse Field Ambulance decamped and, together with around 40,000 troops that Sir Archibald Wavell described as comprising 'possibly the biggest night march that ever took place in war' began to make its way towards a rendezvous with one of the great pages in Australia's military tome – Beersheba. But more on that in the following chapter.

The day after the Battle of Beersheba on 31 October 1917, the 4th Light Horse Field Ambulance was bombed by a German Taube. Hamilton recorded the event:

> Just before sunset, the [stretcher] bearers returned from watering their horses ... 16 men with two horses each. As they dismounted, a German Taube came over – for the third time in 24 hours! With the setting sun behind him, and flying very low, it was impossible to see him until he was right overhead. I then saw the observer leaning out of the cockpit and the bomb leave the plane a few hundred feet up. The bomb burst on impact with the hard ground ... a direct hit on our bearer lines! He then turned and machine-gunned the camp, which added to the confusion. In the black dust and smoke, horses were rearing and neighing, while a few galloped madly away. Men were running and shrieking. Grabbed my medical haversack and ran about 20 yards to reach Brownjohn. His left leg had been blown off ... bleeding badly. His hand was also wounded. Staff Sergeant Stewart came running and together we got a tourniquet on his thigh in about 90 seconds ... Others were attending Oates, right arm blown off, and Hay with his left buttock cut clean away. I found Hamlyn being dressed, with a bad wound over his heart, and in great pain. Gave him a shot of morphia. Cogan, Brown and Whitfield also slightly wounded. Bill Taylor was one of the worst types of casualty – shell shock. Apparently standing between two horses, only a few feet from the bomb, he was not hit. But we placed him on a stretcher, a pathetic, incoherent, weeping wreck, unable to walk.

In the aftermath of Beersheba, Hamilton and his unit moved northwards again. On 4 November they rode eight hours to Tel el Farah. On the 5th they were bombarded all day long by Turkish artillery and on the 7th crossed the Beersheba–Gaza–Jerusalem railway line while all the time moving through emptied Turkish lines littered with dead horses, abandoned tents, hospital stations, caches of ammunition, and all the equipment and flotsam of war. By 8 November they were only 8 miles east of Gaza, which only the day before had finally been captured by the Egyptian Expeditionary Force on its third attempt. Still the wounded kept coming.

At 0200 hours on 12 November while camped at Ijseir, a small town about 65 km southwest of Jerusalem, Hamilton was woken when a wounded trooper – Private William Francis Holmes of the 11th Light Horse Regiment – was brought in suffering from a horribly mutilated leg. The doctors were called; they would have to amputate. There was little time for poor Holmes to prepare himself for the ordeal he was about to endure. Within minutes his artery had been opened at the groin, forceps placed on it to stem the bleeding, and scalpels and a bone saw did the rest. When it was done Holmes, who had been placed on a raised-up stretcher, was kept warm through the cold desert night by a primus stove beneath him and dozens of hot water bottles that had been donated by his mates and filled with water boiled in the unit's only kettle and constantly refilled throughout the night.

The men of the 4th Light Horse Field Ambulance were busy during the day too. They'd rise at dawn, have a wash if there was time, tend to the patients they'd stitched up the night before and evacuate others by 0900 hours. After that they'd have breakfast, strike tents, load their limbers and camels and be ready to be on the move by 1000 hours. But it was always after dusk that the real work began. That's when the day's fighting was generally done. Sometimes the wounded began to arrive in the unit's dressing stations in the late afternoon. Field ambulance dressing stations – those first points of arrival after a soldier is hit in the field – were human dry docks, filled with an endless parade of miserable, battered hulks swept up in the backwash of conflict. For those suffering from shell shock these were hardly places of respite: a defenceless, exposed assemblage of tents with artillery fire blasting holes in the earth around them and shells screaming in overhead. And always with more wounded coming in, swelling the chorus of anguish. Always more wounded.

On 17 November 1917, as the Anzac Mounted Division was busy closing in on Jaffa, Parick Hamilton was encamped just 32 km east of Jerusalem. He had ridden his camel 240 km since leaving Tel el Farah on 25 October, and now all of southern Palestine was in Allied hands. General Allenby strolled into Jerusalem on 11 December, and the final days of 1917 passed uneventfully for the men of the 4th Light Horse Field Ambulance.

In January 1918 the entire Anzac Mounted Division was ordered back down the coast to Belah, south of Gaza, for a well-deserved bit of rest and relaxation. The journey took the 4th Light Horse Field Ambulance eleven days, and when they got there they were replenished with twenty-eight fresh reinforcements from the Australian Army Medical Corps. It had been a long, arduous campaign and it must have seemed for Patrick Hamilton that a lifetime had passed since he joined the unit at Ferry Post on the Suez Canal back in February 1917. The turnover since in personnel had been close to 100 per cent. Hamilton was one of the very few who had managed to stay the course.

On 1 April 1918 they were on the move north again, past Gaza and up the coast to Deiran, a few miles out of Jaffa, and on 23 April the 4th Light Horse Field Ambulance at last entered Jerusalem through the Jaffa Gate, with two horsemen riding abreast through its ancient streets and alleyways. Their ride was an unhurried one – taking three hours for a ride that would have taken only minutes at the gallop. They exited through another gate on the other side of the city, rode past the Garden of Gethsemane and the Mount of Olives, and camped a few miles beyond the city walls in the Judean hills. Hamilton described the scene: 'Over 6000 mounted troops, with their machine gun sections, engineers, ambulances, supplies and transport, complete in every detail. Tough, efficient, splendidly equipped, battle-hardened ... a magnificent body of men and horses.'

The first two phases of the 4th Light Horse Field Ambulance's deployment – Sinai and southern Palestine – were now behind them. The last phase – the push north to Damascus – would see Patick Hamilton witness a shell pass 6 feet over the head of his commander's horse ('the only time I ever saw a shell in flight') and, on 1 May, the near-destruction of his entire unit during the abortive raid on Es Salt, a Turkish stronghold on the east side of the Jordan River. His unit was strung out and exposed along a ridge when the Turks launched a surprise attack. The fight saw the loss of four ambulances, the wagon carrying all of their hospital gear including their surgical equipment, a water cart, twenty-eight transport horses and twelve men – all of whom were captured.

Falling back towards the headquarters of the 4th Light Horse Brigade the unit reorganised itself thanks to the arrival of some borrowed ambulances from the 5th British Mounted Yeomanry Brigade. It was shortly after this incident that the unit was given the nickname 'The Fighting Fourth'. It was an apt title. On 8 May Hamilton decided to add up his unit's casualties since its inception: four killed and eight wounded by a bomb at Beersheba, twelve captured during the Es Salt raid, and on 7 May – the day before Hamilton made his list – another four wounded by artillery fire. That was twenty-eight casualties out of ninety men, a rate of almost 30 per cent.

In May of 1918 alone the 4th Light Horse Field Ambulance treated over 1000 malaria cases despite troops being routinely issued with mosquito nets and jabbed with regular doses of quinine. Quinine came with its own annoying assemblage of side effects, including tremors, vomiting, rapid pulse rates, severe headaches, high temperatures, partial deafness and of course diarrhea. The men of the 6th Light Horse Regiment serving in Palestine referred to the men laid low with diarrhea as the 'Diarrhea Kings', those poor souls who inhabited the back areas behind the support trenches, wrapped up in their blankets and as close to the latrines as they could get without being in them.

Patrick Hamilton was bitten so many times by mosquitoes, he wrote, that his legs 'looked like sieves'. For patients suffering malignant malaria, the most severe form of malaria with the highest rates of complications, ice was brought north from Jerusalem in lorries packed with sawdust. The ice was then wrapped in lint and placed round patients who were burning with temperatures as high as 105 degrees. In the month of May 1918 the 4th Light Horse Field Ambulance evacuated 616 men suffering malaria – the equivalent of an entire Light Horse regiment.

Similar statistics can be found in the operational records of all of the Anzac Mounted Division's field ambulance units. In 1918 malaria was responsible for 11 per cent of the invalidity in the EEF, and most of the Australian doctors serving in the EEF had never even seen the disease before. (No one in Australia had ever seen frostbite either. In Turkey and France Australian soldiers suffering from frozen extremities had no idea that the fact they couldn't feel their feet or hands was cause for concern, and as a result by the time they reached hospital their fingers and toes were literally falling off.)

From July to August 1918 the 4th Light Horse Field Ambulance was in the Jordan Valley and the hills north of Jericho, tending to the never-ceasing flow of wounded as well as watering, twice a day, their share of the more than 12,000 horses that the Anzac and Australian mounted divisions had accumulated, leading them to the multitude of canvas troughs that had been placed at intervals along the River Jordan and filled with water pumped from the river by army engineers. Actually it was more of a stampede: 48,000 hooves, all of them pulverising the soil to dust and then splashing through it as though it was puddles. Then the wind would pick it up and form it into endless clouds of choking earth that were so thick and so still Patrick Hamilton could hardly see the tail of the horse in front of him.

In August the division moved from the Jordan Valley to Ludd, about 12 miles from Jaffa on the coast, but before they left they pitched their tents and lit 142 camp fires to trick the Turks into thinking they were still encamped there and not planning their attack along the coast. On 3 September Hamilton took ten days leave and spent it at the Windsor Hotel in Alexandria. 'I had a very enjoyable and easy time in Alexandria,' he later wrote. 'Went sight-seeing and did a lot of shopping. Had a tunic made to order, boots, leggings ... and spurs nickled over. We are not supposed to do this, but it saves a lot of time polishing the issue spurs, and they look very smart. Played tennis on three days at the French Tennis Club.'

He returned to his unit on 14 September, promoted to medical sergeant in charge, and transferred to the Tent Division. He was now responsible for three things: the daily 'sick parade', including the handing out of medication and deciding who needed evacuating or admitting to hospital or being sent back to a unit; the smooth running of up to four hospital tents, each holding as many as fourteen patients; and most importantly the treatment of the wounded, including the redressing of all wounds and the performing of emergency surgery. Four days later he was on what would be the 4th Light Horse Field Ambulance's final advance of the war, and it was during its push north up the coast towards the Sea of Galilee that he came to know how it felt to be on a stretcher himself. But it wasn't the result of malaria or cholera. Patrick Hamilton was one of the first cases in Palestine to fall victim to an outbreak of a new kind of pneumonia that would sweep across the world and claim millions of lives – Spanish Flu.

A patient of the 4th British Cavalry Divisional Receiving Station, Hamilton was wracked with a nasty, persistent cough, back pain, a temperature of 40 degrees Celcius, and a professional disgust at the lack of sanitation that surrounded him. Toilets overflowed with excrement, and there seemed to be no attempt to separate the sick from the wounded. 'The chap next to me on a stretcher is wounded, with a bullet through his throat! I hate to think of what could happen to him if he catches my wog and cough.'

It turned out that Hamilton would be one of the lucky ones. He survived his influenza and was evacuated back to Gaza on a troop train on 27 September 1918. His war was over. On 1 October he arrived at the 24th British Stationary Hospital in Kantara, the day the 14th British Cavalry Brigade of the Desert Mounted Corps, the Camel Corps and T. E. Lawrence, and the 10th Australian Light Horse Brigade, among others, entered the streets of the final prize, Damascus. In the twelve days prior to the Allied forces entering the Syrian capital the combined Australian and New Zealand field ambulance units received 11,300 sick – more than 50 per cent of the corps' entire strength. Almost all were victims of malaria and pneumonic influenza.

Patrick Hamilton was going home. On Christmas Eve he received orders to leave his unit and make his way to a medical camp at Moascar near Ismaïlia. In his four days there he had medical and dental checks, organised his private papers, read a book and some magazines, played what tennis he was able to, caught up with old friends, and was told on New Year's Eve he'd be leaving for home the next morning. On 1 January 1919 he caught a train to Suez, hopped a lorry to Port Tewfik, and boarded a tug that took him from the docks to the hospital ship *Aeneas*, at anchor in the harbour with a cargo of 800 wounded diggers, all veterans of the Western Front. As Hamilton approached the gangplank those on its starboard decks looked at his unfamiliar leggings, breeches and emu plumes that adorned him as he made his way on board, but nobody said anything. They were all together now, on a ship that would be taking them south down the Red Sea on a 10,000-mile journey home, leaving the heat and the dust and the misery of war behind them.

Chapter Seven
The Hush-Hush Army

After the long spell of tent life mid the dust, heat, flies and mosquitoes of Magil, the mud, cold and rain at Es Sinn, and the long, practically forced march to Baghdad, the first glimpse of Sinbad's hometown, with its blue-tinted domes and minarets, was something to be remembered; but what a disillusionment on entering the town. One wondered how even the thousands of pariah dogs, the scavengers of the town, existed in such filth and dirt. However, after the first disappointment, the thought of living between four solid walls with a permanent roof overhead was a comfort not to be despised.

– Keast Burke, *With Horse and Morse in Mesopotamia*, 1927

Had there ever been, before or since, a grander adventure than the one had by the 670 Australians who were sent to serve with the Mesopotamian Expeditionary Force (MEF) or with the even more 'exotic' Dunsterforce in Persia, Armenia and Russia? Consider it: far-flung lands of which we knew nothing but the legends we read as children – the land of Aladdin and Sinbad and 1001 nights and of genies in bottles. And into this legend-laden land we tossed signallers, soldiers and the men of our famous Half Flight. Here was a recipe for yarns and adventure-telling the like of which would have few equals in the annals of military folklore, and yet the Mesopotamian theatre stubbornly remains the least-known battlefield that Australians were ever sent to fight in. So if you ever catch yourself lamenting the fact that the campaigns in Palestine, Sinai, Lebanon and Syria still take a back seat to the conflict on the Western Front, spare a thought for the boys of the MEF. After the unsuccessful assault on Ctesiphon by British and Indian troops in November 1915 (the wounded totalled almost 3000 men, 700 per cent more than anticipated) the MEF's commander, General Charles Townshend, retreated back into Kut, which sat neatly in one of the Tigris River's tight U-shaped bends. Kut, however, was far from the most pleasant town in Mesopotamia in which to be encircled. Its buildings were made almost entirely from dung and mud, with each freshly produced dung slab a potential new cornerstone. The streets were mud as well, into which flowed raw sewage from its houses, and the whole place was infested with flies. It was, according to the diary of one British officer, the single most unsanitary town in all of Mesopotamia. But after months of setbacks the Turks had succeeded in pushing the MEF from Ctesiphon back into Kut, then promptly surrounded the 8000-strong garrison and laid siege to it on 7 December 1915. And among those encircled were nine mechanics of the Australian Flying Corp's Half Flight.

It seemed an odd decision by Townshend to remain in Kut and make a fight of it instead of continuing his retreat to a more defensible position further south. He'd later claim that his troops were tired and low on morale, but various exchanges with the Turks during their retreat into Kut suggested otherwise. Why not just continue the march southwards towards British forces and safety? One explanation is the idea of making a stand against overwhelming odds appealed to the man, who may have considered it a way of etching his name in the history books, though no real evidence comes to us that his decision was born out of any such misplaced heroics.

Kut's principal defensive structure was a polygonal fort at the pensinsula's neck. Townshend built earthworks and lines of trenches while at the same time demolishing blockhouses lest they be used as rangefinders by the besieging Turkish artillery. The siege was made all the more difficult for the Turks by the quality of Mesopotamia's mud that, when baked hard under the Arabian sun, could even stop a bullet, according to Harry Coghill Bishop's immensely readable 1920 book *A Kut Prisoner*:

> *The mud of Mesopotamia deserves mention in this connection. It is as disagreeable as, and rather more glutinous than, most other brands of the same substance, and when baked dry by the sun is singularly impenetrable to rifle bullets. All the rules found in military pocket-books were quite upset by it, some eight inches of the best variety being quite enough to stop any bullet. For the same reason, trench digging in some places was very slow and tedious work, as the ground at that time was dry and hard, seeming more like cast iron than anything else.*

Townshend also ordered the construction of a series of fortified redoubts, and when he was done had succeeded in increasing Kut's defensive perimeter to over 2400 metres. By the time the Turks had encircled Kut, despite countless bombardments and frontal assaults, they were unable to breach its defences. Two days after an assault on the town's old fort on Christmas Eve resulted in 2000 Turkish casualties, a truce was called and the Turkish commander, Nur-ud-Din, diverted the majority of his troops south with the aim of blocking British efforts to break through and relieve their besieged comrades. He then waited patiently for the Allied garrison to run out of water.

And that is more or less what happened. The siege dragged on until 29 April 1916 when, due mostly to a lack of water, the Allied garrison surrendered. Kut would be held by the Turks until February 1917, when an Allied offensive was successful in retaking the town, too late though to have prevented three out of every four of the Turks' 13,000 British and Indian prisoners from being marched by their captors on a series of horrific 1100-km treks across the desert back to Turkey – the infamous Kut Death March.

There were forty-four Allied flying corps mechanics present at Kut on the day it fell to the Turks, including eight Australians. Only two of them, Corporal James Sloss and air mechanic K. L. Hudson, a motor mechanic from Tasmania, survived. Sloss was on the third march out of Kut and was sent to Afion Kara Hissar in Turkey's central Anatolian plain, the village and its former Armenian church now a POW camp and the home of fellow POW Captain Thomas White. The camp was set below a mountainous rocky outcrop, which explained the origins of its name – opium black rock. An officer's camp at the beginning of the war, its climate was extreme – deep, heavy snows and piercing winds in winter, and unbearable heat in summer. The opium poppies, the village's primary source of income, encircled the town and flowered in an eye-catching mix of mauve and white in the spring and summer, but the colour did little to disguise the sadness of the place. The Armenian male population had been forcibly removed, victims of Turkey's genocidal anti-Armenian policies, leaving the women and children to haunt the local souks, competing with local beggars for whatever scraps of food they could find.

Sloss didn't arrive at Afion until April 1917 and would be described by Thomas White, who had served with him in the Half Flight, as 'greatly altered, wearing a pair of dark glasses ... to cover an inflamed eye'. Hudson, on the other hand, had long been a resident of this old Armenian town-turned-POW-camp, having arrived with an earlier batch of Kut survivors in late 1916, of which White wrote when he witnessed them trudge into camp:

It was pitiable to watch their progress, staggering along like drunken men, stumbling and falling, being sometimes bravely helped to their feet by their comrades almost as feeble, then tottering along a few paces further before dropping again ... it was exasperating beyond measure not to be able to render any assistance to them.

When discharged from the hospital after his arrival, Hudson smuggled a note to White describing his lamentable condition, and White responded by sending him some clothes from his own 'scanty' wardrobe, as well as some tinned food. Hudson wrote an account of the Kut march:

I belonged to the second last party to leave Baghdad ... the rations for this trip of sixty miles were six biscuits, two lbs of coarse flour, one cake of bread ... during this march twenty-seven men dropped out to die through weakness caused by hunger and thirst. I know of three who went mad, and the guard knocked them out with rifle butts and then half buried them under the sand.

For the final journey to Afion they were packed into railway cars fifty at a time:

Most of the day and all night the doors of these closed trucks were kept locked, and as almost every man was suffering from fever, dysentery and diarrhea, the state of affairs can be imagined. After three days and nights of such travelling five men in my wagon were found to be dead when the doors were opened.

The British academic Leonard Woolley, himself a survivor of the Kut march who would go on to find fame as an archaeologist for his discoveries at Ur in 1922 and one of the first to propose that the Biblical flood was merely a localised event, left us his own eloquent recollections of the horror, which he titled *The Roadmakers*:

Famished and spent across the waste, beast like you
    drove us on,
And clubbed to death the stragglers by the way,
Our sick men in the lazar huts you left to die alone,
And you robbed the very dying as they lay.
Naked and starved we built you roads and tunnelled
    through your hills,
And you flogged us when we fainted at our work.
Fevered beneath the sun we toiled, wracked by winter
    chills,
Till death released us, kindlier than the Turk.

Those Australian airmen who did not survive the march, who died a lonely and wretched death in the sands of Mesopotamia, were air mechanic W. C. Rayment, a heating engineer from Melbourne; Corporal T. M. Soley, a motor mechanic from Colac in Victoria; air mechanic L. T. Williams, a carpenter and joiner also from Colac; air mechanic W. H. Lord, a brass moulder from Melbourne; air mechanic J. Munro, a chauffeur from Darlinghurst in Sydney; air mechanic David Curran, born in faraway Downpatrick, a picturesque little village in County Down, Ireland; and air mechanic F. L. Adams from Christchurch, New Zealand.

You can learn a little of David Curran if you go to the records of the Australia Red Cross Society Wounded and Missing Bureau Enquiry Files, 1914–18 War. Though he left no written record of his ordeal, extracts from a plaintive letter written by his mother in Belfast dated 27 December 1918 to Thomas White – almost two and a half years after her son's death – make for sobering reading:

I was thinking perhaps … you might possibly know some Australian soldier who might be coming to Belfast and who would be able to give us a full and true account of my poor Son's fate. If the sad news is true that he died whilst a

Prisoner of War in Turkey, it would relieve my mind a little to get some particulars regarding cause of death etc ... You will kindly excuse me troubling you so much in the matter, but I am so anxious to get all information I possibly can about my Son.

If we could get into touch with anyone who was taken prisoner at the Battle of Kut and who could give us a full account of my poor Son's fate up to the time of his death we would feel very grateful indeed. We know you will assist us all you can.

The report of his death was finally made official some months later:

Curran died in June or July 1916 in hospital in Nisi-bin. He suffered badly from fever on the desert march and from exhaustion and exposure followed by malarial fever, for which he had practically no treatment. Formerly he was a strong, powerful man, but became a walking skeleton.

At Kut the conditions and brutality of the war in Mesopotamia reached their zenith. By the end of the siege its defenders were surviving on 3 ounces of bread and a pound and a quarter of horse flesh per day. Some chewed the ends of their fingers until they bled. And the Mesopotamian winter was typically freezing, with anything that could be burned for heat being burned, save for a collection of ornate wooden front doors buried in a hole in the ground by an unidentified group with a weakness for architecture. Mostly, though, anything that could burn became almost as sought after as food. A piece of stale Turkish bread unearthed by a British medical officer was thought priceless simply because it could burn. Despite an outbreak of anthrax among the Kut livestock, men scavenged their way through pits full of offal in the hope of finding the heart of a mule or a horse's liver. Towards the end of the siege stomach complaints were killing up to half a dozen men a day.

The Turks entered Kut on 29 April 1916, and the first thing they did was shoot 250 of its resident Arab population and hang the Sheikh of Kut and his son. Numerous other bodies were seen swinging from palm trees along the town's waterfront. Although the terms of the capitulation said nothing of being sent on a forced march, that is exactly what the Turks did, forcing the sick and emaciated garrison to Baghdad, 160 km away, and from there to Anatolia. The ration according to one account was a single goat for every 400 men, and medical facilities were non-existent. So-called hospital camps had no medicines and fed their patients two spoonfuls of barley porridge at breakfast and another two at night. The sick lay on the ground with no bedding and were often naked. The patients buried their own dead using what little strength they had left. 'We were driven along like beasts,' Sloss of the Half Flight later recalled. Sloss had tied his wrists to the back of a cart during the Kut march because he knew that to drop out and fall behind meant certain death. Some poor souls were buried by Arab gendarmes while still moving; others who crawled to the edges of streams had flies going in and out of their open mouths as they died. 'Only super men,' wrote Thomas White in his diary after seeing the first columns limp into his POW camp at Afion, 'could have lived through the agonies of being driven like barbarian captives of the ancients over seven hundred miles of mountain and desert.'

Unlike the POW camps preferred by their German allies, the Turks chose to keep their prisoners in specially adapted houses and buildings on Turkish soil, often in the Armenian quarters of their towns and cities, which had plenty of vacancies thanks to the program of genocide the Turks had perpetrated against their resident Armenian communities since early 1915. And although European condemnation saw the slaughter finally end in the summer of 1915, Turkish soldiers continued to kill Armenians with impunity until the end of the war.

Naturally the Turks were happy to avail themselves of the free labour that having a large prison population afforded, with work camps established for the most part along railheads, which were vital lines of communications in and out of Mesopotamia and Palestine. Railroad-linked construction projects abounded throughout eastern Turkey, particularly in the Cilician Mountains. And because the Turks didn't place the same emphasis on camp hygiene as their Teutonic allies, outbreaks of typhus, cholera and dysentery were never far away.

Of all the death marches in Australian military history it is the march from Kut across the deserts of Mesopotamia that is mentioned the least, no doubt because not only did it involve comparably few Australians, it also took place in one of the loneliest uncharted wastelands our diggers ever endured. For Corporal James Sloss, however, for whom thoughts of escape were constantly being entertained, there was still a long road to be travelled. Sent to work on a railroad in Turkey's Taurus Mountains in April 1917 Sloss, together with three Britons, escaped from his work camp 48 km from the Gulf of Alexandretta and managed to find his way, undetected, to the coast. Unable to locate a boat, however, and having already run out of food while on the run they were forced to give themselves up. Sloss was imprisoned for three and a half months, contracted typhus then was sent back to the Taurus Mountains to continue his road building before being transferred to a mechanics' workshop where he spent his time effecting repairs to the Turks' fleet of German-made staff cars – a job that gave Sloss plenty of time to devise the one piece of equipment that had foiled his first escape attempt: a boat.

Sloss and his fellow mechanics – two Australian veterans of Gallipoli, two Britons and two French sailors – fashioned an ingeniously designed collapsible boat made from canvas and hoop iron sequestered from old wooden barrels. The boat measured 3.6 m by 1 m and would have had to be carried in sections more than 120 km to the coast, and from there sailed probably to Cyprus. Unfortunately for Sloss, an altercation with a German officer saw him transferred to another camp before the attempt could be made. By the time he was returned to the camp the others had made the attempt without him, were caught, and that was the end of that.

Was there ever a more low-key arrival of troops onto a foreign shore than the men of the 1st Pack Wireless Signal Troop in Mesopotamia? Not only were there no red-tabs (a British slang term for officers) to greet them when they disembarked the *Teesta* on 19 March 1916, there was an interminable two-hour delay at the half-finished docks before a march through dusty streets to Ashar, 100 km south-east of Basra on the Gulf Coast. In Ashar they were taken to a local Y.M.C.A. and given biscuits and cups of tea. They then marched through a succession of camps, dragging their kits behind them, until finally collapsing into a hut vacated by a unit of the Indian artillery, followed by an idle week until their wireless sets arrived, brought into camp mounted on the back of hand-drawn wooden carts. Welcome to Mesopotamia.

The 1st Pack Wireless Signal Troop was formed in January 1916, the Australian government's response to a request from India for technicians and signalmen to aid its Expeditionary Force D in Mesopotamia. The New Zealand government drew together operators, mechanics and linesmen from their telegraphic service – each of whom were given just four weeks of musketry, visual signalling and buzzer training – while Australia provided drivers, signallers and operators from the Sydney-based Marconi School and the Signal Depots at Sydney's Moore Park, and Broadmeadows in Melbourne.

The first New Zealand troop didn't arrive until 18 April, but the real work for the Australians began on 1 April when they were given their horses – seventy-four splendid, though unbroken, Australian Walers courtesy of the remount depot for that 'just arrived gang of Australian Bushmen'. These horses were so wild it proved a fight even to attach nosebags to them! Technicians were now jockeys, stablehands, and horse trainers! With each signal station comprising seven operators and six drivers, all having to be mounted, those signalmen who'd never been on a horse before were taught in the rough in a riding school where 'no one cared whether you stuck on or came off three times in ten minutes, or whether you were on board or not when your mount bolted for the far horizon'. They loved their horses no less than our Light Horsemen did in Egypt, giving them water in the middle of the day and drinking from the bottom of canvas water bags only after the horses first had their fill. 'We drank with relish from the bottom of canvas buckets,' one signalman wrote, 'the drops which the animals could not reach.'

The initial deployment of the first wireless station from Basra to the 15th Division – on 25 April 1916, the Second Anzac Day – was a happy day for the wireless boys but a sad one for the Allies, coming as it did only days before the British garrison upriver in Kut raised the white flag of surrender. In the weeks that followed wireless stations were being dispatched all along the Tigris and Euphrates rivers: one by boat to Nasiriyah, another to Samawa and another to Khamisiyah. The Turkish cipher messages were at first all but indecipherable to our wireless operators but they took little time in recognising hostile stations and their call signs. The arrival of a captain G. L. Clausen, a linguist from the Somerset Light Infantry, made certain the messages were accurately decoded.

Deploying upriver was an arduous task, but by the time the first troop of Australians arrived in Nasiriyah, a 'land of gardens and mud forts and chieftains divided amongst themselves' 240 km inland from Basra, the wild horses of 1 April were able to walk along a metre-wide plank for 6 metres as they disembarked from their barge behind their new owners, and were now the pride and joy of the corps.

Back home in Australia the loved ones and relatives of this fledgling force had almost no concept of the environment into which their men had been sent, and were none the wiser when initial correspondence began filtering back from diggers describing their experiences. 'A vast quagmire,' one would say. 'A desert with continual dust storms,' said another. Someone might describe the local Arabs as hostile, as only too happy to sell you a chicken at noon just to steal it back from you in the evening, while another would wax lyrical of traditional Arabian hospitality. One would say it's too hot; another, too cold. Heat stroke during the day, frostbite at night. Loved ones in Australia may well have been confused as to what their men were facing, but at least they would not have to grieve over them. Every member of the Australian and New Zealand wireless and signalling corps came home.

The tools of their trade were the wireless units known as pack sets and wagon sets. The pack set got its name because it was light enough to be carried on the back of a mule or a horse, although 'light' is hardly the word the poor animals would have chosen to call it. Hauled along in five separate boxes called 'loads', load #1 contained an air-cooled 2 ¾ horsepower petrol engine and alternator; load #2 consisted of the sending and receiving mechanisms; load #3 had the rigging gear for the 3-metre-high radio masts; load #4 had the masts themselves (made from tubular steel); and load #5 had a litany of spare parts, plus oil and petrol. A well-drilled unit could unpack all this and establish an operating pack set in any terrain in less than eight minutes. Wagon sets, carried on two limbered wagons each drawn by teams of up to six horses and having towering, 21 metre masts, took a little longer!

Although not engaged in any combat role, the men of the

wireless units were often in the front lines, enveloped within the din and shrapnel of war as advanced guards skirmished with Turkish forces sometimes only a grenade's throw away. One unnamed correspondent from G Station describes an altercation with Turkish troops and cavalry on the Hai River south of Kut in late 1916:

> *It is realised we will soon be blown to pieces, so the order is given to retire. Our aerial masts are now conspicuous on the vacant plain, and the next five minutes are lively. We decide to evacuate when a staff officer is seen galloping towards us, storming because we have been left to the mercy of the Turkish gunners. All records in wireless dismantling are smashed within the next few minutes. High explosives land all round us as we make off at full gallop. One shell lobs close enough to cover us with dirt. Luckily no one is hit and our horses need no spurs. An aeroplane working with us develops engine trouble and lands on our left, and the Turks, realising it, change their fire over.*

Everywhere the wireless units were sent they were wary of marauding Arabs who were forever hovering about their flanks waiting to take advantage of an engagement or moment of confusion so they could swoop down and plunder clothing and material from the dead or wounded. Arabs were partial to Australian and British corpses, which they considered far more likely to possess valuable pickings than their Turkish counterparts.

On 11 March 1917, British troops entered Baghdad, that city 'with minarets and domes covered with gold as thick as your finger'. Other minor engagements would follow, but by September, when the Turks began to divert the bulk of their army to Palestine to address more pressing strategic requirements, and particularly after the fall of Beersheba in

October, the struggle for Mesopotamia was effectively over – much to the joy of our signallers and their very Australian sense of battlefield humour. As one operator wrote:

> *Early on the morning of March 11 we came in sight of Baghdad Railway Station. Many were the jokes that were passed – one would go to the ticket window and ask for a ticket to Berlin; others would parade up and down the platform calling out the name 'Baghdad' and telling imaginary passengers to change for all sorts of places! It was the first real railway station we had seen for years, so our fooling was pardonable. But we had no train! The Turks had taken the last one at two that morning.*

After the capture of Baghdad the Australian and New Zealand wireless corps relocated along with many British units to Samarrah, where 'no trace of vegetation relieved the dusty glare of the desert', and spent so much time swimming in the Tigris River there – some men up to three or four times every day – that it was joked they were in danger of turning into Tigris salmon. Water polo, diving, sprints along the river's edge and swimming with their horses before lunch was generally followed in the afternoon by a spate of letter writing, card playing and arguing before a final dip in the river after tea. One Australian, known only as 'old Bill', fashioned a spear from a stick of bamboo and took to standing chest-deep in the river while others threw bait around him in the hope of luring a reasonably sized fish. Overhead, Turkish aircraft visited most days and were routinely shot at, though only one poor sod was ever brought down, and even that was probably the result of a lucky and somewhat disinterested shot. There were concerts too, courtesy of a miniature organ somehow procured by a driver who used to organise church fetes back home. Enlisted men read extracts from *The Sentimental Bloke*, and 'Too-ra-loo-raloo' was sung over and over again, accompanied by banging on assorted plates and tin cups. Diary entries, such as this one by a member of Australia's Cavalry Divisional Signal Squadron, increasingly summed up the mood of the idle men:

> *It is quickly becoming a problem how to put in the long hours between breakfast and sunset; mostly we spend about eighteen hours out of the twenty-four in an endeavour to reach the remaining six quicker than is horologically possible.*

With winter came rugby, and impromptu games began to be organised between a united Australia–New Zealand team and members of various British units. One match saw hundreds of men on the field, many of them drunk after a rousing dinner, all surging back and forth across the field like a single living organism. Pity the poor signaller who managed to get his hands on the ball, which was rarely seen, as he was immediately smothered by fifty or sixty tacklers. No one recalled ever seeing an umpire, and the dozen or so stretcher-bearers present were kept as busy as they'd been in the entire war. More games ensued: an Australia versus 'The Rest' match on 1 January 1918, officers versus enlisted men, Australia versus the Royal Air Force, Australia versus the British 7th Cavalry Brigade, and Australia versus the Duke of Cornwall's Light Infantry (Australia 16; Duke of Cornwall 5) when spectators intervened to bring down players on the verge of scoring tries. No doubt there would have been an Australia versus the Turks game if such forms existed that could have arranged it. During these times the war seemed further away in the face of that spirit of comradeship that always seems to be at its most irrepressible and poignant in times of war.

When the armistice was declared A, B and C troops of the Australia and New Zealand wireless corps embarked for the voyage home, but D Troop's luck had run out. They stayed on and inherited 'The Billet' – Kurdistan in northern

Mesopotamia – now under British rule in the new peace and a region described by Keast Burke as a country 'whose only vegetation is a few stunted shrubs', and within which 'wherever a small pocket of workable soil occurs in a valley there is to be found a community of wild, lawless men who pasture just enough sheep and goats and till just enough of the soil to ... maintain a feud with two or three neighbours'.

Free of the constraints of Ottoman rule, these feudal Kurdish tribesmen were becoming assertive and increasingly hostile, with British attempts to treat them as equals viewed as nothing more than a sign of imperial weakness. Skirmishes began to break out everywhere, as if maintaining communications in the region's mountainous terrain wasn't work enough! And signallers didn't like gunfire – wireless stations were always the last things to be dismantled in a retreat.

It was October 1919 before British wireless squadrons came to relieve the Anzacs. The men of D Troop must have wondered if the Australian government had forgotten about them. The fact was, though, that AIF agents in Bombay had been working tirelessly for their release, but the oil-rich region was strategically too important to be abandoned. When the British finally gathered enough of their own men to man two standby stations, D Troop made their way first to Baghdad, then on to Kut.

The road home was a long haul. On 22 October they piled into five trucks and by 0300 hrs the next day they could see the arc lights of the Kut Supply Depot. Three days later, with all upriver traffic halted to allow D Troop unfettered passage, their steamer, the *P.S. 51*, reached Kurna where the men spent the next eight days in their own specially prepared camp outside Basra. From there they marched to the wharf of the 3rd British General Hospital (where they'd disembarked two years earlier), and boarded the hospital ship *Varela*, which arrived in Karachi on 9 November. There it unloaded

Indian convalescents. The *Varela* then sailed for Bombay, where D Troop spent another three weeks in a camp before boarding the *Medic* on 1 December. Nineteen days later the men sighted Albany, and then Adelaide and finally Melbourne on 20 December 1919. Of all of the men and women we sent overseas to fight for England in the Great War, it was these men of D Troop who were the very last to come home.

In early 1918 Allied strategists began to assemble a secret army. The mission, it was being whispered – and whispered only to those few who were being considered for it – would be dangerous. The men being short-listed, about 150 officers and 300 NCOs, would come from the ranks of British, Australian, Canadian, New Zealand and South African servicemen who had, at an absolute minimum, one full year of front line service. They would all be heavily decorated – some five times over – and were all 'individualists'. You know, the do-or-die type. One man being considered was Canadian Lieutenant Colonel John Warden, commander of the 102nd Canadian Infantry Battalion. And he was cautioned not to do it. 'You'd be throwing away your military career if you embark on this folly,' a friend told him. Well, that was okay – Warden was getting tired of constant run-ins with his superiors anyway, and was looking for a fresh challenge. So he volunteered, even though he had no idea what he was volunteering for, where he'd be going or what he was meant to do when he got there. Warden was intrigued. There was something different about things this time – the secrecy was over the top, even for the military. All he knew is that whatever it was, he wanted to be a part of it. In fact, if he'd known what he was being considered for he'd have volunteered sooner – they all would have, in a heartbeat, and thousands more too – if they knew that in the decades to come the adventures that this soon-to-be close-knit group was about to experience would be likened by historians to the exploits of Lawrence of Arabia himself.

In 1918 British strategists became increasingly concerned about possible Turkish inroads into the oil-rich Caucasus as well as threats to British interests in Persia – modern day Iran. It was decided that a small mobile force should be sent to the region to help safeguard British interests there. The man appointed to lead this new force was Major General Lionel Dunsterville. He was supplied with all the money and assistance he would need and lost no time in assembling only those deemed tough enough, decorated enough, and experienced enough to be a part of it. His list included forty members of the AIF. General William 'Birdie' Birdwood, the Commander of the Australian Corps and the British commander who had swam almost every day in the waters of Gallipoli's Anzac Cove in full view of the Turkish guns just to show his men that he was prepared to share in the dangers, received a letter – personally delivered to him by Colonel Byron – on 3 January 1918 asking for a list of volunteers that would form the nucleus of a new special force. The letter made it clear how important the mission was seen to be, at least in some circles:

> We well realise how difficult it is for you to spare good officers, and especially the kind of officers we want, but from Colonel Byron's explanation you will realise what a big question is involved – nothing more or less than the defence of India and the security of our whole position in the East. If we can only stem the rot in the Caucasus and on the Persian frontier and interpose a barrier against the vast German-Turkish propaganda of their Pan-Turanian scheme, which threatens to inflame the whole of Central Asia including Afghanistan, our minds will be at rest as regards Mesopotamia and India.

The initial list of twenty officers Birdwood supplied was described as the 'cream of the cream' of Australian regimental leaders and was so impressive that within days he received another request for forty NCOs 'of similar quality'. The force was slowly coming together, with the volunteers (Australian, Canadian, New Zealander, South African and British) all living within sight of the Tower of London and meeting daily for briefings. They all had to buy their own kits, and weren't told of their destination until 28 January – the day before they sailed – when they were joined by eleven Russian interpreters. When the group left London on 29 January for Mesopotamia via France, Italy and Egypt, they were yet to meet the man who would lead them into the great unknown.

Lionel Dunsterville was born on 9 November 1865, and attended a private boys' school – the United Services College in North Devon – with author Rudyard Kipling and was the inspiration for Stalky in Kipling's novel *Stalky & Co.* He entered the British Army in 1884 and later transferred to the Indian Army where he served on the Northwest Frontier in the lands beyond the Khyber Pass, that centuries-old invasion route for every conqueror from Darius I of Persia to Genghis Khan and to the Sikhs under Ranjit Singh at the end of the 1700s. He also spoke fluent Russian, a fact he would later acknowledge was a key factor in his selection.

The Dunsterforce was a special forces unit raised decades before anyone thought of having special forces units. They would go on to suffer all of the usual diseases – malaria, cholera, sandfly fever and dysentery. They would dodge the bullets of tribesmen, dine with sheiks, fight alongside Russian Cossacks opposed to the Bolshevik revolution, capture Turkish deserters and German spies and assassins, help Armenians flee the Turkish genocide, incur the ire of local mullahs after flagrantly violating Islamic customs, come to the aid of American missionaries and, most significantly in the opinion of historians, be seen as saviours by tens of thousands of Persians made refugees in their own country thanks to a monstrous drought and the vagaries of foreign armies.

The military objectives of the Dunsterforce were, from the very beginning, fuzzy at best – to enter Persia and then the Caucasus via the Caspian Sea, to link up with the region's disaffected Cossacks and other Russians as well as local Armenians and together secure the Trans-Caucasian railway that ran from the Caspian to the Black Sea, prevent any attempt the Turks might make to seize the oilfields near the city of Baku, and bring to an end any German–Ottoman thoughts of advancing eastwards to India. Normally the Russians could be relied upon to do this sort of work in their own backyard, but Czar Nicolas II had been deposed by the Bolsheviks who then signed a separate accord with the Central Powers, an act that had demoralised the Russian Army which had been eyeballing the Turks in the Caucasus and Persia. Now with the turmoil in Russia, Turkey was in a position to reclaim some of the territories it had lost. Enter Lionel Dunsterville and his multinational mix of high achievers – a unit that some were already referring to as the Dunsterforce but which others preferred to call, the Hush-Hush Army.

The force assembled in Basra and set off into Persia. Although Persia was officially neutral, it had been fought over by Turkish and Russian forces since the commencement of the war until the capture of Baghdad ended Turkish influence there. No one in the Dunsterforce was prepared for what they would see along the way: thousands of starving souls on the sides of the roads, the result of a severe and bitter drought that began in mid-1917 and showed no sign of ending any time soon. An Australian officer, Captain Stanley George Savige, described the mass of starving Persians he saw at Kermanshah, 525 km west of Tehran:

Knots of starving inhabitants were seen scattered across the valley actually eating grass, and every step in the city brought one face to face with a living skeleton. Those strong enough begged or watched for their opportunity to

*steal. Those too weak to stand lay dying in the streets ...
mothers clung to their dying, and in many cases, dead
children. Children crowded round the dead body of a
parent, while many were so weak that a touch would fell
them to the ground, from which they could not rise without
assistance.*

Stanley Savige was born in Morwell, Victoria, on 26 June
1890 and enlisted in the AIF on 6 March 1915. He was a veteran
of Gallipoli and Pozières, where he was promoted to captain.
Wounded at Flers in November 1916 he contracted influenza
but recovered to fight again at Warlencourt, Grevillers, and
Bullecourt and was awarded the Military Cross. He then
volunteered for the Dunsterforce, and was typical of the calibre
of recruit Dunsterville was looking for. In September of 1923,
while working for the Returned Soldiers' and Sailors' Woollen
& Worsted Co-operative Manufacturing Company in Geelong,
Victoria, he founded Legacy.

Savige and the rest of the Dunsterforce saw more
carnage and human misery on the way to and from their
objectives than they ever did fighting. For almost three years
crop production in western Persia had been interrupted by
either poor or no rains. 'Whole villages,' Savige wrote, 'were
without inhabitants. First the Turk, then the Russians,
had swept the country bare of what it nourished ... and the
government, represented by the Shah and thieving ministers,
had cornered all the grain.' Stationed west of Hamadan with
orders to keep the roads south of the Caucasus clear, Savige's
role became more that of humanitarian than soldier. Patrols
through the region to deliver machine guns and material to the
fighting were overwhelmed by refugees and locals; women beat
their chests with gratitude upon sighting Savige's patrols and
kissed his hands for delivering them from the cruelty of the
Turks, while the Persian men would fire their guns into the air,
shouting jubilantly: 'The English, the English!'

Savige received a DSO for his actions at Sain Kaleh. The citation read:

> *For conspicuous gallantry and devotion to duty during the retirement of refugees from Sain Kaleh to Tikkan Tappah between 26th and 28th July 1918; also at Chalkaman on the 5th and 6th August 1918. He was in command of a small party sent to protect the rear of the column of refugees who were being hard pressed by the enemy. By his energy, resource and able dispositions the hostile troops, many of whom were mounted, were kept at a distance, although in greatly superior force. He hung on to position after position until nearly surrounded, but on each occasion extricated his command most skilfully. His cool determination and fine example under fire inspired his men and put heart into the almost panic stricken refugees, thereby averting what might have been a very serious situation.*

Savige's account of his time with the Dunsterforce is the most thorough document that has come down to us detailing the Australian involvement in this fascinating and peripheral Great War theatre. It is a pity, however, that there are no extant diaries from the more than forty Australians who volunteered, but we do at least know their names and can remember them and imagine what they witnessed in these distant places that were so far removed from the familiar battlefields we know so well.

Historians have largely neglected the role Australians and the other non-British participants played in the Dunsterforce, mostly because of the paucity of reliable primary material that has come down to us. Charles Bean didn't even mention the Dunsterforce in his *Official History*. The fact our soldiers served in British units, under British flags, and were wearing British uniforms certainly didn't help foster a sense of national identity or participation. The records of the units they served in are British too. They reside in British libraries and museums and are written by British authors in such a way as to fail to discriminate between nationalities – everyone in the Dunsterforce was a de facto Englishman, and while names are of course mentioned, no effort is made to determine if the person was Australian, Canadian, South African or otherwise. But a photograph taken at Mekinah near Basra in Mesopotamia in February 1918 prior to the force setting out across Persia proves we were there! Nine Australians are pictured in the photograph: Captain William Francis McIver, originally of the 50th Battalion; Captain Eric George Scott-Olsen, 55th Battalion, MC; Captain Ewen Colclough Cameron, 4th Machine Gun Battalion; Lieutenant Richard Henry Hooper, 58th Battalion, MC; Lieutenant Roy Barrett Withers, 13th Battalion, DCM; Captain Earle Norbury Seary, 50th Battalion; Captain Clarence Frank Mills, 4th Field Office Engineers, MC; Lieutenant John Harold Ashley Sorrel, 45th Battalion, MM; and Captain Francis William Lord, 1st Divisional Ammunition Column, MM.

Of the list above only Lieutenant Roy Withers seems to have an extended biography. Born in Callan Park, New South Wales, Withers left Sydney as a private on 6 September 1915 and saw service on the Western Front. After being promoted to corporal he showed conspicuous gallantry while under fire by repelling an enemy raiding party single-handed and securing his unit's exposed flank. For his bravery he was awarded a DCM and promoted to lieutenant, after which he volunteered for special duty with the Dunsterforce. Withers survived the war and returned to Sydney on 19 December 1918.

The original objectives of the Dunsterforce had been all but abandoned by August 1918, due in part to the fact that a mere 900 men, no matter how formidable, were never going to alter the strategic balance in the region. Britain's commander in Mesopotamia, Lieutenant General W. R. Marshall, also never supported the concept of Caucasian intervention and didn't like the fact that Dunsterville was circumventing his own authority by reporting directly to London. It was petulant opposition that Dunsterville could well have done without. There were logistical issues too. Keeping the far-flung force properly supplied was always problematic. When the force's Armoured Car Brigade, for instance, finally arrived from Russia months behind schedule they came with few spare parts, insufficient supplies of lubricant and with Rubberine tyres that were perfectly fine in the cold of the Russian Arctic but solidified in the Persian heat and led to an epidemic of broken rear axles.

In the end the Dunsterforce mission narrowed into one singular objective: the defence of Baku in the face of mounting Turkish opposition. To have any hope of achieving this, the local Armenian and Russian forces had to be moulded into an effective fighting force. And to help achieve this the experience of two Australians was called upon: Captain W. F. Lord formerly of the 1st Division, a student teacher from East Malvern in Melbourne who would help with artillery training; and Captain E. Cameron formerly of the 13th Machine Gun Company, a farmer and grazier from Wellcamp in Queensland, who would assist with the infantry.

The Dunsterforce had grown to more than 900 men with the inclusion of the 39th Midland Infantry Brigade, in addition to its 6000 Armenian and 3000 Russian troops. But they were up against a Turkish force of 7000 at Baku supported by around 5000 Tartars with field guns and cavalry. Their numbers were comparable, but the fighting spirit of the two opposing armies was not. On 26 August when the Turks began their assault on the city the Russian and Armenian lines immediately began to crumble. Lieutenant-Colonel John Warden, formerly of the 102nd Canadian Infantry Battalion, complained bitterly to Dunsterville about not having a staff car so he could properly patrol his 50-kilometre-long perimeter and having to do it on foot, but the lack of proper vehicles was the least of Dunsterville's problems. He was highly critical of the will to fight shown by the Russians and Armenians: 'We came here to help your men to fight the Turks, not to do all the fighting, with your men as onlookers!' he told the Baku Revolutionary Committee that ran the day-to-day affairs of the city. 'In no case have I seen your troops, when ordered to attack, do anything but retire.'

The siege continued for two weeks and the final assault came on 14 September. The situation was hopeless. Dunsterville ordered the sick and wounded to be loaded onto two waiting ships, and after a fighting retreat around seventy officers and 800 men steamed out of the beleaguered city. In the rush to get out an Australian, Sergeant A. Bullen, a lorry driver from Narrabri in central New South Wales, and a New Zealander, H. B. Suttor, a grazier from Napier and also of the 7th Light Horse, both of whom had only arrived in Baku the night before and astonishingly hadn't been made aware of the coming withdrawal, were left behind and had to make their own way out of the city with other refugees in the bowels of a cargo ship that took them across the Caspian Sea to the city of Krasnovodsk in present-day Turkmenistan.

John Warden remained highly critical of Dunsterville's command. 'I never expected to witness such chaos among the British military, especially the regulars. Baku could have been held by good, sound management and organisation. To keep four new armoured cars and never put them in action when we were being driven in and then leave them on the dock was in my opinion criminal.' Stanley Savige, however, was a little more forgiving and tended to view the successes of the Dunsterforce in broader terms:

> The work carried out by the members of the force was varied, from valuable administrative tasks to daring achievements in the battlefield, and all have striven to do their utmost, even in spheres of work for which they

were never prepared and they would never have chosen for themselves. Officers and N.C.O.s have been called upon to superintend famine relief work, to assist in road construction, to police towns, to drill and instruct levies and Armenian troops, and to lend a ready hand in many tasks that were not, in themselves, congenial. Apart from any military results achieved, the members of the force have had the proud privilege of showing the various races in the lands through which they passed, the pattern of the finest army of present times. The effect of their demeanour and their behaviour has been such as to enhance the reputation of the British race in the eyes of all with whom they had dealings.

The Dunsterforce operated as both a military and humanitarian unit in an ethnic powder keg of a region in the final months of a terrible war, used as a pawn in the so-called 'Great Game' – that odd phrase given to the decades-long geopolitical struggle between Britain and Russia. A book chronicling all of the Australian stories that unfolded under its banner over the nine months of its existence would be both a challenge and a joy to tackle. But there should be no great rush to write it. Let its mysteries endure, there are so few of them left in the world. I'm sure the 'Dunsters' would be happy with this. Never has a military force seemed so content with ambiguity and tall tales as Lionel Dunsterville's Hush-Hush Army, happy to stay wrapped in the enigmatic cloak it wore so well.

Chapter Eight
Bromide and Brushstrokes

None but those who have endeavoured can realise the insurmountable difficulties of portraying a modern battle by the camera. To include the event on a single negative I have tried and tried, but the results are hopeless. Everything is on such a vast scale. Figures are scattered, the atmosphere is dense with haze and smoke, shells will not burst where required. Yet the whole elements of a picture are there, could they but be brought together and condensed.

– Frank Hurley, photographer & filmmaker

Artistic renderings of war are almost as old as war itself. The Battlefield Palette, a cosmetician's palette from Egypt pre-3100 BCE used to grind ingredients for use in cosmetics has survived fifty centuries, albeit in two fragments. One shows a battlefield scene with a lion and a vulture preying on dead human bodies that seem to have fallen in battle, while the other depicts two bound captives. The Alexander Mosaic – a floor mosaic uncovered beneath the ash of Pompeii – shows in great detail Alexander the Great defeating the Persians at the Battle of Issus. Christian art during the Medieval period tended to avoid portraying battle scenes, but during the Renaissance artists turned out thousands of sketches and paintings and sculptures showing everything from the design of fortresses, siege towers and anything that could be termed a weapon through to the glorification of military figures and battle scenes that were both contemporary and historic. In the sixteenth century war art became less formulaic and began to move away from idealised representations of conflict thanks to artists such as Urs Graf, the Swiss painter, printmaker and one-time mercenary whose drawings and etchings showed soldiers as ordinary people doing the best they could in less than heroic settings. By the seventeenth century tapestries depicting war became popular forms of sanctioned and commissioned military art, while Napoleon provided Europe's artists with no end of opportunities to advance the genre.

With the invention of photography in the 1830s came a new kind of war art. The world's first war photographer was a surgeon in the Bengal Army, John McCosh. McCosh captured images from the Second Sikh War in 1848–49 that included artillery lines and emplacements, various assemblages of commanding officers, and most significantly of the horrendous aftermath of armed conflict. But it was Carol Szathmari, however, the Austro–Hungarian painter who is considered the first person to ever take pictures in the heat of battle, the world's first true war correspondent. Szathmari was often in the thick of battle during the first twelve months of the Russian–Turkish War (later known as the Crimean War) in 1853, and even had his own wagon for the developing of his glass plates, a wagon that was often the target of Turkish artillery. The American photographer Mathew Brady first brought the horror of the Civil War to the American people with his Battle of Antietam exhibition in New York in October 1862. Eleven years after that seminal date in the history of war photography, Vernon Smith was born in a small town in Tasmania.

It's frustrating how little we know about the life of Vernon Smith, a man who slipped out of our nation's historic narrative as quickly as he slipped into it. Born in the small community of Upper Flowerdale in north-west Tasmania in 1873, or thereabouts as no records have been found to confirm it, Vernon was the son of James Smith, the owner of a butter factory and a man with some kind of an interest in photography himself – an interest he passed on to his son. Vernon briefly helped manage his father's business but left in his early twenties to became a schoolteacher. Then in 1899 he joined the 2nd Tasmanian (Bushmen's) Contingent and departed for Cape Town to fight in the Boer War. But before he left – who knows, perhaps as he was stumbling his way out the front door with his duffel bag over his shoulder? – he grabbed his precious 1895 model Kodak Pocket Camera, a birthday gift from his father.

Kodak's 1895 Pocket Camera wasn't all that much different from its original 1885 model camera. It still had its unremarkable rectangular shape and plain round viewfinder, and still came bound in either a black or red leather case with room for a few extra rolls of film. It could take twelve photos on a single daylight spool that produced 2" x 1½" negatives. The camera was worth about two days' wages, and the whole thing measured just 4 x 3 x 2¼ inches, small enough to fit in his pocket. In South Africa Vernon Smith took more than 460 photographs, mostly of burning buildings, abandoned railway sidings and the twisted, gnarled and smoking aftermath of war. He also photographed many of the long journeys his unit made through the South African veldt, either by train or on horseback, images that were so characteristic of our soldiers' experience there. Almost all of the photographs survive to this day and are the most comprehensive visual record of Australia's Boer War campaign we have.

After the war Vernon returned to Tasmania, went back to teaching and married his girlfriend, Annie. The pair purchased a farm in 1904 and then, in 1913, one year before the outbreak of another war, Vernon Smith died. Australia didn't know it, but it had lost its very first war artist.

James Francis (Frank) Hurley was an adventurous Australian

and visionary artist. In 1914 he accompanied Ernest Shackleton to the South Pole, returning with vivid colour images of their grand, history-making traverse. In France during World War I, he worked alongside soldiers in the trenches and above the parapets.

He was an accomplished and pioneering photographer. Frustrated that his photography failed to capture adequately the visually complex and deadly panoramas of the war as it unfolded around him, he began experimenting with 'composite images' – condensing the battlefield and all that it contained into one picture through the overlaying of multiple negatives. It seemed to him to be the only way to convey all that he saw. Charles Bean, set-in-concrete traditionalist that he was, thought the idea of composite imaging was terrible, and denounced Hurley's photographs as fakes. What chance an historian would think anything else?

Hurley was appointed an official war photographer by Charles Bean and the Australian High Commission in 1917. Modelled after similar ventures that had been undertaken by the British and Canadian governments, the commissioning of artists to go into battle has been a part of every armed conflict in which Australians have been present ever since, and is now the longest-running and largest-commissioning art program in our nation's history. Hurley had two stints in the Middle East. The first, from December 1917 to March 1918, was spent in Palestine where he joined the Australian Mounted Division. Hurley was happy to follow the Light Horsemen after the horrors he'd witnessed in France, a place he described simply as 'hell'. Hurley's second visit, during World War II, was an extended tour that lasted six years and took him to Egypt, Jordan, Libya, Palestine, Lebanon and Syria. Lennard Bickel, the noted Australian journalist and author, wrote that he always felt Hurley 'spent the happiest days of his life in the Middle East'. Hurley never felt the need to contradict him.

Hurley wanted to convey the truth of war and our diggers'

daily experience on the ground. Many considered his pictures of dead and wounded soldiers lying in the midst of doctored battlefields to be grossly inappropriate. But Pozières was not Antarctica. For Hurley, focusing on a single moment in time provided only a glimpse of the horror of war. Photographs should be able to tell a story, they should excite the emotions and assist in the expression of ideas. After all, in 1915 the Italian futurist Gino Severini had painted *Train in Action*, a cubist combination of balletic curves and acute angles with the human form reduced to the same metallic components as a train. Why couldn't a photographer be equally abstract?

Artists have always sought to interpret what they see. If only Charles Bean knew what interpretations were coming. Through Australia's subsequent wars – World War II, Korea, Vietnam, our various peacekeeping roles, Iraq and Afghanistan, war artists have increasingly been given the freedom to interpret what they have seen and to represent war without the spectre of bureaucratic interference. They deserve that licence too because they have stared into the unblinking eyes of war, into what Joseph Conrad once called that 'appalling face of a glimpsed truth', and it is the artist's job to give that face its deathly expression.

The 'controversial' composite images of Frank Hurley were really nothing more than a tentative beginning, the start of a legacy of subjectivity – such as the series of naked sittings agreed to by our soldiers in Afghanistan in 2012 for artist Ben Quilty – that would do so much to reflect and give shape to our contemporary view of war. War artists are not only the chroniclers of a common, distant past. They are also helping us to come to terms with the here and now.

Charles Bean first put forward the idea that artists should be approached and commissioned to record our men at war, and it all began without fanfare in May 1917 with the establishment of the Australian War Records Section (AWRS) in the Public Records Office in Chancery Lane, London. Administered through the Australian High Commission, the AWRS mushroomed over eighteen months into a department with a staff of over 600 people. They would be kept busy over the following two years as more than 25,000 objects – from photographs, manuals, unit diaries, film and those first works of art to aeroplanes, heavy weapons and even tanks – were gathered together and returned to Australia, an impressive collection of the spoils of war. The collection formed the nucleus of what would become the Australian War Memorial, our national museum of war built in part because the Australian government knew that Britain was organising a museum of its own and didn't want the cream of our accumulated artefacts hauled off to London and deposited in a storage room somewhere in Lambeth Road!

Early volunteers wielded brushes rather than cameras and were gathered from lands both familiar and distant. Some, like Louis McCubbin and Will Longstaff, came straight off the front lines of the Western Front, while others – such as Arthur Streeton and John Longstaff, who went on to win the Archibald Prize five times – were drawn from the thousands of expatriate Australians living in England at the time war was declared. William Dyson and Arthur Streeton were given the rank of Honorary Lieutenant to help them navigate their way to the front and overcome any bureaucratic or logistic entanglements along the way. They were paid £1 a week over three months for their trouble, during which time they were expected to produce twenty-five works, no less! Dyson, a cartoonist whose satirical caricatures had already brought him international recognition, was the first of our artists to be sent into battle, arriving at the front in December 1916 and then deciding to remain there, as a civilian and so unpaid, for five months to fulfill the brief he had been given to 'interpret, in a series of drawings, for national preservation, the sentiments and special Australian characteristics of the Australian army'.

The talented Sydney-born graphic artist and former David Jones furniture designer, Frederick Leist, produced more than 150 evocative watercolours of devastated villages in France and Belguim, many of which he composed on grey paper to accentuate the overwhelming sense of gloom and despair he felt while 'dodging shells and mustard gas'.

Our war artists were sent mostly to Europe, which was understandable considering that was where the bulk of the fighting was. Streeton concentrated mostly on landscapes and still-lives of everyday commonplace moments, consciously avoiding recording anything that showed the horror of human suffering. George Lambert, who arrived in Australia from Russia in 1887 when still a teenager, was approached by both the Canadian and Australian governments to be a war artist in 1917. He too looked at ways of somehow muting the horrors and the stark realism of battle. His famous paintings of the Gallipoli landings and our charge at The Nek were composed of subdued pinks and greens that showed our diggers almost indistinguishable in tone from the environment that was engulfing them, as if it were swallowing them up.

Several artists who painted moments from the Great War, such as George Coates, were appointed retrospectively. Coates was born in Melbourne, studied at the North Melbourne School of Design and attended evening classes run by none other that Frederick McCubbin. In 1913 he was elected a full member of the Societe Nationale des Beaux Arts in Paris. A first-rate swimmer and excellent boxer, he enlisted as a ward orderly and served in the 3rd London General Hospital, but was so disturbed by the horrors he'd seen he was discharged in April 1919, classified as 'no longer physically fit for war service'. He returned home to his painting, and it wasn't until 1921 that he was invited to become a war artist. Dismissive of impressionism, Coates' works remained firmly representational. His sensitive portraits – including one of fellow war artist John Longstaff – were crafted in harmonious, low tones that displayed a painstaking approach to detail.

Much of the work of our war artists was done in the drawing rooms, studios and in the fields and villages of England, France and Belgium, with the echoes of battles and the memory of Europe's scarred landscapes still hanging in the air, still fresh and raw. But it would be wrong to think they were only asked to commemorate the bloodiest, the most famous or the most gallant. Often they were asked to paint other places, far less muddy and less familiar places. Obscure places. Sandier places.

Harold Septimus Power was born in Dunedin, New Zealand on 31 December 1877, but moved to Melbourne with his parents when he was still a child. He failed to excel at school, where he spent most of his time impulsively colouring in textbooks, and at the age of fourteen ran away from home to live in the Victorian bush where he began to sketch and paint animals – particularly horses – and everyday rural life. He returned briefly to Melbourne where he found work as a carriage painter, but left again, this time for Adelaide, where he met the great German-born painter Hans Heysen, famous for his watercolours of Australian gum trees and his arid landscapes of the Flinders Ranges. Power worked as an illustrator for various Adelaide newspapers before leaving for Paris in 1905 to study at the Academie Julian.

Appointed to be an official war artist in 1917, Power would go on to become our finest equine artist, though many of his paintings were overly sentimental depictions of the harmony between man and nature. Despite working mostly alongside our troops in Europe, Power produced two works deserving of mention here: *Camel Corps at Maghaba 23 Dec 1916* (1922), and the magnificent *Ziza* (1935), a giant oil on canvas measuring 2.5 m by 1.5 m depicting the most unlikely of scenes – that of a 5000-strong Turkish garrison and

Australians from the 5th Light Horse Brigade at rest together in the desert.

With *Ziza*, Power highlighted the futility of war. The scene depicts soldiers of war, sitting together with weapons downed. That these two groups of men should be fighting one another seems, as a consequence of the image, absurd. The painting is a reminder that it is not people who go to war; that is what governments do. What was always likely to be little more than a historic anomaly, an encounter in Palestine well away from the scrutiny of every last vignette that accompanied the fighting in Europe, suddenly becomes a singular message of hope. Even in the midst of war, war is not inevitable.

By September 1918 the Ottoman Empire was crumbling. Ordered to fall back in the face of the British assault on Amman, remnants of the Ottoman Fourth Army retreated towards a rail junction at Deraa, harassed all the way by the Arab Northern Army. Columns of Turkish troops, their pace slowed by their sick and injured, were strung out along the Hejaz railway that ran north to Amman. The sight of the enemy so exposed proved too much for the local Arabs, many of whom had suffered under Ottoman rule, and straggling and exposed Turks were soon shot dead and looted. The Turks responded by killing the inhabitants of the villages through which they passed.

As the Turks continued their retreat north towards Amman a force of between 5000 and 6000 had, in the ensuing confusion, somehow become unaccounted for – 'lost' to British reconnaissance – and the task of finding them was given to the Australian and New Zealand Mounted Division. Finding the missing Turks was of course only going to be a matter of time – it wasn't easy for thousands of retreating soldiers to stay hidden, especially in a desert environment – but the task was made easier still after the capture of a lone Turkish soldier by the 2nd Australian Light Horse Brigade on 27 September. The missing 5000, the prisoner said, were encamped around a small railway siding named Ziza in the Jordan Valley. The next day, two squadrons of the Australian 5th Light Horse Regiment under the command of Lieutenant Colonel Donald Cameron set off to find them.

And find them they did, at rest at Ziza Station. Instead of wanting a fight, however, the Turkish commander Colonel Ali Bey – already having been told in a British pamphlet drop that the water wells to the north were all dry and that he might as well surrender – sent a white flag to Cameron and asked to arrange a meeting. During the meeting Cameron cancelled an air strike on the Turkish positions that had been scheduled for that afternoon. Grateful for this act of kindness, Bey cautioned that he felt Cameron's regiment would not be large enough to deter a probable Arab assault by Beni Sakhr tribesmen in the hills surrounding Ziza, and promptly offered to launch an attack himself. It was a tempting offer. The Australians and New Zealanders had little affection for Arabs, whom they thought more suited to pillaging and cowardice than fighting. They considered them savages interested only in attacking units smaller than their own, and would dig up the dead to strip them of valuables.

To the Arabs, Cameron's arrival suggested that an Anzac attack on the Turkish positions was imminent, a belief that only swelled the number of tribesmen who were, according to one diarist, 'prowling like jackals' in anticipation of the spoils. But there would be no spoils this day. When appraised of the numbers of Arabs he could be facing, Cameron contacted Major General Edward Chaytor and requested he send his 2nd Brigade from Amman. Cameron then got word to the assembled Arabs – estimated to number close to 10,000 – that if they attacked the Turkish troops then he and his 5th Light Horse would, in turn, attack them. At 1600 hours on 28 September, Cameron pencilled in his diary:

At 1600 I sent a message, by Arabs, to the Bedouins

gathering around the position to the effect that if they attempted to attack the Turks I would attack them. This had the desired effect and they began to withdraw. Although throughout the day the situation appeared at times somewhat critical, fortunately my men did not fire one shot at the Bedouins.

Fearing that it might not be so easy to deter an Arab attack launched after dark, Brigadier General Granville de la Ryrie, who had arrived earlier that afternoon from Amman, issued a remarkable order. He told his officers to peacefully and without aggression deploy their squads at intervals *throughout the Turkish positions.* One can only imagine the soldiers' expressions as the two armies were, in effect, mingled into a single intimidating unit. De la Ryrie's order was astonishing enough, but more so after the mutual slaughter at Gallipoli, Maghaba, Rafa, Gaza and the rest. Following on from de la Ryrie's order, Australians and Turks were busily making their introductions in the Turkish trenches, and preparing to bed down for the night. 'For once all enmities were forgiven,' wrote Lieutenant Colonel John Richardson, the commander of the 7th Light Horse. 'Our men and the Turks boiled their quarts and made chapattis over the same fires.'

The night passed uneventfully – if one could call such a gathering uneventful – until the morning, when a small number of Arabs tried to infiltrate the Turkish lines from the west. They were forced back by New South Welshmen of 'C' Squadron 7th Light Horse with the assistance of a number of Turkish machine-gunners, firing alongside one another at a common threat! When a detachment of New Zealand Mounted Rifles arrived later that morning, they were astounded to see Australians and Turks emerging from the same trenches to greet them! When Cameron returned to Amman with two battalions of fully armed Turks walking alongside him the defenders of the city, in the words of author and Ziza researcher

Damien Fenton, 'thought they were seeing things'.

A quite decent photograph of Major General Edward Chaytor and the commander of the Turkish forces, Colonel Ali Bey, posing uncomfortably side by side on folding chairs can be viewed at the Australian War Memorial. It's a typically starchy photo of the time, and their demeanour leaves no doubt as to who is the victor and who is the vanquished. But the portrait conveys little in the way of information. It falls to Power's glorious rendering to provide us with the only record of the meeting that really matters, and the monumental canvas is a testament to the capacity of every war artist to achieve with an image what cannot be done with a pen.

The Russian-born Australian George Lambert was aged in his forties and living in London when he unsuccessfully attempted to enlist with the AIF and instead joined the Volunteer Training Corps, a home defence militia for men either above military age or otherwise engaged in work deemed too important for them to be sent off to war. Lambert had been an exceptional portrait artist and painter of allegorical images before he was appointed an Australian war artist in November 1917. He set sail from London for Palestine on Christmas Day 1917 and in January 1918 was packed off to Egypt, but despite arriving too late for the Egyptian and Sinai campaigns he was nonetheless prolific, composing more than 130 sketches during his time. From these sketches he went on to produce a treasure trove of works of varying size and scope, including the 23 cm by 28 cm miniature *The Australian Lighthorse Remount Camp at Moascar* (1918), a work given impetus by his good friend Banjo Patterson, who happened to be in charge of the Remounts Section in question, to his 123 cm by 247 cm *Charge at Beersheba* (1920). Lambert had heard of the charge months after it happened from the men of the 4th Light Horse Brigade who were happy to stage a re-enactment for him at the Moascar

Remount Yard so he could see something of the chaotic nature of the charge.

He first began sketching *Charge at Beersheba* using a pencil, rubbing his fingers along the lines to create tone, and continued working on it through until 1920 when he started the canvas. The painting would bring the famous scene to life, following the slow and deliberate processes of the studio tradition. Lambert had a special affinity for, and relationship with, the Light Horse – hardly surprising, considering his swarthy looks and athletic build would have seen him easily mix with the strapping men of the Light Horse regiments. He was one of a very few artists ever to visit Gallipoli when he joined a historical visit to the peninsula in November 1919 (and painted twenty-five canvases as a result), and left London for Damascus in May 1919 so he could personally witness the Light Horse's demobilisation.

Charge at Beersheba depicts a major flashpoint of the war, but the fact is that the majority of war art preserves incidents and vignettes, preparations, aftermaths and errant shells – like the ones that fell much too close to two sand carts at Romani in the western Sinai in August 1917.

In the midst of the Battle of Romani two sand carts of the 2nd Light Horse Field Ambulance had been dispatched to bring back from no-man's-land a number of severely wounded men. The sand carts used by our field ambulance units in the Sinai were an adaptation of wagons that had been used throughout Upper Egypt for decades, but were cumbersome when pulled through heavy sand when four horses were needed instead of the usual two, a fact that often required a man to act as a rider on one of the lead horses. As the two sand carts were returning to their lines with their wounded cargo, Turkish artillery opened fire on them, causing the horses in the leading cart to break into a gallop. One of the attending stretcher-bearers, mindful of having to keep the wounded as still as possible, rode his own horse to the front of the lead cart, signalled 'walk' to the horses, and was able to steady them. It was a moment the men of the 2nd Light Horse Field Ambulance never forgot, and in 1919 George Lambert was asked to depict the incident on canvas. He travelled to Egypt where the incident was re-enacted for him at Kantara. The result, *An Incident at Romani*, is like much of the war art we now have from the two world wars: precious reminders of heroic moments from our nation's past.

In the midst of digging a trench on the outskirts of Tobruk during World War II, twenty-nine-year-old William Dargie was tapped on the shoulder and handed a telegram. He later recalled, 'as I tore it open he asked "Good news or bad?" I said I had won some bloody prize, and he said "Oh," and very sensibly added "How much?"' The 'bloody prize' Dargie had won was the most prestigious prize in Australian art, the 1941 Archibald Prize, awarded in his absence for his portrait of Sir James Elder KBE, the Director of the National Bank of Australia. The fact the win may have been illegitimate – as Dargie, who was on service for the Australian government as an official war artist, hadn't been in Australia to properly lodge all of the paperwork – hardly matters. Anyway he probably wouldn't have missed it: he went on to claim seven more Archibalds, a record that stands to this day.

Dargie was criticised by modernist painters who loathed his work and felt it unworthy of the Archibald. They thought his work pedestrian. A young art critic named Robert Hughes (later art critic for *TIME* magazine) considered Dargie's portraits to be so drenched in realism that he 'sought to reconstruct with infinite labour what the camera can do in a tenth of a second'. Dargie in turn considered much contemporary art to be snobbish and the 'refuge of reactionaries'. What cannot be disputed, though, is his contribution to the body of our war art. Dargie was appointed an official war artist on 6 October

1941 and sent to the Middle East on what would be the start of a mammoth five-year appointment that took him to Lebanon, Libya, New Guinea, India, Greece and Crete and won him his second Archibald for his portrait of Corporal Jim Gordon VC of 2/31st Battalion, a man Dargie considered the 'perfect model for a typical digger ... not the smiling, happy-go-lucky digger of legend but the slightly older-than-young man, with a definite sense of responsibility'.

During the Australian 7th Division's advance on Vichy French–held Beirut on 9 July 1941 Gordon's unit was ordered to seize a ridge near the villages of Amatour and Badarane above the town of Jezzine. It was a difficult objective. Gordon's unit had been pinned down by machine-gun fire when the then-Private Gordon, on his own initiative, left his unit and began a slow, solitary crawl forward over a series of terraces towards an enemy machine-gun post. When he got close enough he stood to his feet and charged it head-on. Using only his bayonet he killed the post's four Senegalese conscripts in an act so audacious it completely demoralised the enemy, after which Gordon's company was able to advance and capture the ridge. For his bravery Jim Gordon was awarded the Victoria Cross.

The campaign in Syria and Lebanon, two countries that had been French protectorates since 1919, has been called the last battle in history fought between Britain and France and the foreign legionnaires and Senegalese, Algerian and other troops from France's fading colonial empire who were in the pay of Marshall Petain's Vichy government. Petain and the rest of his traitorous French quislings had made a separate peace with Germany after the Battle of France in July 1940 and fought alongside the Axis powers against the Allies until the liberation of Paris in August 1944. For the Australians, British and even the French themselves it must have seemed like madness that comrades from the Great War, not to mention the French still being citizens of a country the Allies were fighting to free from Nazi occupation, were here trying to kill one another. The commander of the British and Australian forces in Lebanon, Major General John Lavarack, even wrote to his superiors in a desperate plea to bring the conflict to an end through diplomacy. 'To both Frenchmen and Australians,' he wrote, 'the idea of comrades from the last war fighting against one another is repellent and distasteful, and a useless waste of good men.'

The Australian and British battalions continued advancing to Beirut, pressing on through terrain so gruelling our infantry had to fashion makeshift stretchers for their own wounded, using their rifles and pullovers that 'sagged so much it was like carrying a man in a bag', all because the Cypriot muleteers Lavarack had to get our wounded to clearing stations couldn't convince their animals to climb along its narrow ridges and traverse its precipitous ravines. The fighting was intense. Hilltops changed hands almost every night with most of the fighting done in the dark by men of both sides who were so hungry they stole food from enemy corpses. The whole campaign made a mockery of British hopes that Vichy forces would only put up token resistance. The enemy had air superiority, more troops, and two-thirds of an armoured division to call on and were operating in a country where the topography suited defence. But the Allies ploughed on, and the Australian 7th Division fought its way up the coast road to Beirut, which fell on 12 July and delivered Lebanon (and Syria, which fell in late June) back into the hands of the French General Charles de Gaulle. William Dargie's portrait of Jim Gordon is another example of how a war artist can keep alive the memory of campaigns and actions that otherwise are perennially overlooked, and all too easily forgotten.

I said to the corporals, 'Righto! Scotty, Brian, John,' and off we went. Up to now it had been dark and cold, and down

in our wadi we had felt sheltered and somehow protected. But as we moved into the exposed ground our artillery commenced firing. The Italians replied and almost at once the air was filled with the crash and scream of shells. The dark was broken by the flash of explosions, while the sky above us was criss-crossed with phosphorescent tracks of the tracer.

    – H. B. Gullett, *Not as a Duty Only*

The above is a reference to D Company 2/6th Battalion as it was preparing for its assault on Post 11, the strongest defensive position in the Italian line that defended the town of Bardia, Libya, on 5 January 1941. Post 11 was the last garrison to fall in the three-day siege, which involved six Australian battalions from the 16th and 17th Australian Brigades, the 7th Royal Tank Regiment and supporting artillery. Damien Parer, the great Australian photographer and filmmaker, was there in the midst of it all and even went in alongside the troops, at times filming the charge ahead of the men themselves! The assault on Bardia was an unqualified success. Captured were 40,000 Italian prisoners, 400 artillery pieces, 130 tanks and hundreds of support vehicles. Australian losses were 130 killed and 325 wounded. 'Never,' said the British Foreign Secretary Anthony Eden in a letter to Prime Minister Winston Churchill, 'had so much been surrendered to so many by so few.'

To celebrate the twenty-five-year anniversary of the battle in 1966, the Australian artist Ivor Hele was asked to compose a painting. His work *Bardia* was completed in 1967 and captures in its mass of dead and wounded the bloody struggle for the control of Post 11. Gullett, who has just regained consciousness after having been wounded, is at the centre of the painting, being assisted by Private Harold Brockley, a driver who had abandoned his position in the back so he could join in the fight. Behind them are two brothers, Claude and Bernie Damm. Claude Damm would soon be dead, killed by a bullet wound to the chest. Every figure in the painting has a name. It contains nothing that is superfluous.

Hele's masterpiece hangs today in the Australian War Memorial in Canberra, but it is not his only image of the attack on Bardia. Hele was there when it happened as an official war artist and made many fine drawings of the men of the 2/6th Battalion. His *Digger With Captured Breda Gun* is a crayon drawing showing an unidentified soldier with a captured 6.5 mm Italian machine gun and itself is a reminder that the Australians quickly developed a reputation in North Africa as scavengers of abandoned enemy weapons. His sensitive portrayal showing the gaunt expression of a wearied digger at Tobruk, *Australian Soldier, Libya*, was identified years later by the man's daughter as being that of her father, Sergeant Frank Robert Collins. *Nazi, Sollum*, the portrait of a captured German artilleryman, was composed with a red crayon on woven paper in May 1941. It took over two hours to complete, and Hele would later remark how impressed he was by the German's ability to sit motionless and to maintain, despite now being a POW, a remarkable air of dignity. *Head Study (Lyndon Dadswell)* is a charcoal on paper of one of Australia's most acclaimed sculptors, who had himself been appointed a war artist after having enlisted in the 2nd Division AIF and seen service in Greece, Libya and Syria. Dadswell was in Syria in June 1941 when he received a wound that seriously impeded his vision, and it was during his period of recuperation that he was offered his artist's commission. For a while the two men shared a studio in Heliopolis, Cairo, where Dadswell composed six highly abstract figures that were quite unlike anything that had ever been done by an Australian sculptor. Dadswell returned to Australia in March 1942 and resigned his commission nine months later. Ivor Hele remained in the Middle East and went on to become the most prolific artist in the history of the AWM's war artist program. In New Guinea he painted our troops fighting the Japanese; in Korea he spent five months in its freezing mud. More than 500 of his works are now housed at the Australian War Memorial.

In August '2013 Afghanistan: The Australian Story', a collection of words and images from veterans, their families and also our ubiquitous war artists went on display at the Australian War Memorial. Our commitment in Afghanistan continued the tradition of the AWM war artist that saw, among others, the Archibald Prize–winning artist Ben Quilty dispatched to Kabul, Kandahar and Tarin Kowt in 2011. Quilty, wanting to express the physicality of the servicemen and -women there, painted his subjects naked. But rather than creating heroic-looking figures with confident expressions and an air of conquest he instead used their bodies to reveal their vulnerabilities and anxieties through portraits such as *Captain Kate Porter, after Afghanistan* (2012) and *Captain S, after Afghanistan* (2012), images that show at once strength and frailty. The subjects were encouraged to select poses that they felt reflected an aspect of their Afghan experience, and during the sittings spoke openly about their feelings and attitudes that result in raw truths that were the product of an honest and uncommon bond between artist and subject.

Quilty's experience also had an unexpected effect and ongoing legacy upon the artist, bringing home to him the reality of how the trauma of war can manifest itself in the minds of our soldiers long after they have returned home. Post-Traumatic Stress Disorder (PTSD) is now being addressed as a form of injury every bit as valid as a physical wound, and Quilty is determined to do what he can to make sure the unseen effects of war are recognised and support provided.

> *I hope that [the paintings] tell the story of these people and what they will deal with for the rest of their lives ... in some ways they're about the experience of being under*

*intense pressure and sadness and courageousness,
but really the aftermath of that, which is just the story
they've given me ... I've watched three of them come
down with PTSD since I got back, and that's a crushing
thing to have watched and something that I'd never
anticipated ... I met [Air Commodore] John Oddie on my
way into Afghanistan ... I instantly saw him to be a very
sensitive, quietly spoken, very warm and friendly man,
and I promised him I'd find him when I got back. And I
was warned off seeing him when I got back. People in
the defence force suggested that I stay away from him
because he was having a difficult time emotionally, and
that's exactly why I wanted to go and see him and talk
to him. I met many of the young men who were having a
very difficult time in Afghanistan, and then a lot of men
when I got back who were having an equally difficult time,
and I just knew that John wanted me to tell his story as
well ... and it was a very powerful feeling to be given the
trust of someone like John, who's commanded thousands
of people and lost people under his command and been
through wars, many wars, through the past 25 years.*

Oddie, the only subject who refused to pose nude,
nevertheless saw his portrait as being a representation of
all those who served, not just of himself, and he welcomes
the renewed awareness in society of the 'hidden' wounds of
returned soldiers that artists like Quilty are succeeding in
highlighting.

*I think what Ben is doing is rekindling for me the potential
understanding between society ... within which we are
grown, we are nurtured, with support of which we serve
and into which we return after service ... that society,
its understanding, hopefully has been rekindled ... and
so I think what Ben's doing is bringing back the true*

underlying emotion of service and its relationship with our
society, which has perhaps waned a bit in recent years
but is now firmly back on the table with Ben's leadership.

Post-Traumatic Stress Disorder is insidious. It makes
the past the present. Traumatic events remain traumatic, they
refuse the brain's processing of memories during REM sleep
into those safe places where they can be properly stowed. One
antidote for this is cognitive therapy, by which sufferers can
gain a measure of control over the past event by dealing with
it rationally and understanding it on an intellectual level that
allows them to confront it with less emotion and more reason.
But applying this approach to returned soldiers, ensuring
that the money is spent and the processes put in place
to meet the needs of our servicemen and -women has been
slow to evolve. Artists like Ben Quilty and exhibitions such
as 'Afghanistan: The Australian Story' highlight the need for
increased understanding and intervention. It also represents
the continual evolution of a proud tradition, and paving a road
that will take future generations of war artists down some very
interesting paths.

Chapter Nine
The Eveless Paradise

*Daylight came, and to men who had sometimes despaired of
ever seeing the end of the sands of Sinai, it was like a dawn.
The country was undulating; it was green, and horses tugged
impatiently at their bits in their eagerness to taste grass once
more. Around the patches of young crops poppies showed in
splashes of scarlet. The horseman passed a mud hut with
melon vines and tomato plants, and there were orchards of
apricot trees laden with young fruit. Skylarks rose from beside
the road and fluttered upwards, singing. At sunrise the order
came to dismount, and the Bushman solemnly rolled in the
green grass. He had done that before, after the break of an old-
man drought in Australia.*

– George Berrie upon entering Palestine, Morale, 1949

The prospect of being granted leave in southern Palestine
in 1917 didn't come close to eliciting the sort of
promise and expectations for our troops as it did for those
in Belgium and France. Melons, apricots and tomatoes
there may have been, but there was an alarming shortage
of other things, such as hotels, restaurants, bars and the
sort of establishments of 'varying reputations' that many
of our diggers had been so drawn to back in Cairo. There
also seemed to be an odd shortage of available, unattached
women – a vexing issue not only in this Great War but
in World War II as well. In 1940 the AIF distributed a
pamphlet warning our diggers of the pitfalls of beginning a
conversation with an Arab or Palestinian woman – providing

they could find one. The pamphlet was somehow picked up by the Australian press, and reproduced in part in the 29 November 1940 edition of Brisbane's *Courier-Mail*: 'Arab women are kept severely apart from all men except their husbands, and are easily scared of Australians, so don't look at or speak to any women. They are regarded as inferior to men and you shouldn't even notice their presence.'

While this disturbing situation didn't prevent some soldiers – mostly British, for whom the heat of Palestine must have surely been a revelation – from becoming so enamoured with the place that many decided to register as settlers at war's end, the dearth of feminine company for our 'scary' diggers resulted in an unorthodox nickname for the starkly beautiful, gender-lopsided land in which they now found themselves. They called it the Eveless Paradise.

When British Empire troops began piling up along the Sinai–Palestine border late in November 1917 they had every right to be chock-full of confidence for the fight that lay ahead. Not only had they repulsed the Turkish assault on the canal, they had pushed them inexorably back across the Sinai, winning battle after battle. The canal was safe. Now they sat poised, well supplied and with stomachs full, ready to continue the fight and push their foe northward through Palestine, out of Jerusalem and on up into Syria. Who knows, maybe all the way to the borders of Turkey itself! There was a sense of pride, even of manifest destiny among the more religious. But the Turks had been battling courageously too, striving to make do with some truly calamitous deficiencies in material and manpower that had made the task of preserving the Ottoman Empire in the region all but impossible before the first shot of the war had even been fired.

Turkey had lost the bulk of its artillery pieces in the Balkan Wars of 1912–13, a brutal conflict that devastated the regular Ottoman Army to such an extent that by the time the Great War broke out those artillery pieces had only been replenished on the most modest of scales. The majority of Turkish divisions were woefully short of their full complements of howitzers, and those they still had were a less-than-ideal mix of French Schneiders, German Krupps, and Austro–Hungarian Skodas. The machine-gun situation was equally lamentable for the Turks, who estimated they were short 200,000 pieces. And to make matters worse there was an ammunition shortage as well, which saw each rifleman allocated just 150 rounds (not counting the 200 or so per soldier that were stockpiled in corps depots), a wholly inadequate number of bullets with which to fight a war. Turkey also relied entirely upon its ally, Germany, for air power while its own navy, because of British naval dominance in the Mediterranean, was confined to the irrelevant backwaters of the Black Sea. There was a chronic shortage of doctors and medical supplies, and field hospitals were almost never at full strength. The army's ability to mobilise its forces was also compromised by a critical shortage of both draught animals and supply wagons.

Turkey suffered casualties in excess of 250,000 in 1912–13, almost half of its combat infantry divisions – a disaster of incalculable proportions. Entire armies had been shattered, and as a result training programs and weapons procurement had come to a virtual standstill. That Turkey entered the Great War at all in light of what it had suffered fairly defies comprehension. But when your empire stretches back over centuries it can be difficult to give it up lightly, whatever the hardships. The aforementioned Balkan Wars were the cause of much of this depletion of men and material, making the task of the Allied forces just that little bit easier. But as Ion Idriess wrote in *Desert Column*, 'Every man in his own fashion – by praise or jest or grim curse – expressed admiration for the willingness, the determination, and the bitter stubbornness of the Turk.' Perhaps because of an awareness of just how tough they were doing it, by and large the Australians bore no enmity towards them. Yes they were the enemy but unlike their German allies, the Turks were not considered to be bent upon the destruction of our very way of life, a common anti-German theme.

The Battle of Rafa on the Sinai–Palestine border on 9 January 1917 had completed the taking of Sinai by the Egyptian Expeditionary Force. The Turks had fallen back into Palestine and were fortifying a defensive line that began at Gaza on the coast and went inland to Beersheba. Morale within the Light Horse and the EEF was high. After the victories at El Arish, Magdhaba and Rafa, Lieutenant General Harry Chauvel, the commander of the Australian and New Zealand mounted divisions, was given a knighthood and being described in some quarters as 'the finest cavalry general of the century'. With the railway and water pipeline now effectively laid all the way to the border, the month of February was consumed with the transporting of all manner of arms and supplies eastward that, by March, had transformed Rafa into an inspiring sea of well-fed and -supplied soldiery. All of them looked toward Gaza and the 15,000 Turks who were waiting for them. Everybody in the EEF was excited. They were now so close to the border with Palestine that they could see it with their own eyes. Even their horses weren't immune to the electricity that was in the air:

> *Towards dawn we could feel a difference in our horse's stride, and dismounting more than once in the dark our feet found firm ground and brushed something – could be wet grass – that brought back recollection of by-gone days. And daybreak came ... clad in the softest green, with the darker sheen of the young wheat crop frequently showing, speckled with the scarlet and yellow of the poppy and anemone, they lay before our dazzled gaze. The glorious breeze of the spring morning came like a harbinger of peace breathing on paradise, or so it seemed to many men*

after a year amid the desolation of the Sinai desert.
– George Berrie, *Under Furred Hats*

Sitting on a ridge line overlooking Gaza in the early hours of 26 March 1917 George Berrie could clearly see into the outskirts of the town, and looked on as the hundreds of men of the 53rd Welsh Infantry Division advanced on foot towards a redoubt on the left flank of the Turkish line. Even though shell after shell burst upon it the redoubt held, such was the skill of the Turkish soldier in burrowing himself deep into the earth. As he watched the advance of what he described as those 'young, fresh, and eager' Welsh recruits, Berrie calculated they had about a mile to go before they could, in his words, 'begin to put up an argument'. But his optimism started to fade the more he surveyed the no-man's-land into which they were advancing, and he began to sense that in fact they were marching to a likely oblivion. And so it was. With a half mile to go the trap revealed itself when rows of Turkish machine gunners opened fire. 'In a few minutes,' Berrie later wrote 'it was all over. The Turkish gunners could see no living thing left to fire at.'

'There are five thousand graves in the cemetery at Gaza,' Berrie wrote in *Morale* almost thirty years later. 'And Welshmen fill most of them.' The Welsh advance on the Turkish lines at Gaza was typical of the EEF's first attempts to take the garrison. It had been a disaster, despite the New Zealand Mounted Rifles Brigade having fought their way through the outskirts of the town in tough combat amid cactus hedges and rifle pits occupied by Turkish infantry. By dusk the Anzac Mounted Division had also fought their way into the city along with the 22nd Mounted Brigade – a yeomanry brigade of the British Army – both having come up alongside the New Zealanders and then together pushed onwards.

By 1830 hours the Wellington Mounted Rifle Regiment and the 2nd Light Horse Brigade were well within the northern limits of the city, but what they were encountering was anything but the meagre remains of those Turkish divisions that had been so thoroughly routed in recent battles. The resistance was well organised, stubborn and, to make matters worse, significant Turkish reinforcements were on their way. But the New Zealanders and the 2nd Light Horse pressed on, ignorant of the developments around them, only knowing that they were gaining the upper hand over their enemy. Headquarters, however, had already made the decision: if Gaza couldn't be taken by nightfall they would withdraw.

With nightfall approaching and British infantry losses elsewhere continuing to grow, the order was given to withdraw. It came as a shock to the Anzac Mounted Division, who felt they held the advantage. After all they'd captured almost 500 prisoners, including a divisional commander, and were on the offensive. No wonder then the New Zealanders were heard to mutter in the days to come that Gaza was as close to the sweet smell of victory as the sting of defeat ever got.

George Berrie of the 6th Light Horse, who watched the battle unfold, had his own theory as to why things didn't go according to plan:

> By one of those unlucky strokes of fortune, the whole enterprise was handicapped by a very heavy fog, which did not lift until well into the forenoon. The delay ... proved fatal to the frontal attack launched by the infantry. Gallantly all day they attempted to force the difficult redoubts commanding the southern and eastern quarters, and they suffered very heavily in attempting to storm positions with the bayonet. The Turks had chosen their positions well. For miles on all fronts the gentle slopes were absolutely coverless. Not one yard of the general advance could be made, once within range, except under a hail of shrapnel and withering bursts of machine gun fire.

Oliver Hogue, writing in *The Cameliers*, also agreed with Berrie's assessment regarding visibility that day:

Great enterprises can hang on little incidents. A fall of rain or a passing mist may decide the fate of a nation ... had there been no mist on the morning of 26th March the first battle of Gaza would have been won. Spreading like a pall over the battlefield before dawn, it did not clear off till eight o'clock.

The withdrawal from Gaza was a sad affair. Antony Bluett described the troops as they marched away with Gaza at their backs as resembling a kind of 'slumbering, ghostly army, moving like automata'. And the other thing those there that day remember about the retreat was how deathly quiet it was, the only sounds those of the soft *pad-pad* of camel hooves, the creaking of their cacolets as they carried home the swaying wounded, and the dreary crunching of wagon wheels along the rutted ground. By contrast, on their way out of Gaza, the Wellington Mounted Rifles proudly had in tow two captured and no doubt cumbersome Krupp 75 mm field guns which, if nothing else, showed that their retreat must have been a relaxed and casual one, knowing they'd had the enemy licked even if they didn't claim victory that day.

As the Palestine campaign moved northwards over the next twelve months, the Allied forces accumulated ever more war booty from the retreating Turks. One of the more sought-after items were the Turks' German-made Krupp field guns, which had become a staple part of every Ottoman Army since the government purchased its first shipment of 736 pieces from Friedrich Krupp's Essen factory in 1903. Every gun was numbered, conveniently allowing each to be precisely dated, and our Light Horsemen souvenired them whenever and wherever they could, organising for their return to Australia where they were distributed to communities throughout the country as trophies of war. Today the guns are everywhere: #164 is in the Gallipoli Display at the Australian War Memorial; #284, captured at Ziza in Jordan by the 5th Light Horse on 1 October 1918, is at the Light Horse Museum in Gympie, Queensland; #134, captured by the 22nd Light Horse regiment, is in a private collection in Launceston, Tasmania; while #35, captured by the 1st Light Horse near Amman, Jordan on 25 September 1917, can be seen at the Royal Military College, Duntroon.

The men of the 6th Light Horse spent the month of May 1917 resting in the small beachside village of Marakeb in Palestine. An interesting pastime emerged: that of keeping one's eye out for Turkish spies. Rumours were rife that Turkish secret service agents were lurking about dressed as – depending upon who was telling the story – anyone from Bedouins to British officers. The pastime was given added fuel when someone decided that a Distinguished Conduct Medal (DCM) might well be in the offing for anyone capable of seeing through their dastardly disguises and bringing them in.

It's a matter of record that not a single spy, if there ever were any to begin with, was ever corralled at Marakeb. But there was an 'incident'. Walking with his section late one evening an Australian sergeant whose name is sadly lost to history saw a red-tabbed British officer walking towards him. The sergeant saluted him – which seems to have startled the officer as the British were not used to receiving salutes from Anzacs – and in no time the officer found himself surrounded by four suspicious troopers. The sergeant asked him to state his business, and the officer replied in tones considered to have been unnecessarily sarcastic. The officer then became agitated, a further indication that all, perhaps, was not as it seemed, and the next thing he found himself being bundled off in the direction of an orderly room. Along the way he had the words of the sergeant in his ears, warning him that he had better come along quickly and quietly, and that it was hoped the use of force would not be necessary. What happened in the orderly room will always be a matter of some conjecture. Suffice to say that an hour or so later the officer left the room in apparent good health with two convictions regarding the men of the 6th Light Horse: that they had their fair quota of quite mad sergeants, and that they had very recently and generously been provided with a fair supply of some very good Scotch whisky. The colonel's adjutant had by this time arrived, and proceeded to escort his officer back to his camp, ensuring that he would not fall in among another band of Australian brigands – or off his horse.

In October 1917 the Ottoman Seventh Army – comprised of 4400 riflemen, sixty-eight machine guns, twenty-eight artillery pieces and two aeroplanes – were embedded in Beersheba, the eastern-most point of the Turks' Gaza–Beersheba defensive line. They knew an attack was coming, although they had no idea when. The trick to taking Beersheba, everyone agreed, was surprise. For Chauvel that meant getting six entire brigades and all of their accoutrements – camels, mules, porters and the rest – to the very outskirts of Beersheba right under the nose of the enemy before an attack could be mounted. 'Getting there' was quite a feat.

The massive movement of mounted troops from their camps along the coast began on 28 October. They rode their increasingly thirsty horses through unfamiliar desert in the black of night. Lance Sergeant Patrick Hamilton of the 4th Light Horse Field Ambulance recorded the journey in his diary:

> *Joined the sand cart ambulances last night. Moved out from Esani at dusk. A complete full moon but rotten slow trip. Transport blocked up for miles, halting every*

few minutes. Thousands of camels in convoys. Reached Khalasa, 12 miles out, about 1PM, and turned in ... then stood all day to avoid being seen from the air. Boiled billy and had a good meal of curry and fried onions with Bill Taylor and Norm Challis. Moved out at dusk and travelled all night without a rest. Reached Asluj 12 miles out. Then pushed on fast. A rough ride, covering another 15 miles.

Hamilton's 'rough ride' was only made possible because water wells had been found to support the infantry on their march from the coast. Reconnaissance patrols had told Chauvel there was only water at Esani, too far west to be of any use, but Chauvel refused to accept that and after questioning local Arabs and poring through the records of the Palestine Exploration Fund (an organisation set up under the patronage of Queen Victoria in 1865 to study the archaeology and history of Palestine) it was discovered that wells existed south-west of Beersheba at Asluj. The wells were known to the Turks, who filled them with rubble before they retreated. The 2nd Light Horse Brigade worked for two weeks to clear the wells, without which there would have been no Charge of the Light Brigade. The work of clearing the wells was so vital to the planned attack that even General Sir Edmund Allenby himself, who had replaced Murray as commander of the EEF, rode out from his headquarters to see for himself how the work was progressing.

Our Light Horsemen assembled for their charge in the late afternoon of 31 October 1917, and Chauvel's orders were difficult to misinterpret: 'Capture Beersheba today, in order to secure water and take prisoners.' The wells had been there since Biblical times and had grown in number from seven to seventeen and were still, as they were then, the only wells between Beersheba and Gaza, 40 km to the west. Taking Beersheba, it was hoped, would first secure the Allies water and second help draw enemy troops and equipment away from the Turkish garrison at Gaza, and thus weaken its defences for the impending third assault on the stronghold.

The 4th Brigade was a part of the Imperial Mounted Brigade, which had been raised in Egypt in February 1917 from the 3rd Light Horse Brigade and two British brigades. Renamed the Australian Mounted Division, its horsemen were well aware of the importance of water, the unfettered supply of which was vital to the continuance of the entire Palestine campaign. Under normal circumstances Chauvel would have used the British and 3rd brigades for the charge, but they were not in their positions and the time it would have taken to get them where they needed to be was time that Chauvel did not have.

Many of the 4th Brigade (comprising the 4th Victorian and 12th New South Wales regiments) were 'originals' – deployed with the Light Horse since leaving Australia in 1914 – and were veterans of Gallipoli. They were under the command of Brigadier General William Grant, a farmer and more than competent bushman from the Darling Downs in Queensland who had been promoted to his new rank just weeks earlier and only given command of the 4th Brigade on 1 September. The men suspected they'd be used in a charge at Beersheba and, though they didn't have swords, had been sharpening their bayonets for days in anticipation of what was to come. Grant would form his men and horses into three lines, each with 400 metres between them, their sharpened bayonets reflecting the late afternoon sun. Waiting behind a small ridge overlooking the Turkish positions they waited, as artillery from the British Notts Battery of the Royal Horse Artillery opened fire on the enemy lines. Then they began to advance for what would be the last great and successful cavalry charge in military history, with the 4th on the left side and the 12th on the right. Their objective was 6.5 km away.

Beersheba was not taken by a single charge or even a single brigade, though the charge was the pivotal act in the whole drama. If the charge had not happened the town would not have fallen on 31 October. It was 60,000 EEF infantry and other cavalry that made the charge possible, pitted against just 4400 defenders, some of whom had begun to flee on the Hebron road to the north-east not long after the morning hostilities began. By the time the 4th Brigade began its advance from the south-east, much had already happened. At 0555 hours British artillery opened fire on the enemy trenches to the town's south-west in a preliminary barrage. At 0700 hours the Desert Mounted Corps sent patrols forward and the minarets of the city could easily be seen before them. At 0830 hours infantry of the British XX Corps captured objectives to the south and south-west, and at 1000 hours the Somerset Battery opened fire on Tel el Saba, a rock-strewn hill that had to be taken before any charge from the south-east could even be considered. By the end of the morning English, Scottish and Welsh units had suffered 1200 casualties, including as many as 400 killed. Five gruelling hours later at 1500 hours the New Zealand Mounted Rifles succeeded in capturing Tel el Saba, and at 1530 hours, with not a lot of daylight left with which to achieve victory, Brigadier General William Grant, the commander of the British 5th Mounted Brigade; Brigadier General P. Fitzgerald; Major General Hodgson, the commander of the Australian Mounted Division and Grant's superior; and Lieutenant General Harry Chauvel were engaged in a very brief, and very historic, conversation.

Fitzgerald and Grant both wanted to make the charge. Grant pleaded with Chauvel, saying his men were best placed to do it, but Fitzgerald countered, saying only his men carried sabres, the traditional weapon of the cavalry. But time was running out, and Grant's men were closer to the town in a wadi, where they had been resting. Chauvel took only moments to make his decision. He looked at Hodgson and said, 'Put Grant straight at it,' and before Fitzgerald could sheathe his sabre Grant was on his horse and galloping in the direction of his regiment. 'Men you're fighting for water,' he said when he gave his orders to the 12th Light Horse. 'There's no water between this side of Beersheba and Esani. Use your bayonets as swords. I wish you the best of luck.'

At 4.10 pm the 4th Brigade saddled up, bayonets in hand, and began to ride. They came over to the top of the ridge and saw before them the gentle slope that was all that stood between them and their objective. There was no natural cover, and visibility was poor – a pall of fine dust already hung in the air, a consequence of battle. They broke from a trot into a gallop, and after that they just thundered their way forward, with the second and third lines galloping through the clogging dust kicked up by the hundreds of hooves pounding away in front of them. It all happened so fast the defenders had neither the time to destroy the wells nor to adjust the sights on their rifles. The horsemen were coming so fast the bullets flew over their heads, and by the time the Turks readjusted their sights the horses were a hundred yards closer still, and so still the bullets went too high! And anyway they weren't doing what mounted troops were *supposed* to do: they didn't dismount and charge on foot. History records Grant ordering his men to charge cavalry-style – to continue charging without dismounting. But many of the brigade's horses had by this time gone two days without any water, and their riders were of the mind that when they got that first smell of water in their nostrils, slowing them down for a dismount would have required an uncommon degree of horsemanship!

The horses and men in the front line were hit the hardest by enemy fire, but those that followed suffered few casualties, camouflaged by the huge plume of dust being provided by those in front. The 4th Regiment galloped head-on into the Turks and some leaped over the trenches while others fell into them, horse and all. Most left their horses there and went at the Turks on foot. Some took cover behind dead horses, firing their revolvers until they were out of ammunition. The

12th Regiment encountered fewer obstacles and cut a less harrowing swathe through the Turkish lines. In fact most of the 12th Regiment made it straight through into the town. As Private Walter Mundell Keddie wrote in his diary:

> We were all at the gallop yelling like mad – some had bayonets in their hands, others their rifle – then it was a full stretch gallop at the trenches – the last 200 yards or so was good going and those horses put on pace – and next we were jumping the trenches with the Turks underneath – and when over the trenches we went straight for the town.

Antony Bluett, who was in Beersheba that day with his Honourable Artillery, wrote that the Australians burst upon the Turkish lines 'like a tornado' and that the defenders, paralysed by the audacity of the charge, 'made a mere travesty of resistance in comparison with their stubbornness during the day'. Thirty-one Light Horsemen were killed and thirty-six wounded on 31 October 1917. One of those who died during the charge was a stretcher-bearer and former Test cricketer who chose the wrong moment to peer out over the top of a parapet and was shot in the head by a sniper's bullet. Albert Cotter was thirty-three years old when he died. Between 1904 and 1912 he played twenty-one Tests for Australia and took eighty-nine wickets at an average of 28.64. On the 1905 tour of England he took 124 wickets in all tests and first-class matches at 19.84, including 12 for 34 against Worcestershire. His slinging action would stir controversy today, but for his time he was astonishingly quick. Shortly before he was shot he took some dirt and water and made a muddy cricket ball, tossed it to one of his fellow stretcher-bearers and said: 'That's my last bowl. Something's going to happen.'

On the morning of the charge, Patrick Hamilton of the 4th Light Horse Field Ambulance climbed a small hill 5 kilometres from Beersheba to witness the city's encirclement. He could see the artillery shelling the Turkish lines, softening them up.

By this time Beersheba was all but surrounded, and there he stayed till late afternoon, alone in his witnessing of history, when he was called down to assemble in a flat area that seemed to run all the way into town. There he helped set up camp alongside an Anzac Casualty Clearing Station and everyone in his unit began helping themselves to a 'rough tea' and waited for the wounded to arrive. They were still unpacking when the first seven truckloads arrived.

Hour after brutal hour the surgery went on – from 2000 hours to 0200 hours the next morning. Stretcher-bearers swapped over the stitched up or dead for the still bleeding. At dawn two enemy bombers flew over and dropped bombs to the left and the right of the hospital tents. But the pace never slackened. Patients got a good breakfast and even Norm Challis couldn't wipe the smile off his face. 'It was the real thing,' he said exuberantly, describing how he'd followed the men of the 4th Brigade in on their charge, picking up the wounded as he went. The 4th Light Horse Field Ambulance treated forty-five wounded after the charge, five of whom died of their wounds.

Norm Challis's exuberance didn't last. At sunset the next day, 1 November 1917, a German Taube flew over the 4th Light Horse Field Ambulance bearer lines and its bomber let go his bombs in the direction of the big red crosses of the sand carts before machine gunning what he could. The horses panicked and broke from their lines, and men were running and yelling everywhere. One man had his left leg blown off, and six horses lay on their sides, their insides on the ground beside them. Then someone called out 'Norm!' But Norm Challis was dead.

It remained to be seen how long the Turks could hold Gaza now that Beersheba had fallen, with fresh defences at Sheria and Tel el Khuweilfe to the north of Beersheba having to be readied. The Turkish defenders at Gaza knew an assault was coming, but how the city's ancient foundations – the building blocks of antiquity – must have groaned at the thought of yet another invader! Gaza began life as an Egyptian fortification around 3300 BCE only to become, a thousand years later, an abandoned ruin visited only by nomadic pastoralists. It rose again in 1500 BCE, but had disappeared again by the end of the Bronze Age. The Egyptians later revived it as an administrative centre, and it remained in Egyptian hands for 350 years until the Philistines wrestled it away. It was ruled by the Israelites and the Assyrians, it flourished under the Persians, and it was the last bastion to fall to Alexander the Great as he conquered his way south to Egypt. It was incorporated into the Roman Empire in 63 BCE and became so prosperous it was governed by a 500-member senate. The Romans were followed by the Byzantines, and then came Islam, and the city's churches were turned into mosques. Islamic dynasties that no one remembers – such as the Tulunics and the Fatimids – came and went, and when the Crusaders arrived at its gates in 1100 they found an uninhabited city, again in ruins after the population had fled in anticipation of their arrival. The Mamluks followed the Crusaders and restored it as the capital of a new province, and in 1299 the Mongols burnt it to the ground. A series of sultanates followed, and in 1516 the city was incorporated into the Ottoman Empire. Then on the night of the 1st and 2nd of November 1917, the British and her allies kicked the Ottomans out in the Third Battle of Gaza.

With the fall of Gaza the Turkish front in southern Palestine had collapsed. All eyes were now on Jerusalem, and the troops repeated: 'All roads lead to Jerusalem.' It was a grand phrase appropriate for a grand city – but the roads would fail to be worthy of their destination. They were goat tracks mostly, tracks that often led over precipices and required the agility of a mountain goat to traverse. In reality there was only one road to Jerusalem from the south, an exceptionally beautiful road that began at the port city of Jaffa and passed through orange groves that stretched as far as the eye could see. It was one of the world's most-travelled routes, used by conquerors and farmers, merchants and artisans, mothers and children, and now by the men of the 2nd and 3rd Australian Light Horse.

The consuming of bully beef was something of a ritual for George Berrie of the 6th Light Horse. Berrie detested the 'deadly sameness of the stringy, fatless beef', even when taken out of their tins and cooked up as rissoles by the regiment's well-intentioned cook. Often made a smidgen more interesting with the addition of 'doubtful' onions before being fried in bacon fat they nevertheless proved 'tasty enough to win a war on'. This culinary breakthrough however didn't stop him from experimenting with whatever ingredients he could occasion upon, and as it turned out he did such a good job that his fellow Light Horsemen begged him to remove the cook by whatever means necessary and take up the cooking cudgels himself! In *Morale*, writing in the third person, Berrie described his approach to army cuisine:

> *He opened three tins of beef, minced the contents up with the onions, and rolled them well in the flour. Then he flattened the mixture and fried bits of it at a time in his dixie. The fame of his enterprise soon spread as the noses of passers-by smelt him out, and when he carried the piled-up dixie into the supports, his section was waiting for him gog-eyed and open-mouthed. By the time the last rissole crumb had disappeared, the whole troop was imploring the Bushman to take on the cooking, and to win the war by saving their lives instead of trying to take Jackos. There might have been something in that, but the Bushman didn't see it.*

While advancing north from Gaza, George Berrie arrived at what had been the cookhouse for a nearby Turkish military outpost and spied something hiding behind an abandoned pile of utensils: a plucked fowl! He carefully picked it up and placed it in his haversack. Fully realising there was a possibility the fleeing Turks poisoned the poor bird, Berrie nevertheless considered it a risk worth taking for the sake of some lovely strips of grilled chicken.

Still, there exists something of a myth about what the average digger in the AIF was fed, particularly in the Great War. 'Bully beef, biscuits and black tea' is the mantra that often emerges in accounts of what filled their stomachs and kept them on the march. Bully beef – canned corned beef, which often turned into a kind of paste while still in the tin thanks to the desert heat – isn't hard to find references to in books and diaries detailing the supposed diet of our Anzacs. But their diets were considerably more complex than the legendary tales of bully beef would suggest. Incidents of scurvy, for example, were non-existent among our troops thanks to the unfettered supply lines from Egypt to the front lines. The men in the EEF were fed a quite well-balanced diet by a catering service that didn't exist before the war and that, by war's end, was making the boast that the Australian soldier was the best fed of any in the world. Indeed, a typical ration for our diggers on the voyage home included fresh meat six times a week, a daily quota of bread, rice, vegetables, potatoes, butter, oatmeal, raisins, cheese, jam and tea as well as a weekly treat of mustard, pickles and vinegar.

The Jordan Valley in the summer of 1917 proved a miserable time for all those who served there thanks to the heat and the powder-like dust that got into everything. As Patrick Hamilton wrote in his diary:

> *The dust is of the finest, penetrating variety. Take, for example, any bowl of solution on the hospital table. Cover*

*the bowl with a fly net, over that put a four-folded piece of
damp linen, and over the whole of the table and contents
put a thick sheet. Yet invariably the solution collects a dust
cloud on its surface within an hour.*

But even worse than the heat or the dust were the swarms
of mosquitoes. While it was an exaggeration to say – as it did in
the British military's *Handbook to Palestine & Syria* – that 'no
European has ever survived a summer in the Jordan Valley',
the mosquito menace and the malaria they carried proved to be
nothing short of calamitous and no effort was spared to reduce
the ability of the mosquito to breed. Along every waterway
trees were cleared, either by hand or by burning, to expose the
water to sunlight. Canalisation – the cutting of small canals
using stones reinforced with puddled clay – confined water in
narrow, deep channels to prevent stagnation and encourage
swift currents. Entire swamps were drained in this way, and
when the canals ceased to flow they were quickly filled in to
prevent the spread of the disease. But as bad as it was for the
Allies one can only guess what malaria had been doing to the
Turks, whose diet and standard of medical care were poor and
whose undernourished bodies would have offered the disease
scant resistance.

General Edmund Allenby marched into Jerusalem on 11
December 1917 and for T. E. Lawrence, at Allenby's side for the
official entry into the ancient city and dressed in a borrowed
cap and belt, it was the most significant moment of the entire
war – an odd point of view considering the city had no real
strategic value. But what it lacked in strategic value it more
than made up for in symbolism. Its religious aspects, however,
were largely lost on our Light Horsemen who never admitted
to having any particular religious zeal and who by and large
showed little more than a casual tourist's interest in the great

pilgrimage sites of Christendom. Their interest was in the fight to come – to ride down from Jerusalem to Jericho and into the Jordan Valley to the north, and on to Damascus. Allenby used the next two months to reorganise his supply lines and rest his men, then in late February broke out into the area west of the Jordan River and attacked Amman in March, an ill-conceived raid against a superior, entrenched enemy that cost the Anzac Mounted Division 177 lives – more than were lost at Romani. Nothing that happened in the Sinai or Palestine so affected the morale of the Light Horse. And if that weren't enough, two more assaults on Amman would follow, not because the place was of any real strategic significance but because Allenby knew that when the time came to break out and head north along the western Plain of Sharon towards Damascus, he wanted the enemy looking nervously to the east. In the months ahead, feints and diversions would be the order of the day, until the real business started in September.

In September 1918 the Turks had more than 100,000 men spread between Damascus and their forward positions to the west of the River Jordan, but significantly only some 30,000 men dug in on the front line itself, and of those only 20,000 were stationed between the river and the coast, with almost all the Turkish cavalry further away still, to the east in Trans-Jordan. It was a defensive line full of holes, inadequately manned and hopelessly out-gunned. Against this Allenby had a significant advantage in both infantry and artillery, but most spectacularly in cavalry with 12,000 men compared to the Turks' 2000. As Antony Bluett wrote in *With our Army in Palestine*, the push north towards Damascus began in the late afternoon of 18 September:

> *At dusk on the night of September 18th the orange-groves began to erupt, and for eight hours horse and foot in orderly columns marched silently forward, the infantry to their battle positions and the cavalry to the beach between*

Arsuf and Jaffa, there to wait till the breach had been made. At half-past four the next morning the shattering roar of artillery proclaimed that the offensive had begun, and at dawn the infantry attacked the Turkish positions, swept over those nearest the coast at the first onslaught, and then swung eastwards.

Allenby had opened fire on the opposing Ottoman Fourth Army with 384 atillery pieces – an average of one gun every 45 metres. British infantry overran Turkish defences in no time and within a day two opposing armies had been virtually encircled. Nazareth, 40 kilometres to the north, fell on 20 September and Nablus and Samaria the following day. Turkish divisions everywhere were losing formation. The panic and the flight was such that it took just twenty-three Australians of the 9th Light Horse to capture 2800 Turks as they retreated north through the narrow mountain pass on the Nablus–Jenin road. As Lieutenant H. H. Stephen of the 9th Light Horse wrote:

They had no idea we were there, and came along in batches of 100 or so. The road ran between high hills, passed over a bridge, and then on to about ten acres of clear flat ground. So we allowed the enemy to pass over the bridge, then bail them up and disarm them, and then turn them out to the flat. There was a great amount of booty.

Allenby and Chauvel, at a meeting at Megiddo on 22 September, couldn't believe their luck. What had happened to the expected Turko–German counterattack? It could have come anywhere between Acre and Beisan and split the offensive in half, but there was nothing. In place of the heavy casualties Allenby had allowed for there were barely any. There had been no delays, no unexpected setbacks, and what's more the enemy was surrendering in droves. At Jenin 10,000 Turks emerged from the surrounding hills after being chased out of Samaria by British infantry and gave up without a struggle when they were charged by the 9th and 10th Light Horse regiments.

There were a few token battles fought, such as the brief stand by German and Turkish defenders at Semakh along the southern shoreline of Lake Tiberius. The 11th and 12th Light Horse regiments had charged their positions in the pre-dawn darkness only to run into a barrage of machine-gun fire. The Light Horsemen dismounted and a day of fierce fighting ensued. The next morning, with the help of some Australian machine gunners, Semakh was overrun and its defenders either killed or taken prisoner. But Semakh was the exception.

The men of the 10th Light Horse were the only AIF regiment from Western Australia. They had fought at Gallipoli at The Nek, were there at the battles of Romani and Magdhaba, helped to break the Turkish line at Gaza and Beersheba, and pushed the Turks out of much of the Jordan Valley. Like so many of our Light Horsemen they had ridden a long way in the last three years, but unlike our other Light Horse regiments the men of the 10th had come to believe they had no peer within either their own army or anyone else's for winning on the battlefield. And there was still one last great chapter to be written. In August the 10th Light Horse was one of the few regiments to be re-equipped with their old swords and rifle boots and retrained in the traditional role of orthodox cavalry. They felt they were about to be chosen to lead a great charge, and the path to Damascus lay open before them. It was an affront that the oldest continually inhabited city on the planet remained a symbol of Turkish resistance, and the 10th Light Horse Regiment wanted to be the ones to kick them out.

It was an event that would become known as the Great Ride. But it wasn't just a case of galloping all the way to Damascus and winning the war. Army logistics are a nightmare at the best of times, and managing the needs of all of the competing units and their modes of transport would not be easy. The Allies had some 10,000 horses that required 80 tonnes of straw, 50 tonnes of hay, 50 tonnes of oats and more than 300 tonnes of fresh fodder *every day*. Add to that 38,000 camels, 42,000 mules and 12,000 donkeys. And then there were the men – the Light Horsemen and the infantry and the artillery regiments and the medics – 69,000 men in total. Who would go and who would stay behind, and who would be chosen to spearhead the attack and get to Damascus before the annual rains came in November?

It was a ride through a largely unknown landscape. Mountain passes had to be seized before they were occupied by the enemy, and nobody knew the precise routes (which were mostly little more than tracks) along which they would need to travel. There were no reliable small-scale maps either, and the only inkling officers had of what awaited them were sketchy briefings that were long on rhetoric and bereft of specifics. It wasn't until a meeting at Jenin on 25 September between Allenby and his corps commanders that things began to take shape. General George Barrow and his 4th British Cavalry would thrust 70 kilometres north from Beisan to Deraa and join with a force of Arab irregulars and destroy what was left of the decimated Ottoman Fourth Army, then combine his forces with Chauvel's mounted divisions and push north.

When Allenby's forces broke through the Turkish defences at the Battle of Megiddo the cavalry raced ahead – as far as 100 kilometres in something like fifty-five hours – and cut off the Turkish retreat. On 28 September Henry Gullett, Australia's official historian in Palestine, reported that Australian cavalry had forded the Jordan at several places under cover of darkness and taken a hundred Turkish prisoners while as many of the enemy as were able, both Turkish and German, were seen escaping in motor lorries along the road to Damascus. And then came a squadron of Western Australians, the 10th Light Horse, charging through in the dark and 'flinging themselves from their horses' as they attacked the enemy with bayonets. Artillery units, too impatient to wait for engineers to repair damaged bridges, flung their horses and equipment and themselves over boulder-strewn riverbeds. Supply lines stretched all the way from Jaffa and were somehow managing to keep pace with the advance, with rations and horse fodder always there when man and horse needed them. As Gullett wrote:

> It was an interminable column winding along mountain roads represents a fantastic association of the ancient east and the modern west, an imposing fleet of motor lorries followed by hundreds of horse and mule-drawn vehicles, then camels and thousands of white donkeys. Ceaselessly and almost sleeplessly this wonderful procession goes up behind our Light horsemen, along the dusty road to Damascus.

Damascus fell to the Allies on 1 October. It was long a source of debate as to which was the first unit to enter the ancient city, but according to Gullett the 10th Light Horse had gotten their wish to take the city.

> The first troops into the city were the Light horsemen from Western Australia, who also had the distinction of being the first mounted troops to enter Jerusalem last December. The Western Australians found their way into Damascus by accident, and their ride was one of the most dramatic and picturesque incidents of the whole campaign.

Picturesque indeed. The 3rd Light Horse Brigade, comprising the 8th, 9th and 10th Light Horse regiments, had spent the night of 30 September camped in the Adana Gorge on the Beirut Road to the west of the city. *The War Diary of the 10th Light Horse* records their orders to strike out for the Aleppo road at dawn on the following morning, 1 October:

> *At 20:00 orders were received to bivouac for the night and be ready to move off at daylight, 10th Regiment to be in the advance ... Regt moved out at 05:00 ... advance troops pushed on at the trot to Dumar railway station where a troop train loaded with troops but without an engine was standing in the station. On the main road immediately opposite the station about 800 Turks were formed up. These with the troops on the train threw up their hands when called upon to do so by Lieutenant McGregor who with troops was advancing with drawn swords ... a further batch of mostly Germans were captured in a stone house by the river.*

Unable to see their way to the Aleppo road through the mass of wounded Turks and Germans and hundreds of transport vehicles and animals both dead and dying it was clear they would have to go through the heart of the city itself. So the 10th pressed on in the pre-dawn light led by their commanding officer Major A. C. N. 'Harry' Olden, a dentist from Narrogin north of Albany who knew an opportunity when he saw one. An advance scouting party was passing through the outskirts of the city, moving silently along a riverbank. With the river on one side of them and a long mud-brick wall on the other they were surprised by a sudden burst of Turkish gunfire. Nobody was wounded, but the commander of the advance party thought it time for his Western Australians to mount up, draw their swords and charge. Thousands of Turks were still at their barracks 300 yards away, the only troops between the 10th and the city. But they gave themselves up, and minutes later the city was theirs. Pomegranates were given to passing horsemen, children grabbed at stirrups and ran alongside the column hanging on to bridle-reins. As Gullett later wrote in

The Australian Imperial Force in Sinai and Palestine:

> *They rode, dusty and unshaved, their big hats battered and drooping through the tumultuous populace ... with the same easy casual bearing and the same quiet self-confidence that are the distinctive characteristics of their country tracks at home. They ate their grapes and smoked their cigars, and missed no pretty eyes at the windows. But they showed no excitement or elation. The streets of old Damascus were but a stage in the long path of war. They have become true soldiers of fortune.*

Upon entering Damascus, huge crowds assembled and cheered and fired rifles in celebration. At 0630 hours on 1 October 1918 Major Olden and the advance guard of the 10th Light Horse officially accepted the Turkish surrender, a fact of war and of history that should give pause to anyone who uncritically accepts the assertion of T. E. Lawrence in his autobiographical and only slightly fictional book *Seven Pillars of Wisdom* that it was he who got there first. The 3rd Light Horse Brigade later continued the pursuit of the hapless Turks along the road north to the city of Homs, which fell on the 16th, and finally to Aleppo – the northernmost extent of the Allied advance – which fell on 25 September. Turkey surrendered six days later.

Since the move on Damascus began on 19 September the Desert Mounted Corps had taken almost 50,000 prisoners including more than 650 officers. An army-sized cache of guns, small arms, transport vehicles, aeroplanes and airfields and wireless units and stores of all conceivable items had been plundered from the enemy in just thirteen days after years of stubborn resistance, a rout on a scale almost without parallel in modern warfare.

On 14 October, two weeks after the fall of Damascus (and ultimately just sixteen days before Turkey's capitulation), Gullett filed the following description of life in the Allied encampments that were dispersed throughout the ancient city:

> After thirteen days on bully and biscuit it is good to know fresh meat and bread again; the mutton is of the best and the bread, if dark and coarse and heavy, is still a long way ahead of biscuit. We were too late for the famous Damascus apricots, but there are grapes for the multitude, and pears and apples and pomegranates and also raisins and other dried fruits ... best of all every camp is within sight and sound of many running waters.
>
> As I write the wide leafage of poplars and vineyards and orchards are touched with the early tints of autumn. The garden about the house where I am living for a few days with an Australian regiment is animated with the life of a Light Horse camp. The horses are not, as you might think, tied up to the trees, nor is the garden in the least danger of destruction. It is extraordinary what discipline will do, and in orchard areas occupied for weeks by a brigade of our cavalry not ten pounds worth of damage has been caused. Billies are boiling on scores of little fires made of pine wood boxes from a great enemy supply dump captured nearby, and for breakfast there is bacon and eggs and grilled tomatoes ... and after breakfast every man who smokes lights a cigar or Turkish cigarette of good quality ...
>
> Perhaps the most alluring and disappointing loot of all is the Turkish paper money. Like all the money it should be at once handed in when captured. But its value is so low that a good deal of it is to be found in the regiments, and nobody takes much notice. After Jenin I met a Light Horseman with his horse's nosebag crammed full of Turkish notes of high face value. 'Like some?' he

asked, pulling out a fistfull. 'It's pretty stuff, but it's no use to a man.'

When the time came for our Light Horsemen to come home many had become so attached to their horses that some shot them rather than leave them behind among a people whose preferred mount was the camel. Horses were at best beasts of burden in Palestine and through much of North Africa, and at worst a possible source of nutrition. In Europe in 1918 our Anzacs sold or simply gave their horses to French and Belgian farmers who were in desperate need of them to re-plough crater-filled and long-abandoned fields. But in Egypt and Palestine it was a different matter.

Much has been made of the affection the Light Horseman had for his horse, and no doubt the recollections told of the difficulty in parting with an animal that had seen you through thick and thin from the Suez Canal to Syria are true. But there was a little postwar romanticising going on too when talking of the bond between rider and mount. Those who brought their working farm horses with them from Australia would have seen them first and foremost as beasts of burden, and would likely have had a far more prosaic view of them than some of the Light Horse literature that has come down to us would suggest. Certainly there aren't many references to 'beloved mounts' in war diaries and letters. Horses, after all, required a lot of work, far more than the utilitarian camel for instance. Horses had to be groomed, routinely fed and watered, their bridles and bits and other paraphernalia had to be oiled and cleaned, and then there was the piqueting. 'At last we are without horses, we handed them over yesterday, and I don't think there is a man sorry either,' wrote Trooper Edward Dengate of the 12th Light Horse Regiment who had ridden over the Turkish trenches at Beersheba. While it is possible Dengate's words may have just reflected exuberance at the thought of returning to Australia, it is just as possible he was rejoicing that the day-to-day chores of looking after a horse would soon be behind him.

There were things some of our diggers did in the war that they'd wished they'd never done – things that violated the 'rules of war' and would trouble their consciences long after they returned home. The massacre of Arabs in the village of Surafend in Palestine in December 1918 is only the most obvious example. The war had been over for several weeks when a New Zealand soldier was shot in the chest and killed by an Arab who had been attempting to rob him as he slept. This resulted in his unit exacting vengeful retaliation on the inhabitants of Surafend, the town the man was seen running towards in the dark. Like the Australians the New Zealanders were tired of being shot at and robbed by Arabs, and a British military that refused to take any action for fear of risking a rise in religious tensions in India.

Not all decisions taken by men when in battle reflect their humanity. Not all options are ethical or decent. In *Morale* Berrie related a conversation 'the Bushman' had with one of the men of the 6th Light Horse after the war as they were tossing up the pros and cons of participating in an upcoming Anzac Day march. Berrie didn't much like them.

> *It's hard to keep a decent step when a man sees the old women standing by, the mothers of your fellows, wearing their medals. You have to bite your lip hard when you see them crying. I asked a chap not long ago if he was coming to the march, you'd remember him well enough. Well he said no, and I asked him why. 'I played a rotten game over there,' the old digger said, 'and I know it. The Anzac march is no place for me.'*

When war's end finally came, Berrie was unable to work

up much enthusiasm at the thought of returning home. He knew that on that inevitable day when the regiment was disbanded he would feel abandoned, robbed of what he had come to consider was his spiritual home. He also had a lingering resentment against his own countrymen, only a quarter of whom were actively 'for' the war, with as many against it and the rest lukewarm at best. He knew there would be the initial fervent welcomes when they got back, but also that the novelty of welcoming home troops would soon wear off. He thought of friends lost, of men who had put in for leave but had it refused and died in battle the next day. Berrie vowed that when he got back home he would never march through the streets of an Australian city where he would be forced to listen 'to the mocking lip-service of the anti-conscription mob'.

In the wake of the Great War the world's nations lost no time in both modernising and demobilising their militaries. Within a year of the signing of the armistice on 11 November 1918 the 1st Australian Imperial Force, its numbers already decimated by death and disease, was no more. Our mounted units, once the pride of the nation, were no longer needed, reduced to just two cavalry divisions and a few Light Horse regiments. And no longer were they comprised of experienced veterans but by a Citizen's Military Force (CMF), with only seasoned officers left in key roles. Training in horsemanship was largely abandoned in rural areas, reduced to just a few days every year and an annual six-day camp, and it was obvious to all that the glory days of the Light Horse now resided in history.

Chapter Ten
Tobruk Stories

*These men from the dockside of Sydney and the sheep-
stations of the Riverina presented such a picture of downright
toughness with their gaunt, dirty faces, huge boots, revolvers
stuffed in their pockets, gripping their rifles with huge
shapeless hands, shouting and grinning – always grinning –
that the mere sight of them must have disheartened the enemy
troops. For some days Rome radio had been broadcasting that
the 'Australian barbarians' had been turned loose.*

– Alan Moorehead, war correspondent, 1941

The deserts of the Middle East and North Africa remained untouched by war for two decades until Italy, that most second-rate of colonial powers, attacked Egypt on 13 September 1940. War was again coming to the sands of North Africa and the Western Desert, and the strategic reasons behind the build-up of opposing forces that would soon begin were the same as they were in the Great War. Germany and Italy aimed to cut Allied access to Middle Eastern oilfields and bring the vast reserves into their own sphere of influence, while at the same time severing British ties to its military reserves in the Far East by securing the Suez Canal. By contrast the Allies saw this new war in the desert as an opportunity to open up a new front against Germany and siphon off its men and supplies from the battlefields of Europe.

By attacking Egypt Mussolini had also hoped to gain some imperial prestige in the eyes of his European neighbours, but what followed was an embarrassing rout. British forces mounted a counterattack that took them across the Western Desert in pursuit of the fleeing Italians and into the region of Cyrenaica, the name that had been given to the administrative region of Italian-controlled eastern Libya in 1927. With Mussolini's forces in complete disarray, Hitler gave thought to propping up his ailing ally but baulked when told that at least four Panzer divisions would be needed to achieve a decisive victory. Feeling that the commitment of such a large force could compromise the planned-for invasion of the Soviet Union, Hitler held off for as long as he could until the defeat of the Italian forces in North Africa became so prescient his hand was forced. And so on 11 January 1941 he issued a directive that German forces in operation in the Mediterranean 'should assist for reasons of strategy, politics, and psychology'.

At first the Fuhrer sent only aircraft. The 10th Air Corps, or *Fliegerkorps,* which specialised in coastal operations, was dispatched to Sicily from its base in Norway to counter Royal Navy interference with Axis supply routes between Italy and Malta. But harassing convoys was never going to be enough, and on the morning of 6 February 1941 Hitler summoned to the Reich Chancellory the man he had chosen to be the new commander-in-chief of German troops in Libya – Erwin Johannes Eugen Rommel. Hitler promoted him to *Intragenerational* the very next day, and in the course of that day Rommel began the coalescing of a new *Sperrverband* – a sort of 'blocking force'. This disparate assortment of units soon grew to become the 5th Light Motorized Division, a common designation that would evolve into a name the whole world would in time come to know – the DAK, the *Deutsch Afrika Korps.* The first units of this new fighting force began arriving on Libyan soil on 10 February 1941. Rommel himself first set foot in North Africa just four days later. The Italians were still under Italian command, but the initial German force comprising two divisions operated under Rommel's unfettered leadership. Within two months he had re-taken most of what had been lost in all of Cyrenaica, and Mussolini couldn't have been happier.

In fact he was beside himself. Rommel's arrival had Mussolini babbling to any who'd listen that the two men would one day be standing side by side in the streets of Cairo at the head of a victory parade that would be one of the grandest spectacles the world had ever seen. More than a year later, on 29 June 1942 when victory looked certain Mussolini piloted his own plane to Libya, bringing with him his white Arab charger and eleven other aircraft carrying his administrative staff, personal chef, a retinue of journalists and party leaders in the belief that Rommel was only days away from entering the Egyptian capital. He also brought 200 drums of black shoe polish to burnish the boots of his victorious Italian infantry. But three weeks later on 20 July, looking gaunt and pale, Il Duce took his charger and flew back to Rome. It had become clear that Rommel wasn't going to be entering Cairo any time soon. Officially it was exhaustion caused by a strenuous workload resulting in a bout of amoebic dysentery that sent him home. Unofficially, according to one unnamed government minster in his entourage, the cause was far more commonplace: humiliation.

Tobruk, about 150 kilometres west of the Egyptian border in Libya, was always going to be a series of shit-fights. Its configuration meant even if you bombed it to its foundations supply ships would still be able to drop anchor in its sheltered harbour. Furthermore it sat on the end of a peninsula, which meant it could be well defended by a relatively small number of troops. And it couldn't be bypassed either, because its defenders would easily be able to strike out and disrupt vital lines of supply.

The war in North Africa was like none before it, fought in an environment that forced both armies to adjust to its style, its tempo, its moods. Rainfall evaporated before it hit the ground, and soaring inland temperatures ensured the battle would be fought on the coast, where sea breezes brought relief from the heat. There were some opportunities for tactical opportunism, with the absence of roads and the generally good conditions for vehicle movements meaning units were as free to travel in any direction without hindrance – fuel permitting – in much the same way as a fleet of warships could sail the high seas. But the incessant dust raised by daytime troop movements proved an unwelcome calling card and meant that any hoped-for element of surprise had to be forged in night deployments and unleashed at dawn.

Tobruk had been a strategic point on the North African coastline since antiquity. The Italians began to develop it as a fortress after their invasion in 1911 and it remained the only deepwater harbour between Tripoli and Alexandria. If Rommel could seize it he would shorten his supply lines by over 1500 kilometres, and his goal of reaching Cairo would be that much easier. Tobruk's garrison of 30,000 included 14,000 Australians – three brigades drawn from the 9th Division, a brigade from the 7th Division and the 2/3rd Anti-tank Regiment, most of whom had been chased there from Benghazi with Rommel still snapping at their heels. The worst *khamseen* in recent local memory, however, worked to their advantage, halting the German pursuit and giving the Australians precious time to dig in. 'For two days,' wrote the British naval officer and later author Anthony Heckstall-Smith, 'while the stifling *khamseen* lashed the surface of the desert into a raging sandstorm, wearing anti-gas goggles and with handkerchiefs over their mouths the men of the garrison laboured ceaselessly preparing the perimeter defences.' Sappers laid minefields, infantrymen repaired barbed-wire barricades, anti-tank ditches were cleared of sand, artillery pieces were camouflaged, wireless operators rolled out hundreds of kilometres of telephone wire to scattered outposts and ammunition was distributed throughout the defences, each flanked by steep, rocky wadis impassable to German tanks.

Rather than repeat the mistake of the Italians who had held Tobruk before them and who employed only a single, inadequate line of defence when the Allies arrived in January and booted them out, the 9th Division's commander, Lieutenant General Leslie Morshead, instead adopted a 'depth in defence' approach. First there was his Red Line, consisting of two rows of strong points manned by infantry. Two miles back lay his Blue Line, a minefield covered by artillery fire. Finally, there was a last-ditch line of anti-aircraft guns at the harbour. It was Morshead's multiple line of defence strategy combined with his policy of aggressive forward patrolling that contributed most to Tobruk's successful defence.

On 10 April everyone was done preparing. The *khamseen* had passed, and the defenders for the first time were able to look out from their semi-circular perimeter. What they saw was an inhospitable, rock-laden wasteland with no vegetation of any kind. When the enemy would come with their *blitzkrieg* assault, as Morshead knew they would, he was certain they would expect him to do what the British had done at Dunkirk – abandon their forward positions and fall back. But all that did, Morshead realised after talking to Dunkirk veterans, was to allow the German infantry to follow the tanks in unmolested. What Morshead would do was tell his men to stand fast, allow the tanks to pass the Red Line. When the German infantry came through behind them, the steadfast men of the 9th Division would attack them in the open. This is what happened over the next few days during the so-called 'Easter Battle'.

Rommel, brimming with confidence after defeating the Allies at El Agheila on 24 March, capturing Benghazi on 4 April and the British 3rd Armoured Brigade at Derna two days later, ordered his Panzers forward in much the same way as they had been used in Poland, Belgium and France – in a massive armoured assault, a *blitzkrieg* that would sweep all before them. He expected to be at the sea within seventy-two hours. But this time it would be different. This time his armour didn't breach anything, they were allowed in, and the further in they went the more Morshead's policy of in-depth defence paid off. British and Australian artillery were waiting for them and the German armour paid a heavy price, with 25-pounders hitting them at point-blank range. The Panzers' commander, the seemingly invincible Lieutenant Colonel Gustav Ponath, was killed in the field. As the Germans turned and retreated they again passed through the Red Line perimeter, which hadn't been abandoned, with Australians firing out of their stony trenches. The Red Line's barrage of mortar, Bren and small-calibre fire took a toll on the fleeing infantry. The Easter Battle of 11–14 April was Germany's first defeat of World War II, but now that the battle was over, the seige had begun.

'You *have* to speak to Joe,' a friend of mine with a network of World War II digger connections far in excess of my own told me excitedly over the telephone late one afternoon. 'Joe,' she said, 'has this *fabulous* story about how he and his unit captured *Rommel*! Only problem was, well, they didn't realise it was him and they ... well ... they let him go.'

'What? They ... what? They didn't recognise him?!' I remembered that New Zealander – I can't recall his name – who had Rommel in his binoculars as plain as day, resplendent in his general's uniform, but he was too far away from the Desert Fox to shoot him and didn't have a sniper to call on to make the shot. Anyway my friend went on to explain to me that they were on the front line getting shot at, which is no time to be arranging the domiciling of prisoners. The orders regarding the taking of prisoners on the front line while under fire were clear: send them back down the lines. Obviously they didn't know just who they had, and so that's what they did. 'Well, just promise me you'll speak to him,' said my friend. 'It's a wonderful story, and no one tells it like he can. You have to talk to Joe.'

I met Joe Madeley at his home on the New South Wales Central Coast in February 2013. We'd barely shook hands when he began telling me of his days with the 2/13th Battalion, the first complete unit of Australians to ever fight the Germans in World War II. The 2/13th, unlike other battalions, stayed the *entire* course of the Tobruk siege. Joe's memories weren't confined to the war. 'I flew with Charles Kingsford Smith you know. He landed near our home and it cost me five shillings to go up with him – I was only a youngster and I had to sell an awful lot of rabbit skins to save that five shillings! That was in 1930.' So he not only lived through a historic period of adventure and conflict, he paid five shillings for the chance to sit *alongside* history.

Joe Madeley was born at five minutes past midnight on 29 February 1920. That was a leap year, so his father saw to it that the time was recorded as five minutes before midnight on the 28th so little Joe could have a birthday every year.

I was born on the farm in a place called Coreen, between Albury and Corowa. I could drive a team of horses when I was nine and left school at 14 to work the farm. I was proud dad was a soldier in the First World War with the 15th Field Company Engineers, and I badgered him till he let me enlist.

Joe disembarked from his troopship in the Suez Canal, and after spending a week in the 5th Australian General Hospital in Gaza was ordered to Tobruk, which he couldn't get to quick enough.

I'd never ever fired a Bren gun when I went into action, let alone learned how to put it together and everything ... but we learned quick – we had to! We were told our job was to garrison North Africa ... well that all sounded good but I'd never fired a Bren and had about an hour on the Italian 47-mm Breda anti-tank gun. The gun didn't even have sights on it, and I was told to just point it straight at the target and not fire until the tank was 200 yards away. Now that all sounds fine, but I'm pretty sure the range of those tanks' guns was further than 200 yards.

And what did he know of Tobruk?

Well, I knew it was in the desert, but I didn't know the place was under siege or anything like that. We left Alexandria harbour on the HMS Hero, a little tub, a destroyer or something ... and arrived in Tobruk at night and were sent to the Salient, the worst part. The first thing I learned is never put your head above the parapets in daylight – the Germans had a lot of excellent snipers.

It must have been terrifying.

I wasn't terrified, but nervous, on edge – the slightest sound and I'd jump two foot. Our trenches were just a couple of feet deep too, and you couldn't leave them or you'd be shot. So to relieve myself I'd pee into a bully beef tin and hoy it over the top.'

Joe had a cupboard full of remarkable stories, like the time the Italians launched an artillery bombardment on the Salient and how he dived into a shell hole to escape it – only to have two Germans jump in after him trying to save *themselves* from the bombs of their Italian allies!

We used to do patrols every night – one night at a listening post we'd walk so far, meet the next sentry coming the other way, then turn back – this was in the south-west corner, not as savage as it was up in the Salient. So anyway I was heading back to my trench when all of a sudden this almighty bombardment started. I jumped into the first shell hole I could find, and then the next thing I knew two chaps fell in on top of me and … well they were Germans! Well we fought for a bit, just a bit of shoving really, no one reached for their guns – then more shells started to come over and we ended up hanging on to each other in the bottom of the flamin' hole with all these shells coming over. Then when the barrage stopped we stood up and this big bloody German pointed to where the shells had come from – they came from his own lines – and he said: 'Bloody Italians!' And we just looked at one another and we all shared a grin, then they went their way and I went mine. They were the only words he spoke to me, the only words.

After surviving the shelling, they didn't try to take each other's lives.

We were just all the same, the three of us, all of us there being shelled and trying to stay alive. And anyway when we stood up I realised I'd left my rifle in the bottom of the hole, and I couldn't have reached it anyway. I didn't realise it till I was on my feet, so I couldn't go down for it or else they'd have polished me off.

Then there was the time, you know the great German song 'Lili Marlene', the song that Marlene Dietrich made famous, well at Tobruk we weren't far from the German lines, and there was this one night, a typical night in the desert, well it was a frosty night and it was flat and sounds carry forever. So anyway this one German starts to sing 'Lili Marlene' and then a few of his mates joined in with him, and oh it was a beautiful sound, so clear and you could hear every note, it was as though they were right there with us in the dark. Well I suppose they were weren't they? And when they finished we all clapped, and we all knew the song of course – a pretty song it is, too. Then one of our boys, Peter Robinson, well he started to sing 'Silent Night' – and you know that's a German hymn, originally. Well there was dead silence as his voice rolled out across the blinking desert, because there's just nothing out there to stop it or get in its way and, well, when he finished they all clapped and hoorayed, too. And then we all ducked for cover!

Now I'm not one to glorify war or say it's something when it isn't. It was a miserable time, just miserable. But there were some good moments, too. Like the time Noel Goodworth – he was a stretcher-bearer – the time Noel went out after an armistice was agreed, and patched up Germans and saw German medics patching up our boys as well, he said. The first wounded they came to, they just bandaged up – it didn't matter what uniform they were wearing.

After failing to relieve the siege of Tobruk in June 1941 with Operation Battleaxe, the British tried again on 18 November with Operation Crusader – the aim of which was, like its predecessor, to destroy Rommel's forces and break through to the besieged city. Operation Crusader quickly descended into a confusing series of running tank and infantry battles, but as it ground its way towards Tobruk, the emboldened garrison broke out and managed to capture the high ground of the Ed Duda ridge, east of the city. Joe Madeley was there at Ed Duda that day.

When we advanced on Ed Duda, when we fought our way out of Tobruk to meet up with the New Zealanders we gave covering fire to some British. But then they got knocked back so we charged up the hill and we yelled and screamed and made the Germans think there were bloody thousands of us! Ohhh it was a hell of a mess, very chaotic, as most of those sort of battles are. There were trucks and vehicles of all sorts belonging to the enemy, they were everywhere and we were all amongst 'em.

Then there was this staff car, a German staff car – none of us saw where it'd come from. Anyway Bertie Ferris, he and his section and the car's driver said they were surrendering, but you see you're always told that you haven't got time to muck around or fiddle around with prisoners in the midst of a fight, and the orders were that we had to send 'em to the back lines. So Bert sticks his head in the car and looked around and there were two officers in the front seat and three in the back ... I didn't know that at the time, Bertie told me all this years later. Come to think of it I think Bert got [a Medal of Merit] for that night later on. So anyway Bert sent 'em on to the back of our lines, and they just did what they were told and drove out of sight and away they went. Now, years later in The Rommel Papers, which were Rommel's own personal diaries, he mentioned that on that very day in that place, Ed Duda, that he thought they – the Germans – were still on that rise, and that he had no idea that we'd attacked it, running up onto it screamin' like mad buggers, and he wrote: 'All of a sudden we were surrounded by these big Australians – they must have been the pick of the Australian Army, and one put his head inside and sent us straight on back.'

Now Bertie Ferris was a big bloke, I mean he towered over me an', well, I reckon he'd have been 6'2" or more, and big shoulders too. Oh he was a big lad that's for sure. Anyway Bertie didn't know anything about what Rommel had wrote, or the publishing of the diary – well he had no idea. He told me all this years later, about the officers *in the staff car, and he was telling me that it was dark in that back seat and he couldn't really make out any faces or anything. And then, after Bertie told me the story it would have been another year or more and I was reading Rommel's papers and I thought well that's the same date and the same place, and the same tale as Bertie Ferris told me. Anyway I saw Bertie and I said it looked to me like we had the Desert Fox caught dead to rights on that day and let the bugger go! Bertie said to me 'Oh crikey, don't tell anybody that for Christ's sake, or they'll never forgive me!'*

I couldn't help but wonder if the driver of Rommel's staff car that day was a proud old German named Rudolf Schneider. Joe had met Rudolf at a soldier's reunion in Stuttgart, West Germany, in 1988 and had urged me to visit him while I was in Germany on a forthcoming trip. Rommel had, by most accounts, three drivers during his tenure as commander of the Afrika Korps. Three men whose job it was to drive him in his various command cars to and from the front lines and often hundreds of kilometres into the North African desert. Rudolf was one of these men, and although he wasn't able to shed any light on the account of Rommel's near capture, he was present throughout a meeting between Rommel and a captured New Zealand officer, Brigadier George Clifton, commander of the 6th New Zealand Brigade – a conversation now recognised as the single most significant verbal exchange of the war between a New Zealand officer and an enemy commander.

Clifton had been captured by the X Italian Corps and just a few hours later, after unsuccessfully trying to bluff his captors that a large Allied force was on its way to rescue him, found himself in the presence of the Desert Fox himself.

'Rommel was angry because he thought the New Zealanders responsible for a massacre of German wounded near Mersa Matruh,' Rudolf recalled.

Clifton replied that what had happened were that ... some Germans had only faked being wounded, and then opened fire on the New Zealanders as they passed through them. Rommel accepted Clifton's version as he knew how chaotic night fighting could be ... and then he asked why was New Zealand involved in a war so far from its own shores ... 'Are you here for sport?' I remember him asking. Clifton said that they were there fighting for England, that when you attack one country in the British Empire, you attack them all. Well anyway, Rommel had him locked up, and that was the end of it.

This wouldn't be the last time Rommel and Clifton would meet. After being imprisoned, Clifton managed to escape through a bathroom window and remained at large in the desert for five days before being recaptured by a small group of German officers out hunting gazelle. He was just 16 kilometres from British lines. Dragged back to face Rommel a second time, Clifton reminded him that it was his duty to escape, a warrior's maxim that Rommel himself well understood and accepted. Rommel would later write that he found Clifton to be 'brave ... and very likeable', despite a thinly veiled reference by Clifton to Rommel's increasing girth when Rommel remarked that he, too, would have attempted an escape if he'd been in Clifton's position: 'I'm quite sure you would try, sir,' Clifton replied, 'but I do not think you could have walked as far as I did.' (Clifton had trudged more than 160 kilometres on just a single bottle of water.). 'No,' Rommel replied with a grin. 'I would have stolen a car.'

Despite their obvious camaraderie Rommel threatened to have him shot should he escape again. But to prevent another escape, Rommel sent Clifton to a POW camp in Veano, Italy the very next day. It took eight attempts, but in February 1943 Clifton escaped again. He was then sent to a prison inside the medieval fortress at Gavi in Peidmont – the 'Italian Colditz' –

from which escape was considered impossible. But escape George Clifton did in April 1943, only to be recaptured on a nearby rooftop. At the time of the Italian Armistice in September 1943 he was planning to evacuate *all* of the prisoners at Gavi, but when Germans replaced the Italian guards in the camp he was sent to yet another POW camp in Germany on the outskirts of Frankfurt am Main. He remained there until 22 March 1945 when, during an Allied air raid, he escaped through the camp's wire perimeter, was shot in the thigh (a wound that shortened his leg) and continued on until he stumbled his way into an advance patrol of Americans. After the war Clifton wrote a witty account of his life as a soldier titled *The Happy Hunted.*

In September 2013 I went to Stauchitz, about 70 kilometres north-west of Dresden, where 91-year old Rudolf Schneider still lives in a house he built in the 1950s, largely with his own hands, after teaching himself the arts of bricklaying, joinery and carpentry – 'All the professions that a man needs,' he told me with pride. The house, which sits on a large 4000-square-metre block fifteen minutes from the town centre, into which Rudolf walks every day for lunch at his favourite restaurant, has since been renovated and expanded, and he now shares it with his son and daughter-in-law. We went upstairs into his living room and before I'd even had a chance to sit down he said: 'Barry, I did not belong to the Nazi Party – I believe in God and I am a Christian. My father was a soldier in World War I and when he came home he looked after a farm girl who had long black hair down her back, and I am the result!'

Rudolf Schneider joined the Wehrmacht on 27 March 1941 as an eighteen-year-old and was sent to Iraq before his ability to speak English had him reassigned in July to the *Kampf Staffel Kiehl*, Rommel's personal protection and reconnaissance unit. 'I became one of Rommel's drivers,' he told me.

I was chosen because I knew English and could operate their equipment. I also had a good memory for landscapes, which was important in the desert, and I knew a little about English artillery too. We would drive long distances into the desert and all you would see was sand and stone. Rommel was a very proper German soldier of the 'old school'. He would eat with us, and always wanted to be close to the front lines so he could see with his own eyes what was happening. I was only a young soldier and I only said 'yes sir' on those rare occasions he gave me an order directly – most of my orders were received through his adjutant. But I witnessed many things. I once saw him in an argument with the Italian commander because he was anxious to push a strategic advantage he'd gained. That was very much how Rommel liked to attack – quickly.

Rudolf admired Rommel's integrity and was proud of his service to him.

When propaganda pictures were taken of our unit they hung Swastika flags over our vehicles. When the photographers went away, Rommel ordered them be taken away. He didn't very much like Nazi insignia. 'I am a German soldier,' he would say. Once when we were in the desert on one of our long reconnaissance missions we found a group of German soldiers who we thought were sleeping. When we got closer we saw that their throats had been cut. I found a Gurkha's knife there, too, a kukri – I still have it somewhere.

His living room looked more like a research centre than a home, filled to overflowing with documents, photographs and folders – but all in German!

In 1988 when I met former soldiers and old enemies like

Joe in Stuttgart and talked to them in my poor English, which I began to teach myself in 1938, I decided I'd write everything down that I had seen in World War II. We were all – Germans and Australians – nervous before that [first] reunion and we had two, or was it three, glasses of whisky! Soon we were all friends, reminiscing and asking ourselves why we had to fight one another. There were soldiers there from the US too, and Italy, France, New Zealand – 4000 men in all, I think.

The trip to Stuttgart, which was across the border in West Germany, was made possible because his wife's father lived there. 'Trips like this were difficult for those of us living in the GDR (German Democratic Republic), but were not forbidden.'

I have seen terrible things, Barry. Soon after I was assigned to Rommel I saw a young German soldier with a bayonet through his chest – it was like he had been nailed to the ground. It was a terrible thing for an eighteen-year-old boy to see. At El Alamein I saw a young Australian with a smashed shoulder, it was just completely smashed. He asked me for help, so I took my jacket off and gave it to him, even though I knew he would be dead in a few minutes.

After offering me a piece of *Zwetschgendatschi* (Bavarian plum cake) Rudolf got up again, went to a cabinet and returned with an Iron Cross. It was the first I'd ever seen that hadn't been behind glass, awarded to Rudolf during his time with the *Kampf Staffel Kiehl*, which had become renowned for its daring thrusts deep behind enemy lines. Rudolf was awarded it for his part in a mission that involved the capture of a train and then driving it throughout the night 80 kilometres into British-held territory to blow up a large ammunition depot.

'I was captured near El Alamein in 1943, and spent the

next six years in a POW camp. I returned to (East) Germany in 1949 where my girlfriend, Alfreda, was waiting for me. She waited all those years for me to come home,' he said as he paused to catch his breath. 'We moved here to Stauchitz in 1955, but my English suffered because the East German government didn't like anyone speaking the languages of our Cold War enemies. But in 1988, after meeting your country's soldiers again after so long, well, I began to learn it again.'

Though the documents and letters that Rudolf had in his possession were in German, it was his photographs that most intrigued me. These pictures, now almost seventy years old, looked much like the ones my father had from his own days serving in the Royal Australian Air Force in Darwin. The uniforms were different, sure, but everything else – the awkward poses, the straight haircuts, the amateurish nature of the images that were taken – it was all so familiar. The pictures I was looking at – taken in Libya before the real fighting started – had a German officer relaxing in a hammock between two palm trees, reading a book; two Libyan children having fun on the seat of a German motorcycle; Libyan families – their skin as dark as chocolate – happy and eager to be photographed; an elderly man outside his home proudly holding the reins of his camel; a Libyan man with his daughter on his knee, their handsome faces graced by white smiles that were broad and untroubled and not at all coerced. *Of course* they all sang 'Lili Marlene' and 'Silent Night' to each other across the trenches. It seems to me to have been a totally right and proper thing to do. The surprising part, I always thought – even in war – was the shooting, never the singing.

'I have been a very lucky man,' Rudolf told me as I looked at my watch and regretted the long drive I had ahead of me that night. 'Alfreda and I married and we had three children. But I have never forgotten the war, and the opponents who are now my friends.' And so, armed with yet another slice of Bavarian plum cake, I was on my way. Rudolf walked me to my car then turned towards a small area of lawn where his favourite deckchair awaited. There was a good half hour of sunlight left.

Back in Joe's living room on the New South Wales Central Coast, as I was digesting the implications of his Rommel story, the memories kept coming.

> *You know I was seasick by the time I got out of Sydney Heads? We stopped for three days in Ceylon before we went on, then went to Gaza where we had our camp and our training, just a couple of weeks of it, then we headed to the desert. The siege began late on the evening of 10 April, so the eleventh was the first full day of it. The Salient was the worst part of the whole thing – it was a heck of a mess out front – dead bodies, wounded men everywhere. Our stretcher-bearers went out and their stretcher-bearers went out ...*
>
> *I was from a farm way out in the Riverina ... where there are millions of rabbits and at dusk they all come out to feed, and if you fire one shot then in a split second they've all gone back into their burrows. It was the same there, at Tobruk. We were all sitting up on the holes and then somebody fired a shot and straight away all of us shot back into our burrows!*

'I have a book here,' he said as he reached deep into a pile of German propaganda leaflets he'd souvenired at Tobruk. 'It's called *Alamein: War Without Hate*.'

> *You know the desert war wasn't a 'kill at any cost' war like it was in Europe. Hmmm, well, saying that, one night at Alamein we had to do just that – with rifles and bayonets – on the night of 23 October. We overran an enemy post and the Jerrys were running for their lives and*

we were, well, shooting them down as fast as we could pull our triggers … and you sort of, well, when you're like that you're not human, you can't be or else you'd be dead, I suppose. I remember my mate Keith saying 'This is the way to fight a war … look at 'em run!'

Tom Duncan – he and I were together right through from the start. We both even made Lance Corporal the same day. Anyway at Alamein he was firing away with a Bren gun and got short of ammunition, and we had a chap with us – Jackie Lowe – cos we always had an extra guy who carried the ammo. So I called out to Jack and said 'Race over to Tom, he wants some ammo,' and so up he jumped to go to Tom and he fell straight away. WHACK. It hit him straight in the stomach – and that still gets to me terribly – and he fell, and his stomach was just all hanging out and, ohhhh, he was a hell of a mess. I hopped over to his side, and he was calling out for his mum and I yelled for a stretcher-bearer and tried to get some ammunition and drop it in alongside Tom. And my god he was off his nut too – there was a bloke lying alongside him with a bullet hole right through the centre of his forehead, and I said 'God's sake, who's that?' and Tom said, 'That's Lockie, poor ol' Lockie, they've shot Lockie!' Lockie was our platoon sergeant, and he didn't smoke and he didn't swear, and was one of the greatest blokes you'd ever want to meet – everybody liked him and he always would say 'come on chaps, come on' and he'd be walking around and, ohhh, Lockie was wonderful. Anyway we had to go back and I had to drag Tom out of there cos he was in a bit of a mess with what he'd seen …

The morning of 31 October at Alamein was the last time we attacked, but there were a heck of a lot of booby traps and mines about, and I was up at about 0200 hours in the morning cos one of our fellas had been hit out in the minefield and I'd gone out and brought him in, and the rations had come up about 0200 hours and they wanted someone to go and get the rations. So three of us went to get the rations, and then whoosh, over comes a shell and whacked us all in the legs. So Tom and I got wounded with the same shell and went out in the same flamin' ambulance!

Another night at Alamein we had tracers goin' everywhere and of course there's nine bullets between every tracer, and there were mortar bombs and my mate Keith was next to me and we came from the same town and signed up together and when we left his mother said to me, 'Look after him Joe, he's only a baby.' So when he got hit the first thing I thought about was what his mother would say! I jumped to my feet and, well, he was hit in the foot so I put him on my shoulders, gave him the fireman's lift and I carried him back and stumbled and we fell into a pit and onto barbed wire and I felt a bit of panic. Then I remembered my dad when he told me, 'If you panic, you're dead.' Keith was crying out and I slapped him and said 'For christ's sake quieten down!' And anyway a tank came by and I put him on the back of this tank after threatening them by taking a grenade out of my jacket. Years later Keith asked me in a pub in the Riverina, 'Joe would you really have thrown that grenade?' I said 'I don't know, I was off my bloody head then, but thank god I didn't have to' because along came an engineer's truck driven by a mate I knew from Wagga, and he took Keith to the back lines. There were six of us – a section – that went in that night, but only three came out. I should have been killed. I told Tom later I died three times that first night at Alamein. I should have been killed ...

One night I pulled a tin of bully beef from my haversack and it had a bullet hole right through it – the bullet had passed through the top of the haversack, *through the beef and out again – it only missed me by that much, and a hole in a pair of socks too! Then Tom and I were bombed by American bombers – I had blood coming out of the corner of my mouth, my ears, my nose, and Tom was worse he had blood coming out of his eyes as well and was yelling at those Yankees and using language I'd never heard before ...*

Oh you'll like this – out there facing the Derna Road we were stationed near the ration dump, and one night we thought we'd sneak into the rations dump. So we crawled in under the barb, all the while thinking about sausages, which we quickly found and carried out four cases – there were four of us so a case each – and we left there and crossed the Derna Road going back to our camp. Now bust me, you wouldn't credit it but along came a car full of English Red Caps (military police) – a major, a captain and a lieutenant. 'Don't you take those cases off your shoulders, boys, and if you make a run for it we'll wing ya,' one of 'em said. Anyhow they made a big mistake – they insisted we be hauled up on charges for taking these bloody sausages! They wanted to court-martial us, the four of us. Anyway we had with us a Lieutenant Barton Moore (Old Bull) who later became a Queen's Council and his father before him was a QC too. So a month later we had to front up, and I wrote a letter to Dad and said that if you don't hear from me I'll be in the 'boob' (jail) in Jerusalem.

Anyhow of the four of us I was up first and questioned – and they asked a hundred questions, it took an hour and a half and they still were just on me – Moore suggested to the court that instead of taking a week to go through each defendant, just charge one, and whatever he got went for the four of us. Moore asked which one, and Joe put his hand up. So Joe was charged with stealing four boxes of sausages. Moore said, 'Something's wrong here.

*How can one man carry four cases of sausages?' Anyway
hundreds of cases went missing, so we were scapegoats.
The four cases were there as exhibits, but when they were
opened there were just rocks in them, so someone had
pilfered the exhibits!*

*Another time we were back out on the line, and we
were sent to help in a cookhouse, it was a bakery, but full
of weevils. The trucks came along just on dusk to fill up
and take loaves to the front line – so Joe said to his mate,
'What say we join in' on a line of people taking stacks of
loaves to a truck, so they joined the line and took twelve
loaves of bread with them back to their own lines! It was
about the only time we ever went into town.*

*Our only entertainment was at night time when
enemy bombers would come over and bomb the harbour –
and the bombers, as they left the harbour when they
straightened out, if they had a tail gunner then he'd give
us a bit of a burst as he went over. Ohhh, we'd see the
tracers going through the air and the bombs going off and
they used to drop a lot of flares, or the planes before them
rather, so the bombers could see where to bomb – that was
our entertainment.*

*We were up in Syria after all that for four or five
months, then Rommel came back down and re-took
Tobruk. I went by train from Damascus to Aleppo and saw
some of the seedier sides of town. I was only a lad then
of course, and hadn't been around much as far as women
were concerned. But when we went to a brothel and this
lass came and sat on my knee and she was all over me
like a rash – I still resisted! So when I got home they called
me an 'overseas virgin'! But I'm glad I was. There was
a saying we had for those blokes who went with those
women – it was 'going upstairs'. Years later at reunions
some of the blokes'd be with their wives and they'd say
to each other 'Did you go upstairs?' and of course nobody*

knew what we were talking about. I saw a mate of mine with a venereal disease and, oh Christ, what a mess he was in.

The man credited with coining the phrase 'Desert Rats' was the propagandist Lord Haw-Haw. Haw-Haw's real name was William Joyce, an American-born Irish fascist who broadcast Nazi propaganda as host of the radio show *Germany Calling* from September 1939 to May 1945. Joyce's derisory nickname was originally created to refer to another propagandist broadcaster, Wolf Mittler, Joyce's predecessor on *Germany Calling*. Mittler escaped capture in 1943 by fleeing into Switzerland, but returned to Germany after the war, becoming a radio host in Bavaria and later gave traffic reports for radio station Bayern 3. Joyce had in excess of six million regular listeners inside the UK when he was at the height of his popularity. It was Joyce who used the phrase 'the poor desert rats of Tobruk' to describe the men of our 9th and 7th divisions. The phrase describes as much their tendency to collect equipment from hastily vacated German positions as their extensive network of tunnels. Germans were proving themselves to be an unintentional font of inspiration when it came preserving the spirit of the siege.

When Propaganda Minister Joseph Goebbels derided the flotilla of ships that kept the troops in Tobruk supplied with food and material as being of advanced age and 'piles of scrap iron', the phrase was tweaked and the tiny fleet of Australian destroyers – HMAS *Stuart*, HMAS *Vendetta*, HMAS *Vampire*, HMAS *Voyager* and HMAS *Waterhen* – would forever be known as the Scrap Iron Flotilla. They fought together off the coasts of Greece, Crete, Calabria and Italy, and in 1942 got a new nickname: the Tobruk Ferry Service. During the siege they made a total of 139 runs in and out of the besieged city. *Vendetta* held the record with thirty-nine individual passages –

eleven from Alexandria and nine from Mersa Matruh, and from Tobruk eight to Alexandria and eleven to Mersa Matruh. 'When the Scrap Iron Flotilla came into port,' Joe Madeley told me, 'they could only stay for a short time because they had to be away before sunrise. So if anything wasn't loaded on and they had to go, even if it was at the end of the gangway, up it'd go and they'd be off.' From the end of May until the first week in August the Scrap Iron Flotilla carried 1532 troops to Tobruk, took 2951 away, including wounded and some prisoners of war, and deposited 616 tonnes of supplies. There was no doubt in Joe's mind as to their worth. 'Oh yes, we wouldn't have made it through the seige without 'em.'

John Pocock would never have enlisted in the AIF in July of 1940 if his mother hadn't said he could. 'I was in the NSW Militia (Citizen's Military Force) when I joined,' he told me over coffee and lamingtons in his living room in Goulburn.

> *I was only sixteen. I was a dispatch rider. I rode a motorbike and joined the army with my motorbike, which I bought for five pound, and we got paid threepence a mile – but we had to buy our own petrol! So you know what we did? We'd sit up at night and spin the front wheels so the odometer reading would go up, and we'd get more money.*

How does a sixteen-year-old enlist in the armed forces? 'Oh they were desperate,' John says with a grin. 'I was 5'5" and the minimum height was 5'6", so I sort of stretched myself up, you know. To make the height. I've often said I wished my mother bought me hindsight instead of a yoyo.'

> *I left for the Middle East on the Queen Mary. We were on E deck aft, way down in the bowels of the ship. We'd take our gear up on deck and have a nap on the deck when*

we were allowed. The first few days on the QM I was given the job of delivering messages to the various units all around the ship, and I was lost for about two days, I couldn't find my way back to the orderly room! It was a big ship, but small compared to ships these days I suppose. Around 80,000 tonnes I think. We went to Ceylon, and the ship we were to be transferred to from the QM was 20,000 tonnes, a Dutch ship, I can't remember the name. Anyway it looked like a little toy bobbing around. On that ship we had bunks, and our own toilet, and the food was good. So we had a comfy trip from Ceylon to Port Said.

I couldn't understand the whole place at all. Palestine was our first camp, isolated from the population and an orange orchard right beside the camp, and we were told that Australians from the First World War brought them there! I wasn't too sure I believed that. Our beds were cane, with straw on top, and we'd hide oranges in the straw ... and we were very, ummm, welcomed there too. The people were friendly.

There's no doubting the welcome our diggers received in Palestine. A Dr Chiat, a long-time resident of Tel Aviv who emigrated to Sydney in July 1940, said on arrival to a reporter from *The Argus*:

Everyone made the Australians welcome. Homes were thrown open to them wherever they have been stationed. They are very popular with everyone but particularly with the girls ... under their tutelage the children have learned how to sing 'Roll Out the Barrel'. Young Arabs are now playing two-up with piastres!

We weren't in camp for long and there was trouble. The trouble was I was put in 8th Division Signals, and the only reason my mother let me go to war was because I had an older friend, Bunny, who joined with me, and he went and promised my mum that he'd look after me over there. And so she let me go. But when the 9th Division Signals was formed out of the 8th plus some extra recruits that came in, well one of the blokes they grabbed for the 9th was Bunny, my friend. So I went up to the CO of the 9th, whom I knew – he was in the militia with me back in NSW – and he said, 'Well, I have my quota already, I can't take any more. But I guess if anyone wants to transfer out, I'll let you take his place. So I got the message there'd been a transfer out of the 9th, so I was trudging up the hill to join them and who do you think the bloke was trudging down towards me? It was Bunny! He was coming back to the 8th so he could be with me! So it was all for nothing – he went to 8th and me to the 9th. That of course meant he later went and became a POW in Singapore. He survived, though.

I rode my motorcycle for a while, delivering dispatches and messages and that sort of thing, but what they really needed were drivers. And back in Australia my dad was in the tourist business, and we always had a car and a truck. I could drive a Fagel from age twelve – that was a bus. Dad had the bus run from Warrandyte to Melbourne along a dirt road – of course Warrandyte was in the country in those days, now it's a suburb. When the 7th Division went home we relieved them in Syria and I got my bike back, and from there we were sent to Tobruk. Then I became a dispatch driver in a little Morris truck, delivering stores at the same time. [The Ford and Morris trucks at Tobruk were one-tonners fitted with special oversized tyres, which made them ideal for travelling over sand. They were nicknamed 'Battle Buggies'.]

One night outside Tobruk I'd stopped in my truck and was having a kip, and suddenly these tracer bullets appeared overhead, and I was too stupid to know I was in any danger. Just some Germans doing some strafing.

So I made my way into Tobruk and found my unit, and that night I had to go to the 2/13 HQ and take some boys down to the harbour for their swims – because water was scarce and we were all a bit daggy. We got a container of water a day – half to the kitchen for cooking, and half for the APC – Armpits and Crotch! I went for a lot of swims with the troops, which was fun, except when the Stukas came over. We were often targeted coming down delivering the troops too, but we were schooled for this. We'd stop our trucks, get out and walk to the side. My truck was never hit. You know, I don't think I was ever frightened in Tobruk, never really terrified.

My accommodation was good, really good. I moved into a dugout that some decent Italian must have dug when they were there. It was about as big as my lounge rug here, about 4 feet deep and sandbagged over the top. And there was just me in there with a bedroll, and the odd scorpion and rat ...

I can't recall Tobruk very much; I mean the actual town, I knew the harbour and the beach, though – never had to go near the hospital – I was in my own little world. I was only there three or four months. One day I was taken out on a little yacht called a Zingarella, an Italian fishing boat that was captured by the British in Benghazi ...

In January 1942 I went to the Signals Training Battalion and they made me a wireless operator after I got a distinction at wireless school. That got me an extra three bob a day, which made nine bob a day total, which was big money then and I was sent to El Alamein. In Alamein I had a van, which looked a bit like a pie van, and me and my co-driver used to operate between HQ and the various units twenty-four hours a day – so we worked in shifts. One evening it was my turn on, and I was in the van and my mate was cooking tea at the side of the van, just heating meat and vegies and a cup of tea. Then with no warning a shell landed beside the truck and blew the top of his head off. So I didn't get a meal that night. The Germans were shelling the area and, anyhow he was killed and, ah ... um ... then I got another mate, and we were moved into brigade HQ and I was the Brigadier's wireless operator and we stayed there till we were recalled.

One day I approached my CO and asked for leave to go and visit my dad in Syria – he was in the army field workshops. He told me he couldn't give me leave to go to Syria, but then he said 'I'll give you a week's leave, but you'll have to spend it in the vicinity of Cairo, or Egypt somewhere.' Then he said, 'If I had to see my dad in Syria and was on leave, I'd go to the pommy bloke at the railway station and ask him for a ticket so I could 'go back to my unit'. They'll fall for that. But don't YOU ever do that now, will you?' So I laughed and said, 'No, sir,' and anyway I got to Beirut on the train and looked up my father's unit and we spent a few days together and that was lovely.

Of course coming home I had to do the whole thing in reverse, you know, go pleading to the RTO and ask him for a pass so I could return to my unit, except this time it was true! Anyway I got onto the train and into a private carriage and the only passenger in there was a sheik, and it turned out he had this double life. He was a Muslim in Beirut in Lebanon, but when he was home in Cairo he was a barrister married to a Greek Catholic woman named Diana! He and I became good friends and I'd go to his place. I'd get in the wireless van and claim he was a long way out of Cairo, then I'd turn down the dial till I went off the air, so my unit thought I was out woop-woop, out of range somewhere while all the while I was at the sheik's house enjoying his hospitality. But he had a girl on the side too, so Diana and I would spend time at a houseboat on the Nile called the Arabia, owned by Thomas Cook, the travel company. But it was also used by the Signal Corps.

It was quite nice. Sheik Nasib Wehaba – w-e-h-a-b-a, I think that's how you spell it.

It could be quite boring as a wireless operator, sitting up late at night with nothing happening, not a lot of traffic. So you'd talk to other signalmen down the line, and we used to read these saucy books we bought in Cairo. Of course they're tame by today's standards, but anyway we'd key these stories off to one another. We did it in morse because you could get distance with morse, but transfer it to voice and the distance is halved.

Alex Gurney, the chap who drew the cartoon Bluey & Curley, came to visit one day and sat with us chewing the rag. He used to write down what was said, and then draw a cartoon around the words. He was a lovely chap; he spent a lot of time with us and you wouldn't have known he was anyone special to look at him.

Born in Plymouth, England, in 1902, Alex Gurney came to Australia with his parents as a child and settled in Hobart, Tasmania. By sixteen he was submitting sketches and caricatures to the *Bulletin* and *Melbourne Punch*, and in 1926 moved to Sydney where he worked for a series of newspapers before settling in Adelaide in 1931, where he created a series of comic strips including The Daggs and Fred the Football Fan. Gurney moved to Melbourne in 1933, became the feature cartoonist for the Melbourne *Herald* in 1934, and created Bluey & Curley in 1939, the strip that would bring him fame. Bluey, a Great War veteran, and Curley, a new recruit, provided readers a light-hearted depiction of the Aussie digger who never took himself too seriously. During the war Gurney was an accredited war correspondent and as such visited our troops in the Middle East and New Guinea, one of whom was the fortunate John Pocock. Alex Gurney died in 1955. 'I thought Alex was a helluva good chap and I still remember reading about him the day he died. Very sad.'

At the end of January 1942 John Pocock returned to Melbourne. In August 1944 he joined the Military History and Information Section (MHIS) and was sent to New Guinea and the Solomon Islands. He left the army in August 1945, joined the public service, and later returned to university to become a dentist.

Back at Joe's place on the New South Wales Central Coast we are perusing a few souvenired German propaganda pamphlets that had been dropped by Nazi dive-bombers over El Alamein. They were small – about the size of a postcard –and they had drawings of a platypus and boomerang – the Australian 9th Division's vehicle insignia. One read: 'AUSSIES! The Yankees are having a jolly good time in your country. And you?' Another read: 'DIGGERS! You are defending Alamein ... What about Port Darwin?'

Propaganda like this was harmless enough. In fact it has been argued that it was actually good for the morale of our boys because it unintentionally exposed the frustrations of the Afrika Korps at the Australians' stubborn resistance. At Tobruk one pamphlet read: 'YOU CANNOT ESCAPE. Our dive bombers are waiting to sink your transports. Think of your future and your people at home. Come forward. Show white flags and you will be out of danger. Surrender!' As Joe told me, some diggers were so desperate to souvenir them that they chased them down as far as the barbed wire of no-man's-land!

On 1 August 1941 Broken Hill's *Barrier Miner* newspaper ran a piece suggesting that the Germans, if they really wanted to give their propaganda the best chance of luring over any wavering Australians, should consider a serious re-write and start appealing to all those weaknesses that our diggers and we as a nation wore so proudly on our sleeves: 'AUSSIES' suggested the *Barrier Miner*, 'We have been trying for the past three months and are getting fed up. Come out and give yourselves up. The German beer is the best in the world, and we have millions of gallons here. Our prison camp is the most luxurious in the world with two-up schools every night, trots on Monday afternoons and gee-gees every Tuesday, Thursday and Saturday. It's all yours if you please, please ... let us take Tobruk!'

'I am only seventeen,' the captured German soldier told the reporter from London's *Daily Mail.*

> *They flew me over here from Crete three days ago and put me in the battle. I joined the army only four months ago. I am supposed to be a lorry driver, but they made me a fighting soldier. At 5:15am, when it was still almost dark, the Australians woke us suddenly with a terrible artillery barrage. It was horrible. Then came the tremendous fire of machine guns, and we flattened ourselves against the ground. Suddenly the Australians seemed to be coming at us from all directions. We shot isolated men but there were too many of them. They came at us with tommy guns, machine guns, everything. Something hit me in the arm. Resistance was out of the question – anyway I had to surrender.*

That story was told to a correspondent from London's *Daily Mail* at El Alamein after the assault at Tel el Eisa, a railway siding north-west of El Alamein in July 1942. The correspondent found the youngster sitting on the floor of a dressing station looking shaken and dishevelled. 'The prisoner's cheeks,' the reporter later wrote, 'were smooth and very pale, his lips were full and red, and thick steel-rimmed spectacles rested on his nose.' It's likely he served with either the German Signals Intercept Company 621 or the 164th Light Division, sent in by Rommel to plug holes in the Axis defences opened up by the advance of the Australian 26th Brigade in the wake of the initial air and ground bombardment that lasted seven hours. And what a bombardment! The heaviest to date in the desert campaign, various Afrika Korps diaries described the sound as being reminiscent of the 'drum fire' barrages of the Western Front.

The Australians, fresh from their rest camps in Syria, put the Axis on their collective back feet at Tel el Eisa. With the help of British Valentine tanks and seventy-nine sorties by Wellington and Albacore bombers that dropped over 100 tonnes of explosives on Axis positions it took just a day and a half to knock out around three dozen German tanks and take upwards of 1400 prisoners, a figure that increased to some 6000 in the week and a half that followed as the 26th Brigade broke out of Alamein, advanced along the coast in the direction of Tel el Eisa and captured almost the entire Italian Sabratha Division and a healthy swag of the Trieste Division as well.

One of the diggers who took part in the battle of Tel el Eisa was a young vineyard worker from Adelaide, Thomas Derrick, who left school at fourteen and was by all accounts quite the larrikin. His passions were boxing, Aussie Rules football, cricket and gambling, though not necessarily in that order. After working for nine years in a vineyard in South Australia Derrick departed on a troopship for the Middle East on 17 November 1940 as part of the 2nd/48th Battalion, which would go on to become the AIF's most decorated unit (four Victoria Crosses and eighty other awards and distinctions), an honour Derrick did more than his fair share to help his unit attain when, on 10–11 July 1942 he ran through a gauntlet of German and Italian grenades on his way to single-handedly taking out three machine-gun posts and capturing over 100 prisoners! When German reinforcements arrived and began a counterattack, Derrick destroyed two tanks using sticky grenades.

For his uncommon heroics Tom Derrick was awarded

the Distinguished Conduct Medal and promoted to the rank of sergeant. He then saw further action at El Alamein, taking out more machine-gun posts during a fierce exchange in late October before returning with the 2nd/48th to Australia in February 1943 for jungle warfare training. Sent to New Guinea (from desert to rainforest!), the indefatigable Derrick won for himself a Victoria Cross after scrambling up a near-vertical slope of jungle at Sattelberg on New Guinea's northern Huon Peninsula, under covering fire from his unit, threw a series of grenades from a distance of between just 5 and 7 metres into entrenched Japanese positions and cleared out an astonishing *ten* machine gun posts!

Derrick's luck, however, eventually ran out. After returning to Australia for further training in February 1944 he was posted to Borneo in May 1945 and it was there, while pushing up a hillside on Tarakan Island off the east coast of Borneo, that he was hit across the chest by a burst of machine-gun fire when he raised himself up off of a jungle track to check on the safety of his men. 'I've had it, that's that,' he said. 'Write to Beryl.' Derrick died of his wounds on 24 May.

The siege at Tobruk was the longest in British and Australian military history. One of the key reasons the garrison held out was Major General Leslie Morshead's policy of 'aggressive patrolling'. The no-man's-land between the defenders' trenches and the German lines was not to be considered no-man's-land. It would be thought of as Australian territory. Most patrols took place along the so-called Red Line, Tobruk's 45-kilometre-long front. There were few encounters with Germans who, judging by the incessant jack-hammering and drilling gave the impression they were more intent on digging in than advancing. Raids into the German lines were constant but mostly covert, as Morshead wrote in his diary:

The enemy's positions were deeply penetrated night after night. Considerable casualties were inflicted, mines were either disarmed or shifted onto enemy tracks, or brought back for our own use. Above all, the enemy was kept in a constant state of fear and trepidation, so that he was awake by night and slept by day.

The Australians dominated the night at Tobruk. They withstood two major attempts to storm its defences and in so doing laid to rest the myth of German invincibility. Their active patrolling had won them no-man's-land in the face of an enemy who preferred to remain hidden behind their defences.

Rommel would eventually capture Tobruk, several months after the Australians were withdrawn to Syria for a well-deserved rest and the city garrisoned by fresh troops from Britain and South Africa. Rommel then advanced on to El Alamein, but that was where the tide of battle in North Africa finally turned decisively in the Allies' favour. The Second Battle of El Alamein, which took place over twenty days from 23 October to 11 November 1942, was the first decisive Allied victory of the entire war. Two weeks later church bells were rung in every parish across Britain in honour of the fallen, an outburst of solemnity and joy the like of which prompted author George Orwell to scribble in his diary on 15 November, 'Church bells rung this morning – in celebration for the victory in Egypt, the first time that I have heard them in over two years.'

From Sudan to Afghanistan almost 103,000 men and women of the Australian armed forces have been lost at home and on foreign soils as a result of war service, and every year on Remembrance Day names approved by the Australian War Memorial's Memorial Council are added to the Roll of Honour.

As Mark Twain once wrote, 'It's not the size of the dog

in the fight, it's the size of the fight in the dog.' There has always been the proud boast in regards to the size of our armed forces and the troops we've traditionally put in the field that Australia has always punched above its weight. Sixty-five nations, or thereabouts, have numerically superior armed forces than we do. Just over a quarter of one per cent of our population are engaged full-time in the military, a figure that is far below the UK, the Netherlands, France and Germany. We have never maintained a large peacetime army, a fact that should be consistent with a country with no land borders or adversaries with significant amphibious capability. We do not possess a military that is larger than our small population requires, yet we have over the decades developed a reputation as the soldiers you want when you need to make a stand, and turn the tide.

Acknowledgements

A book that draws so many threads together from so many disparate sources is not easy to write. I am indebted to Joe Madeley – a 'Rat of Tobruk' and one of the famed 2/13 Battalion, the first fully formed Australian unit to face the Germans in World War II – and his fellow 'Rat' John Pocock of the 9th Division Signals. Both provided many priceless insights into the everyday life of the desert soldier. At his home in the small town of Stauchitz, a half hour's drive north of Dresden in Germany, Rudolf Schneider, General Erwin Rommel's personal driver in the North African campaign, welcomed me with a plate of Bavarian plum cake and refused to hide his admiration for his commander, an admiration shared even by Romel's adversaries in a campaign many called a 'war without hate'.

Ray Rauchle – the grandson of George Rauchle, the last survivor of the New South Wales Contingent sent to Sudan in 1885 – welcomed me into his home in Orange in the central west of New South Wales and gave me a copy of a handwritten letter from George to his mother, written on the SS *Australasia* while '500 miles from Aden'.

I want to thank Alan Arnold, the Reference Services Librarian at Campbelltown Library, who allowed me to take books home, most of them rare and a century old, that he really shouldn't have. Also many thanks to the staff at the Kiama & District Historical Society and the Goulburn & District Historical Society.

Use was made of the wealth of material by war correspondents and historians like Charles Bean and Henry

Gullett, without whose accounts we would all be considerably poorer, but the real surprises were those written by the soldiers themselves, some who had a literary turn-of-phrase that would be envied by many an author. Australians like George Berrie and Patrick Hamilton, Thomas White and Keast Burke; Tommies like Antony Bluett; and bit players in this historic drama like Alexander Aaronsohn, a Romanian-born Jew who wrote with genuine flair about his time serving with the Turks in the Great War, providing a rare perspective on battles in a world where history is mostly written by the winners. I would also like to thank Pam Brewster at Hardie Grant for helping make this all possible, and Dale Campisi for his editorial panache.

Lastly a big thank you to the staff of the Australian War Memorial's Research Centre who brought out box after box of documents from their archives and never once complained of tired limbs.

Bibliography

Books

Aaronsohn, Alexander, *With the Turks in Palestine*, Houghton Mifflin, 1916.

Anderson, Fay and Trembath, Richard, *Witnesses to War*, Melbourne University Press, 2011.

Andrews, Eric, *The Anzac Illusion: Anglo-Australian Relations During World War I*, Cambridge University Press, 1993.

Asher, Michael, *Khartoum: The Ultimate Imperial Adventure*, Viking, 2005.

Barrett, James, *The Australian Army Medical Corps in Egypt*, H. K. Lewis & Co., 1920.

Beckett, Ian, *The Making of the First World War*, Yale University Press, 2012.

Berrie, George, *Under Furred Hats*, W. C. Penfold & Co., Sydney, 1919.

Bevan, Scott, *Battle Lines: Australian Artists at War*, Random House, 2004.

Bierman, John and Smith, Colin, *Alamein: War Without Hate*, Penguin, 2002.

Bishop, Harry, *A Kut Prisoner*, John Lane, 1920.

Blundell, John, *Out of the Desert*, Turner Publishing Company, 1999.

Bollard, Robert, *In the Shadows of Gallipoli: The Hidden Story of Australia in WW1*, New South Publishing, 2013.

Brugger, Suzanne, *Australians in Egypt, 1914–1919*, Melbourne University Press, 1980.

Coulthard-Clark, Chris, *Where Australians Fought*, Allen & Unwin, Sydney, 1998.

Cromer, Evelyn, *Modern Egypt*, Macmillan & Co., 1908.

Crotty, David, *A Flying Life: John Duigan and the First Australian Aeroplane*, Museum Victoria, 2010.

Daley, Paul, *Beersheba: A Journey Through Australia's Forgotten War*, Melbourne University Press, 2009.

De Vries, Susanna, *Heroic Australian Women in War*, HarperCollins, 2004.

Dinning, Hector, *By-Ways on Service: Notes from an Australian Journal*, Constable & Company Ltd., London, 1918.

Dinning, Hector, *Nile to Aleppo*, George Allen & Unwin Ltd., London, 1920.

Donovan, Peter, *STORM: An Australian Country Town and World War 1*, Donovan & Associates, 2011.

Dunsterville, Lionel, *The Adventures of Dunsterforce*, E. Arnold, London, 1920.

Egan, Eleanor Franklin, *The War in the Cradle of the World*, Harper & Brothers, 1918.

Erickson, Edward, *Ordered to Die: A History of the Ottoman Army in the First World War*, Greenwood Press, 2001.

Fell, Alison and Hallett, Christine, *First World War Nursing: New Perspectives*, Routledge, 2013.

Gerster, Robin and Pierce, Peter, *On the Warpath: An Anthology of Australian Military Travel*, Melbourne University Publishing, 2004.

Grainger, John, *The Battle for Palestine, 1917*, Boydell Press, 2006.

Grainger, John, *The Battle for Syria, 1918–1920*, Boydell Press, 2013.

Grey, Jeffrey, *A Military History of Australia*, Cambridge University Press, 2008.

Hamilton, Patrick, *Riders of Destiny: the 4th Australian Light Horse Field Ambulance in the Palestine Campaign 1917–18, an Autobiography*, Mostly Unsung Military History Research & Publications, 1995.

Inglis, Kenneth, *Sacred Places: War Memorials in the Australian Landscape*, Melbourne University Press, 1998.

Inglis, Kenneth, *The Rehearsal: Australians at War in the Sudan 1885*, Rigby, 1985.

Johnston, Mark, *Anzacs in the Middle East*, Cambridge University Press, 2013.

Lock, Major H. O., *With the British Army in the Holy Land*, Robert Scott Roxburgh House, 1919.

Massey, W. T., *How Jerusalem Was Won*, Jonathan Ingram & Lazar Liveanu, London, 1919.

Molkentin, Michael, *Fire in the Sky: The Australian Flying Corps in the First World War*, Allen & Unwin, 2010.

Palenski, Ron, *Kiwi Battlefields*, Hachette NZ, 2011.

Perry, Roland, *The Australian Light Horse*, Hachette, 2009.

Peters-Little, Francis, Curthoys, Ann and Docker, John, *Passionate Histories: Myth, Memory, and Indigenous Australia*, ANU E-Press, 2010.

Pocock, Tom, *Alan Moorehead*, Random House, 2011.

Ramsay, Roy, *Hell, Hope and Heroes: Life in the Field Ambulance in World War 1*, Rosenberg Publishing, 2005.

Rees, Peter, *The Other Anzacs: The Extraordinary Story of our World War 1 Nurses*, Allen & Unwin, 2008.

Rosen, Erwin, *In the Foreign Legion*, Duckworth & Co., London, 1910.

Savige, Stanley, *Stalky's Forlorn Hope*, Alexander McCubbin, Melbourne, 1920.

Semple, Clive, *Airway to the East 1918–1920*, Pen & Sword Books, 2012.

Smith, Colin, *England's Last War Against France: Fighting Vichy 1940–1942*, Weidenfeld & Nicolson, 2009.

Stanley, Peter, *Digger Smith and Australia's Great War*, Murdoch Books, 2011.

Stockings, Craig, *Bardia: Myth, Reality, and the Heirs of Anzac*, University of New South Wales Press, 2009.

Stockings, Craig, *Zombie Myths of Australian Military History*, University of New South Wales Press, 2010.

Stone, Barry, *The Diggers' Menagerie*, HarperCollins, 2012.

Thompson, Julian, *Forgotten Voices: Desert Victory,* Ebury Press, 2011.

Trainor, Luke, *British Imperialism and Australian Nationalism,* Cambridge University Press, 1994.

Watson, Bruce, *Desert Battles: From Napoleon to the Gulf War,* Stackpole Books, 1995.

Williams, John, *Anzacs, the Media, and the Great War,* UNSW Press, 1999.

Wilson, Graham, *Bully Beef and Balderdash,* Big Sky Publishing, 2012.

Woodfin, Edward, *Camp and Combat on the Sinai and Palestine Front,* Palgrave Macmillan UK, 2012.

Woodward, David, *Hell in the Holy Land,* The University Press of Kentucky, 2006.

Web sources

www.globalsecurity.org

www.awm.gov.au

www.trove.nla.gov.au

www.throughtheselines.com.au

www.oilgeopolitics.net

www.theaerodrome.com

www.war-experience.org

www.wartimememoriesproject.com